THE REVELS PLAYS

Founder Editor: Clifford Leech 1958–1971
General Editor: David Hoeniger

THE WHITE DEVIL

The White Devil

JOHN WEBSTER

EDITED BY

JOHN RUSSELL BROWN

THE REVELS PLAYS

METHUEN & CO LTD
LONDON

This edition first published 1960
Second edition 1966
Reprinted 1968
SBN 416 61030 7

First published as a University Paperback 1967
Reprinted 1968 and 1970
SBN 416 69890 5

Introduction, Apparatus Criticus, etc.
© 1960 and 1966 John Russell Brown
Type set by the Broadwater Press
Reprinted by lithography in Great Britain
by Latimer Trend Ltd, Whitstable

TO

ELAINE BRUNNER

General Editor's Preface

The aim of this series is to apply to plays by Shakespeare's pre-
decessors, contemporaries, and successors the methods that are
now used in Shakespeare editing. It is indeed out of the success of
the New Arden Shakespeare that the idea of the present series
has emerged, and Professor Una Ellis-Fermor and Dr Harold F.
Brooks have most generously given advice on its planning.

There is neither the hope nor the intention of making each
volume in the series conform in every particular to one pattern.
Each author, each individual play, is likely to present special prob-
lems—of text, of density of collation and commentary, of critical
and historical judgment. Moreover, any scholar engaged in the task
of editing a sixteenth- or seventeenth-century play will recognize
that wholly acceptable editorial principles are only gradually becoming plain. There will, therefore, be no hesitation in modifying
the practice of this series, either in the light of the peculiarities of
any one play or in the light of growing editorial experience. Nevertheless, in certain basic matters the plan of the series is likely to
remain constant.

The introductions will include discussions of the provenance of
the text, the play's stage-history and reputation, its significance as
a contribution to dramatic literature, and its place within the work
of its author. The text will be based on a fresh examination of
the early editions. Modern spelling will be used, and the original
punctuation will be modified where it is likely to cause obscurity;
editorial stage-directions will be enclosed in square brackets.
The collation will aim at making clear the grounds for an editor's
choice in every instance where the original or a frequently accepted
modern reading has been departed from. The annotations will
attempt to explain difficult passages and to provide such comments
and illustrations of usage as the editor considers desirable. Each

volume will include either a glossary or an index to annotations: it is the hope of the editors that in this way the series will ultimately provide some assistance to lexicographers of sixteenth- and seventeenth-century English.

But the series will be inadequately performing its task if it proves acceptable only to readers. The special needs of actors and producers will be borne in mind, particularly in the comments on staging and stage-history. Moreover, in one matter a rigorous uniformity may be expected: no editorial indications of locality will be introduced into the scene-headings. This should emphasize the kind of staging for which the plays were originally intended, and may perhaps suggest the advantage of achieving in a modern theatre some approach to the fluidity of scene and the neutrality of acting-space that Shakespeare's fellows knew. In this connection, it will be observed that the indications of act- and scene-division, except where they derive from the copy-text, are given unobtrusively in square brackets.

A small innovation in line-numbering is being introduced. Stage-directions which occur on separate lines from the text are given the number of the immediately preceding line followed by a decimal point and 1, 2, 3, etc. Thus the line 163.5 indicates the fifth line of a stage-direction following line 163 of the scene. At the beginning of a scene the lines of a stage-direction are numbered 0.1, 0.2, etc.

'The Revels' was a general name for entertainments at court in the late sixteenth and seventeenth centuries, and it was from the Master of the Revels that a licence had to be obtained before any play could be performed in London. The plays to be included in this series therefore found their way to the Revels Office. For a body of dramatic literature that reached its fullest growth in the field of tragedy, the term 'Revels' may appear strange. But perhaps the actor at least will judge it fitting.

CLIFFORD LEECH

Durham, 1958

Contents

Preface

As a student of Webster, I have been most fortunate. The earliest
and greatest of my debts is to Professor F. P. Wilson, who super-
vised my first steps and provided a model of imaginative scholarship; to acknowledge my indebtedness to him is an occasion for
both thankfulness and humility. In succeeding years my colleagues,
students, and friends at Stratford-upon-Avon and Birmingham
have helped me in many ways, and from elsewhere Mr John Crow,
Dr George Hunter, and Professor Fredson Bowers have most
kindly come to my assistance. I am also indebted to Keble Plays,
the dramatic society of my Oxford college, for the opportunity of
producing *The White Devil*; I am most grateful to everyone who
took part in that production.

In preparing and presenting this edition I have received help
from the Research Grants Committee of Birmingham University,
and as my work neared completion I enjoyed three months at
the Folger Shakespeare Library, Washington, D.C., through the
generosity of the Fulbright Commission and the Trustees of the
library. G. P. Putnam's Sons of New York have kindly given permission to reprint the account of Vittoria Accoramboni in *The
Fugger News-Letters*, edited by V. von Klarwill, translated by
Pauline de Chary and published by them in 1924. Finally, I am
most grateful to Mr David Borland, who read my manuscript with
continuous care and saved me from many obscurities and inaccu-
racies, and to Professor Clifford Leech, the general editor of the
Revels Plays, who gave me criticism and advice with generosity and
understanding.

JOHN RUSSELL BROWN

Stratford-upon-Avon,
  January, 1958

Abbreviations

Bentley	G. E. Bentley, *The Jacobean and Caroline Stage* (1941–56), 5 vols.
Boklund	G. Boklund, *The Sources of 'The White Devil'* (Uppsala, 1957).
Eliz. Stage	E. K. Chambers, *The Elizabethan Stage* (1923), 4 vols.
Chapman, *Comedies*	G. Chapman, *Comedies*, ed. T. M. Parrott (1914).
Chapman, *Tragedies*	G. Chapman, *Tragedies*, ed. T. M. Parrott (1910).
Dekker, *Dramatic Wks*	T. Dekker, *Dramatic Works*, ed. F. Bowers (1953–61), 4 vols.
Dekker, *Wks*	T. Dekker, *Non-Dramatic Works*, ed. A. B Grosart (1884–6), 5 vols.
Dent	R. W. Dent, *John Webster's Borrowing* (1960).
Florio	M. de Montaigne, *Essays*, tr. J. Florio, ed. H. Morley (1885).
Greene, *Wks*	R. Greene, *Works*, ed. A. B. Grosart (1881–6), 15 vols.
Honour's Academy	N. de Montreux, *Honour's Academy*, tr. R. Tofte (1610).
Jonson, *Wks*	B. Jonson, *Works*, ed. C. H. Herford and P. and Evelyn Simpson (1925–52), 11 vols.
Libr.	*The Library.*
Lucas	J. Webster, *Works*, ed. F. L. Lucas (1927), 4 vols.
Lyly, *Wks*	J. Lyly, *Works*, ed. R. W. Bond (1902), 3 vols.

Marston, *Wks*	J. Marston, *Plays*, ed. H. Harvey Wood (1934–9), 3 vols.
Middleton, *Wks*	T. Middleton, *Works*, ed. A. H. Bullen (1885–6), 8 vols.
M.L.N.	*Modern Language Notes.*
M.L.R.	*Modern Language Review.*
M.P.	*Modern Philology.*
Moryson, *Itinerary*	F. Moryson, *An Itinerary* (ed., Glasgow, 1907–8), 4 vols.
N. & Q.	*Notes and Queries.*
Nashe, *Wks*	T. Nashe, *Works*, ed. R. B. McKerrow (1904–10), 5 vols.
O.E.D.	*Oxford English Dictionary.*
P.M.L.A.	*Publications of the Modern Language Association of America.*
P.Q.	*Philological Quarterly.*
Pettie	S. Guazzo, *Civil Conversation*, tr. G. Pettie (ed., 1925).
R.E.S.	*The Review of English Studies.*
S.B.	*Studies in Bibliography.*
S.P.	*Studies in Philology.*
Sh.S.	*Shakespeare Survey.*
Sidney, *Wks*	P. Sidney, *Works*, ed. A. Feuillerat (1912–26), 4 vols.
Tilley	M. P. Tilley, *A Dictionary of the Proverbs in England in the Sixteenth and Seventeenth Centuries* (1950).
Wm Shakespeare	E. K. Chambers, *William Shakespeare: a Study of Facts and Problems* (1930), 2 vols.

John Webster's plays are referred to as follows:

A.Q.L.	*Anything for a Quiet Life.*
A.V.	*Appius and Virginia.*
C.C.	*A Cure for a Cuckold.*

D.L.C.	*The Devil's Law Case.*
D.M.	*The Duchess of Malfi.*
N.Ho	*Northward Ho.*
W.D.	*The White Devil.*
W.Ho	*Westward Ho.*
Wyatt	*Sir Thomas Wyatt.*

Quotation from *The White Devil* and *Duchess of Malfi* is from the Revels Plays edition; from Webster's other works, the text is of the first edition, the reference to Lucas' edition or, for some plays written in collaboration, to Bowers' edition of Dekker's *Dramatic Works.*

W. Alexander's plays are referred to as follows:

A.T.	*The Alexandrean Tragedy.*
J.C.	*Julius Caesar.*

Shakespeare's plays and poems are referred to as in C. T. Onions' *A Shakespeare Glossary* (ed. 1941); all quotations from Shakespeare are from the Globe Shakespeare (ed. 1911), unless otherwise stated.

Introduction

Antecedents

The first edition of *The White Devil*, which is dated 1612, is the earliest printed work for which John Webster was wholly responsible, and, unless some other play, now lost, had been written and produced without leaving a trace in theatrical or literary records, it was the first play wholly by Webster to be seen on any stage. Yet by 1612 Webster was at least thirty years old,[1] and had been in practice as a writer for some ten years.

His literary apprenticeship seems to have been irregular as well as lengthy. The first undoubted reference to him in any record is an entry dated 22 May 1602, in the day-book of Philip Henslowe, business man and theatrical impresario. On this day Henslowe lent five pounds to the Admiral's Men, one of his dependent companies of actors, so that they could make an advance payment for a play called *Caesar's Fall*, the sum to be shared among Anthony Mundy, Thomas Middleton, Michael Drayton, and 'webester & the Rest'. This transaction seems to have been completed seven days later when a further three pounds were lent for the 'fulle paymente' of Thomas Dekker, together with Drayton, Middleton, Webster, and Mundy, for 'ther playe' which was by then renamed *Two Shapes*. Henslowe's day-book also shows that in October of the same year Webster collaborated with Dekker, Thomas Heywood, Wentworth Smith, and Henry Chettle on a play called *Lady Jane*, for the Earl of Worcester's Men. Within a fortnight he and Heywood were working on yet another play, *Christmas Comes But Once a Year*, and they were shortly joined by Chettle and Dekker. None of these early

---

[1] The year and circumstances of his birth are unknown; in the dedication of *Monuments of Honour* (1624) he stated that he was born free of the Merchant Taylors' Company.

works has survived in its original form and only *Lady Jane* in an altered form, but we may guess that they did not provide a very promising start for the new dramatist. When he came to write a preface for *The White Devil*, among all his early associates he wished to be compared with only Heywood and Dekker; by then his aspirations were in other directions—towards the 'full and height'ned style' of Chapman, the 'labour'd and understanding works' of Jonson, and the plays of Francis Beaumont, John Fletcher, and Shakespeare.

Early in his literary career Webster found new employment. In 1604, following Middleton's lead, he and Dekker started writing for the boy actors of St Paul's, first *Westward Ho* and then, in the following year, *Northward Ho*; these are city comedies of cuckoldry and intrigue, and both were published in 1607. Webster, but not Dekker, was also fortunate in finding work with the King's Men, writing for them the Induction to John Marston's *The Malcontent* in 1604. But about this time Webster seems to have gone back to his old masters, the Earl of Worcester's Men who, on the accession of James I, had become Queen Anne's Servants. In 1607, *Sir Thomas Wyatt* was published as written by Dekker and Webster and as performed by the actors of this company; this chronicle-play is probably a redaction of the earlier *Lady Jane*, but it was printed in such a 'bad' reported text that no one can now be sure which parts are by Webster, or whether he had any hand in its reshaping.[1] The title-page of *The White Devil* states that it, likewise, was presented by the Queen's Men.

There is only one major uncertainty in what is known of Webster's early career, and that is the date and authorship of the tragedy called *Appius and Virginia*. When this play was first published in 1654, it was ascribed wholly to Webster, but Rupert Brooke, F. L. Lucas, and other critics have seen the hand of Thomas Heywood in a number of its scenes. It might have been written as early as 1603–4, but the weight of evidence is in favour of a date many years after *The White Devil*, in the late twenties or early thirties.[2] What is cer-

[1] Cf. *Eliz. Stage*, III, 294 and Dekker, *Dramatic Wks*, I (1953), 399.
[2] Cf. *Eliz. Stage*, III, 508–9; Lucas, III, 121–45; C. Leech, *John Webster* (1951), pp. 93–4; and Bentley, V, 1246–8.

tain, and, for present purposes, more important, is that Webster had a long and tentative preparation for writing *The White Devil*. Over a period of ten years he had been concerned with only a handful of plays whose texts, or titles merely, have survived, and for these he had always worked in collaboration—if *Appius* is an exception to this, he used his freedom to write scenes in close imitation of another dramatist. Yet drama seems to have taken up all but a few moments of his literary endeavours: his only known non-dramatic writings of this time are verses prefixed to the third part of Mundy's *Palmerin of England* (1602), Stephen Harrison's *Arches of Triumph* (1604), and Thomas Heywood's *Apology for Actors* (1612). It is small wonder that, when *The White Devil* was first produced, a rumour got about that Webster had been 'a long time in finishing this tragedy'.[1]

But however carefully Webster had worked on *The White Devil*, he must have been particularly anxious about its first performance, for it was not the sort of play with which the Queen's Men habitually satisfied their audiences. Their chief theatre, the Red Bull at Clerkenwell, was

> frankly a plain man's playhouse, where clownery, clamor, and spectacle vied with subject matter flattering to the vanity of tradesmen.[2]

Webster provided 'Charges and shouts',[3] ghosts, disguises and deaths, but his play stands apart from all the surviving plays associated with the Queen's Men from 1609 to 1619; it is more carefully worded, more sophisticated and courtly than any of the others. It is obviously different from *Greene's Tu Quoque*, which is specifically a vehicle for a popular clown, or from Heywood's five narrative plays of *The Golden*, *Silver*, *Brazen*, and *Iron Ages*, which are all a continual bustle of action and spectacle. *The Rape of Lucrece*, the only other tragedy besides Marlowe's *Edward II* which was certainly in the repertory, allows the death of its virtuous and homely

---

[1] 'To the Reader'; for what was probably Dekker's comment, see below, p. xx.
[2] L. B. Wright, *Middle-Class Culture in Elizabethan England* (1935), p. 609.
[3] v. iii. 0.1.

heroine to be completely overshadowed by the alarums and battles
which are the climax to the play. In *The White Devil* there is none of
the adventure of *The Four Prentices*, the curious piety of *A Shoe-
maker a Gentleman* or the belief in 'ordinary' people which is shown
in Daborne's *The Poor Man's Comfort*—a pastoral in which the
shepherd's daughter is never discovered to be of noble birth. When
the plays of the Queen's Men were not boisterous and unreflective,
they were usually practical and unsubtle; they had nothing to compare with Flamineo's elaborate cynicism or with Vittoria's courageous pride.

The First Performance

The date of *The White Devil*'s first performance can be determined
to within a month or two. A series of borrowings from Robert
Tofte's *Honour's Academy* (a translation from Nicolas de Montreux's *Bergeries de Juliette*)[1] proves that the play must have been
written some time after the publication of this pastoral in 1610, but
the dedication to Dekker's *If it be not Good, the Devil is in It*, which
was published in 1612, provides evidence for much closer limits.
Addressing the Queen's Men who had performed his own play,
Dekker wrote:

> I wish a *Faire* and *Fortunate Day*, to your *Next New-Play* (for the
> *Makers-sake* and your *Owne*,) because such *Braue Triumphes* of
> *Poesie*, and *Elaborate Industry*, which my *Worthy Friends Muse* hath
> there set forth, deserue a *Theatre* full of very *Muses* themselues to
> be *Spectators*. To that *Faire Day* I wish a *Full, Free* and *Knowing
> Auditor*.

It is almost certain that the '*Worthy Friend*' was Webster and that
the '*Next New-Play*' was *The White Devil*.[2]

A reading of the preface to *The White Devil* reveals some slight
echoes of Dekker's dedication:

> ... it was acted, in so *dull* a time of winter, presented in so *open* and
> *black* a theatre, that it wanted (that which is the only grace and
> setting out of a tragedy) a *full* and *understanding auditory*.

[1] Cf. R. W. Dent, *P.Q.*, xxxv (1956), 418–21.
[2] E. E. Stoll was the first to suggest this identification (cf. *John Webster*
(1905), p. 21), and the present editor strengthened his argument in *P.Q.*,
xxxi (1952), 353–8.

But, of course, were a direct debt to be deduced from this, it would date Webster's preface, not the performance of his play. The relation between Dekker's preface and *The White Devil* depends on other, stronger evidence. First, Webster was likely to have been Dekker's '*Worthy Friend*', for they had collaborated, not only for Henslowe's companies, but also for the Paul's Boys, and Webster was to name Dekker, together with Heywood, in his own preface among other more learned and courtly writers. Secondly, '*Braue Triumphes of Poesie*, and *Elaborate Industry*' fits Webster's contemporary reputation and the reputation of no other dramatist known to have written for the Queen's Men between 1609 and 1619. Thirdly, as shown above, there would have been particular need for a '*Faire* and *Fortunate Day*' and for a '*Full, Free* and *Knowing*'[1] audience when such a play as *The White Devil* was to be performed by the Queen's Men.[2]

Accepting this identification, we can deduce a fairly precise date for Webster's play. Dekker expected the '*New-Play*' to be performed shortly after the publication of his own some time in 1612—that limits the date to 1612 or early 1613. But the first edition of *The White Devil* is itself dated 1612, and its preface says that the first performance had already been given in 'so dull a time of winter'—that still further limits the date to either January to March 1612, or else (allowing for the fact that a book dated 1612 *might* have been

---

[1] I.e., 'full, generous, and intelligent'.

[2] A number of verbal parallels have been noted between the two plays: with *W.D.*, II. i. 49–51, cf.:

> . . . you should put vp such game
> As fits an Eagle, and pursue the fame.
> And not like rauens, kites, or painted Iayes
> So'are high, yet light on dunghills, for stinking preyes.

with *W.D.*, v. vi. 141–4, cf. (in a scene set in hell):

> I am perbold, I am stewd, I am sod in a kettle of brimstone, pottage—it scaldes,—it scaldes,—it scaldes—whooh.

with *W.D.*, v. i. 165–7, cf.:

> Taylors . . . feare not sattin nor all his workes

(Dekker, *Dramatic Works*, ed. R. H. Shepherd (1873), III, 289, 349, and 328).

The Latin tag, '*Flectere si nequeo superos, Acheronta movebo*' is found in the text of *W.D.* at the end of IV. i, and, in precisely the same form, on the title-page of Dekker's play; it is also found in the dedication to Marston's *Antonio and Mellida* (1602), but in a different form.

published as late as 24 March 1613, the last day of the old legal year) some time between late November 1612 and early February 1613. But what is known of the current practice of Nicholas Okes, the printer of *The White Devil*, suggests that this second possibility is extremely unlikely; it would seem that if this particular printer had received the manuscript later than about 10 November 1612, the title-page would, in normal circumstances, have borne the date 1613, not 1612.[1] So we may conclude that *The White Devil* was first performed very early in 1612, probably in February. Nothing that is known about the play conflicts with this suggestion.[2]

Webster's preface says that the play was first performed in 'so open and black a theatre'. This might have been one of two used by the Queen's Men about this time. In a patent of 15 April 1609, their 'nowe vsuall houses' are given as 'the Redd Bull in Clarkenwell and the Curtayne in Hallowell'.[3] At first sight it would seem as if the 'open and black' theatre must have been the Curtain, for this was by far the older of the two and was soon to fall into disuse. But the patent is the last record which definitely links the Queen's Men with this theatre and it is known that by 1612 they were 'vsuallie frequentinge and playinge att the sign of the Redd Bull'.[4] This almost decides the matter, for Webster's preface speaks of 'most of the people that come to that playhouse', and that does not suggest the unusual use of an old theatre for his particular play.

The structure and fittings of the Red Bull have been carefully and imaginatively considered by Professor George Reynolds in his *Staging of Elizabethan Plays at the Red Bull* (1940). Professor Reynolds has shown that the Bull conformed to the general plan of

[1] According to the *Short-Title Catalogue*, every book which bears his imprint and which was entered in the Stationers' Register later than 10 Nov. of any one year between 1608 and 1613, bears on its title-page the date of the year following, or some later year.

[2] For a further literary borrowing and for possible topical allusions, see III. ii. 135 n., III. ii. 89–91 n., v. iii. 183 n., and v. vi. 160 n. Lucas suggested that a sermon called *The White Devil: or the Hypocrite Uncased* which was preached by T. Adams in March 1613 might have been named after a recent play; if so it might have followed either a performance (perhaps a later and more successful one than the first) or else the publication of the quarto.

[3] *Eliz. Stage*, II, 231.

[4] *Ibid.*, II, 237; quoting a law-suit of 1623.

other Jacobean public theatres: it had a main stage projecting into an open yard which was surrounded by galleries; this stage had railings on its outer sides and was at least partly covered by a 'heavens' or roof; it could be entered by three doors at the back and mounted at its corners and through two or more trap-doors; some part of the rear of the stage could be curtained off; there was a balcony, or upper-stage, which could be likewise curtained off, and there were windows overlooking the main stage; there were some permanent, structural pillars or posts, but others could be brought on to the stage for special purposes; there was a mechanical device for ascending and descending to and from the 'heavens'. Such was the theatre in which we must try to imagine the action of Webster's play.

Many of the actors who were members of the Queen's Men early in 1612 are now little more than names, but Richard Perkins stands out as the most famous 'straight' actor among them. When Webster praised his acting in a note to the first edition of *The White Devil*, he was paying an unprecedented tribute; not only is this the first note of its kind in the history of English drama, but it precedes all other testimony to Perkins as an actor by more than ten years. At this time, in his early thirties,[1] Perkins was only at the threshold of his career; he had been a member of Worcester's Men in 1602 but all the other major roles he is known to have played date from after 1626, as, for instance, Sir John Belfare in Shirley's *The Wedding*, the gallant and sometimes villainous Captain Goodlack in the first part of Heywood's *The Fair Maid of the West*, and Barabas in a revival of *The Jew of Malta*. Webster testified that his acting in *The White Devil* crowned 'both the beginning and end'; this means that he almost certainly played Flamineo, for Bracciano, the other major male role, dies more than five hundred lines before the end.

Subsequent Events

Undoubtedly Webster gained in confidence and reputation by *The White Devil*: in the following year, his *Monumental Column* was published together with other elegies on Prince Henry by Hey-

[1] Cf. C. J. Sisson, *Sh.S.*, vii (1954), 59.

wood and Cyril Tourneur; within two years[1] his *Duchess of Malfi* was performed by the King's Men at their 'private', enclosed theatre at Blackfriars and at their much larger, 'public' theatre, the Globe; then followed the lost play, *The Guise*, and probably some contributions to the 1615 edition of Overbury's *Characters*—these included a character of 'An Excellent Actor'. At this time Webster seems to have been a familiar figure with the King's Men, a hostile portrait of him appearing in a description of the Blackfriars' audience:

> But h'st! with him Crabbed (*Websterio*)
> The *Play-wright, Cart-wright*: whether? either! *ho*—
> No further. Looke as yee'd bee look't into:
> Sit as ye woo'd be *Read*: *Lord*! who woo'd know him?
> Was euer man so mangl'd with a *Poem*?
> See how he drawes his mouth awry of late,
> How he scrubs: wrings his wrests: scratches his Pate.
> A *Midwife*! helpe? By his *Braines coitus*,
> Some *Centaure* strange: some huge *Bucephalus*,
> Or *Pallas* (sure) ingendred in his *Braine*,—
> Strike *Vulcan* with thy hammer once again.
>
> This is the *Crittick* that (of all the rest)
> I'de not haue view mee, yet I feare him least,
> Heer's not a word *cursiuely* I haue *Writ*,
> But hee'l *Industriously* examine it.
> And in some 12. monthes hence (or there *about*)
> Set in a shamefull sheete, my errors *out*.
> But what care I [?] it *will* be so obscure,
> That none shall vnderstand him (I am sure.)[2]

Webster's connection with the King's Men continued for some years; *The Duchess* was revived by them at least twice before its publication in 1623, and about 1621 they performed a city comedy at the Blackfriars called *Anything for a Quiet Life* which was probably written by Middleton and Webster.[3]

But Webster was not for long the servant of any one company,

[1] Certainly before 16 Dec. 1614, when William Ostler, who had played Antonio in the first performance, is known to have died.

[2] Written by Henry Fitzjeffrey of Lincoln's Inn; printed in *Certain Elegies done by Sundry Excellent Wits* (1618), F6ᵛ-7.

[3] Cf. Lucas, IV, 65-8.

nor, indeed, did he often work alone. Shortly after 1616, his tragi-comedy, *The Devil's Law Case*, was performed by his old associates the Queen's Men,[1] and then, once again, he seems to have turned almost wholly to writing in collaboration. Certainly in 1624 he wrote *The Late Murder in Whitechapel*, or *Keep the Widow Waking*, in association with John Ford, William Rowley, and his earlier collaborator, Thomas Dekker; the text of this play has not survived but we know that it was acted at the Red Bull and that it dramatized two contemporary news-items, a case of matricide and a forced marriage with a rich widow.[2] Webster may have written *Appius and Virginia* on his own about this time. He certainly wrote a Lord Mayor's Pageant and a few occasional verses,[3] but the only other plays with which his name has been associated were *A Cure for a Cuckold* (written with Rowley and possibly Heywood) and, less certainly, *The Fair Maid of the Inn* (with Massinger and Ford). The end, as the beginning, of Webster's career is hard to trace among the uncertainties of collaboration, lost plays, and plays which have never been very highly regarded. He probably died some time in the sixteen-thirties.[4]

All that we know about Webster's later years suggests a failure of artistic confidence. *The Devil's Law Case* retained satiric and poetic elements from the two tragedies, returned to citizen characters and a city background, and experimented with the new tragi-comic modes of Beaumont and Fletcher; in trying to do all this at one and the same time, the play was original enough, and it has had a few admirers; but, as far as we know, Webster never followed up its experiments. If *Appius and Virginia* was written soon afterwards, it achieved a bare dramatic style of its own, but again it had no suc-

---

[1] Bentley dates earlier; but see *N. & Q.*, n.s., v (1958), 99–100.

[2] Cf. C. J. Sisson, *Lost Plays of Shakespeare's Age* (1936), pp. 80–124.

[3] *Monuments of Honour* (1624), verses prefixed to Cockeram's *Dictionary* (1623) and verses on an engraving, 'The Progeny of the most Renowned Prince James King of Great Britain . . .', which must date after December 1624 (cf. *M.L.N.*, xlvi (1931), 403–5).

[4] Some scholars think that Heywood's reference to him in *The Hierarchy of the Blessed Angels* (licensed 7 Nov. 1634) implies that Webster was dead by that date; Professor C. J. Sisson suggested that he was the John Webster buried at St James', Clerkenwell, on 3 March 1638 (cf. *Lost Plays* (1936), p. 102, and R. G. Howarth, *N. & Q.*, cxcix (1954), 114–15).

cessors. As far as Webster's share is concerned, the collaborative plays are only remarkable for echoes of earlier successes—a clown, a noble or bawdy sentiment, a concealed or surprising motivation, or a cynical stratagem; the most favourably disposed critic has not discerned a development in the series as a whole, nor much to praise in the overall effect of any one play, or of any one plot within their complicated and often untidy structures. Webster's work after *The Duchess of Malfi* shows that he was either unable or unwilling to continue in a similar vein, and that he did not discover a new one in which he could work persistently. The achievements of 1612–14 were not only hardly won, but also precariously won— these are important facts for any one who wishes to appreciate and criticize his two tragedies.

2. WEBSTER'S READING

The Life and Death of Vittoria Accoramboni

The White Devil depicts events which took place in the late sixteenth century. The real-life Vittoria Accoramboni was born in February 1557 at Gubbio, a small town on the Apennines some hundred miles to the north of Rome. The family was an old one, but Claudio and Tarquinia were not rich enough to provide well for their eleven children. Vittoria, however, was very beautiful and at the age of sixteen she was married in Rome to Francesco Peretti, a young nephew of Cardinal Montalto—in Webster's play Peretti is represented by Camillo, and Montalto by Monticelso. About 1580 Vittoria met Paulo Giordano Orsini, Duke of Bracciano; he had been born in 1537, betrothed to Isabella Medici, then a child of eleven, in 1553, and married to her in 1558; there were three children of this marriage, including a son and heir, Virginio, but in 1576 it had become known that Isabella had a lover, Troilo Orsini, and she was consequently murdered, probably by her husband's own hand. In 1581, Bracciano, now enamoured of Vittoria, ordered the murder of Peretti, and then married Vittoria in secret. The Pope, Gregory XIII, directed them to separate, and for the next four years the couple were continually separating and re-uniting, as the Pope commanded and as Bracciano tried both obedience and evasion. Investigations were made into the murder of Peretti and for some time Vittoria was imprisoned in Castle Angelo in Rome. Shortly after her release, Bracciano again married her and held court with her at Bracciano, his fortified palace to the north of Rome. In April 1585, Pope Gregory died, and on the 24th, in the confusion caused by the election of a new Pope, Bracciano was openly married to Vittoria, thereby performing the ceremony for the third time. But on the day they were thus married, an hour or so later, the new Pope was announced, and he was Cardinal Montalto. The new Pope took the name of Sixtus V.

Bracciano soon discovered that he could expect little mercy from the uncle and protector of his wife's former husband, and so he left the city with Vittoria for Venice and then Padua. He was a dangerously corpulent man, with an ulcer in his leg, and on the journey north he became very ill; soon he and his new duchess moved for his health's sake from Padua to Salò on Lake Garda, and he died there on 13 November of the same year. He had made ample provision for Vittoria in his will, but the relatives of his former wife wished to protect the interests of the heir, Virginio. They tried to force a compromise, and when Vittoria refused, they had her murdered in Padua, the assassins being directed by Lodovico Orsini, a kinsman of Bracciano.

Such are the historical facts behind Webster's play, but no one knows the exact form in which Webster heard or read this story. Certainly the outline which recent historians have disentangled[1] can bear little relation to the story as it reached Webster; his play was written only twenty-seven years after Vittoria's death, a time too short for checking facts, debating contradictory evidence, and disclosing hidden motives. Webster must have known the story in one, two, or possibly a small handful of, incomplete, partisan, and inaccurate accounts. There were many such sent across Europe within a few years of the events they described. Dr Gunnar Boklund, in *The Sources of 'The White Devil'* (Uppsala, 1957), has listed a hundred-and-nine early manuscript accounts, now scatter-

[1] Cf. D. Gnoli, *Vittoria Accoramboni* (Florence, 1870), G. Brigante Colonna, *La nepote di Sisto V* (Milan, 1936), and C. Bax, *The Life of the White Devil* (1940).

ed in twenty-seven libraries in Italy, Austria, England, and America,[1] and among all these he has distinguished four main versions and some thirty minor, more or less independent ones. In addition, six historians had told Vittoria's story in print before Webster wrote in 1612, and two pamphlets had been issued, one in English about Pope Sixtus and the other in Italian about Vittoria herself. Not one of these accounts could have given Webster all the details found in *The White Devil*; either an all-sufficient source is yet to be found, or else Webster used two or more sources which bore some resemblance to extant accounts. The latter is the more likely, for gossips and newsmongers are seldom very original; but the possibility of a lost, eccentric account cannot be discounted, especially since a few highly individual versions have already been found.[2]

In the light of Dr Boklund's researches some useful deductions can be made about Webster's putative source. Firstly, it seems highly probable that he knew nothing of Isabella's adultery, of Bracciano's two early marriages to Vittoria, or of the Greek sorceress he maintained in his household. Some scholars have suggested that Webster knew all these facts, and that he consciously suppressed the first two, and from the sorceress took hints for the character of Vittoria's waiting-woman, Zanche the Moor; but Dr Boklund has now shown that no contemporary account of Vittoria mentions any of these facts, and indeed he has argued that no contemporary writer about Vittoria would have been likely to know them. Furthermore Dr Boklund has shown that one of the extant manuscripts departs from history *and* from every other contemporary account in a way in which Webster did, and no one else would have been likely to do. This manuscript is a news-letter written in German for the Fugger banking-house, and now kept in the Nationalbibliothek, Vienna.[3] Originally it must have been translated or adapted from Italian sources of which no trace is now left. It alone, of all the accounts, agrees with Webster in calling Bracciano's heir Giovanni, and not Virginio as he was in fact. In

---

[1] The following account relies on Dr Boklund's discovery and grouping of manuscripts.

[2] E.g., Biblioteca Vaticana, MS. Urb. Lat. 1644; cf. Boklund, pp. 38–9.

[3] MS. 8959.

addition, this news-letter has many unhistorical details in common with *The White Devil* which very few contemporary accounts have as well: it, like Webster's play, says that Isabella lived to be murdered by Bracciano's order at about the same time as he effected the murder of Peretti (Webster's Camillo); it also says that foul play was suspected at Bracciano's death, and that Vittoria was killed, not by hired assassins, but by Lodovico himself. In real life, the new Pope and Isabella's relatives pursued Vittoria and her family after Bracciano's death, but in this Fugger news-letter, as in *The White Devil*, the Pope takes no active part in this and Francisco de Medici (the Duke of Florence and Isabella's brother) seems to be responsible for ordering her death. In its report of her death there are detailed likenesses to Webster's play: the murderers find her at her prayers, and, in agreement with only one other known manuscript, Lodovico asks, 'Do you recognize me?'[1] No other manuscript or printed account corresponds so consistently to *The White Devil*, and so Dr Boklund has claimed that the lost Italian account on which this news-letter was based was probably Webster's main source. An English translation of the news-letter is reprinted as Appendix I of this edition.

If Dr Boklund's theory is correct and the German translation is a reasonably complete version of its original, it would follow that Webster, like its compiler, may have been ignorant of Bracciano's obesity and sickness,[2] and of the rumours that Vittoria attempted suicide while she was in prison, and again after Bracciano's death. It could also be claimed that Webster closely followed the outline of events given in his source, save only that he made Vittoria wholly responsible for instigating the murder of Isabella and Camillo, suppressed its report that she 'did not wish to turn unfaithful' to her first husband, and delayed Bracciano's marriage until after the escape from Rome.

[1] Cf. *W.D.*, v. vi. 1 and 172.

[2] It has been suggested that Webster transferred Bracciano's obesity to Francisco, but the one passage (II. i. 180–1) in which Francisco is called 'corpulent' may be merely a pun on his title of 'Grand Duke', a title given to him in the Fugger news-letter (cf. App. I, p. 189). If Webster really meant Francisco to be grossly fat, he remembered his intention only at this one moment; later Francisco is simply a 'goodly person' (v. i. 94).

Of course, many details of Webster's play must stem from sources other than this comparatively brief account. Dr Boklund has suggested that some came from: *A Letter lately written from Rome, by an Italian Gentleman, . . . Newely translated out of Italian into English by I.F.* [i.e., John Florio] (1585).[1] In Webster's play the new Pope pronounces excommunication on Bracciano and Vittoria, and then, surprisingly, tries to dissuade Lodovico from seeking to avenge Isabella's death, and so disappears from the play. His disappearance is in accordance with the Fugger news-letter and a few other documents, but his quite unhistorical refusal to encourage revenge and his pronouncement of excommunication could have derived from *A Letter* and from no other known account. Here the excommunication is mentioned only as a threat by the old Pope, but the sense is not easy to follow and, in a rapid perusal, one might think that it was the new Pope who so threatened. His refusal to avenge is stated clearly, as a remarkable fact 'contrary to the expectation of all men'. Other oddities in this *Letter* are the imprisonment of Vittoria in a 'monasterie of Nunnes', rather than in Castle Angelo (this is the closest any contemporary account comes to Webster's 'house of convertites'),[2] and its unique report of family councils to try to prevent Bracciano's second marriage (this may have given Webster a hint for the councils of Act II of *The White Devil*).[3]

There are other circumstances in Webster's play which figure prominently in some contemporary accounts of Vittoria but are not mentioned in either of those which have been considered here. These chiefly concern Vittoria's family. From the Fugger news-letter, Webster could only have learnt that Vittoria had a brother, 'a certain Duke Flaminio', who was killed with her; from *A Letter* he could have learnt nothing of these things. But other accounts tell of a second brother, Marcello, who helped to arrange her first husband's death and who was, according to some manuscripts, in the employment of Bracciano. It was also known that Vittoria had

[1] Extracts are reprinted as Appendix II of this edition.
[2] Cf. III. ii. 264.
[3] This would mean that he tightened the action of his play by making Francisco de Medici, and not Cardinal Medici, a chief figure in these councils; Francisco was necessary for later action in the play, whereas the Cardinal could have taken no further part.

a chamber-maid called Caterina Bolognese who likewise helped
Bracciano's schemes, and two accounts might be interpreted as
saying that she died with her mistress at Padua.[1] Vittoria's mother
is likewise mentioned, though she is pictured as aiding Bracciano's
schemes, not seeking to frustrate them as in *The White Devil*. The
last scene of the play has several details which occur in contemporary accounts other than the Fugger news-letter or *A Letter*: some
say specifically that the assassins entered masked as they do in the
play, some that the real-life Vittoria bared her breast and asked for
mercy as Webster's does;[2] some describe the searching of Vittoria's
wound which may have given rise to Flamineo's 'Search my wound
deeper: tent it with the steel That made it'.[3] Isabella's words as she
parts from her husband in the play, '*manet alta mente repostum*' (II.
i. 263), may also have been suggested by one of the contemporary
accounts which picture Lodovico proudly uttering these very
words as he is captured after killing Vittoria; but this correspon-
dence is not quite so striking as may appear today, for in Webster's
day the line from Virgil was a well-known commonplace.[4] Finally it should be noticed that four accounts mention Lodovico's
banishment from Rome (which is presented in the first scene of
Webster's play), and that two mention the investigations into the
murder of Peretti (which might have suggested the arraignment of
Vittoria in the play).

No single manuscript or book which was examined by Dr Boklund could have furnished Webster with all these details; perhaps
some of the correspondences are accidental; perhaps some were
contained in the Italian original of the Fugger news-letter or in a
more comprehensive, now lost, account. All that can be said is that
any manuscript of what Dr Boklund called the 'Claudio Accoramboni' type[5] could have supplied most of them—but, if Webster did
consult one of these, it was probably after fixing the main course of
his play, for such accounts diverge widely in their treatment of
Isabella and in the later stages of their narrative.[6] Or Webster could

---

[1] Cf. Boklund, pp. 94–5.   [2] Cf. v. vi. 216 and 183.
[3] v. vi. 238–9.   [4] So Lucas, I, 87, n. 1.
[5] E.g., British Museum, Egerton MS. 1100; cf. Boklund, pp. 36–8.
[6] They also allude to Bracciano's obesity; cf. p. xxix, n. 2.

have found a brief account of the more important of these details in Cesare Campana's *Delle historie del mondo* (Venice, 1596) or Giovanni Niccolò Doglioni's *Historia venetiana* (Venice, 1598).

Many details of Webster's play have no parallel in contemporary accounts of Vittoria and must have been invented or derived from other sources. Elizabethan and Jacobean drama could have provided many suggestions—for satirical malcontents,[1] for a false death,[2] for ghosts, murders, intrigues, and so forth; it is clear, for instance, that Webster took Cornelia's madness from *King Lear* and *Hamlet*.[3] More details came from a wide reading; Dr Julio may have been suggested by recent English history,[4] and the death-bed rites which Bracciano's assassins mockingly administer were taken from an Erasmus *Colloquy*.[5] References to pirates off the Italian coast and to the Vitelli (wrongly associated with Vittoria's family) could have come from Webster's general reading about Italian affairs.[6] Many details concerning the papal election, including the service of food, the presence and function of ambassadors, the announcement of the new Pope and the blessing of the people, were taken from *A Treatise of the Election of Popes*, translated from the French of H. Bignon and published in London in 1605.[7] This pamphlet, from which extracts are reprinted as Appendix III to this edition, is the one certain, fairly extensive source for *The White Devil*; besides providing picturesque details of action which no account of Vittoria could have supplied, it also has verbal parallels to Webster's play,[8] and describes the procedure which Webster, contradicting Florio's *A Letter*, used for the election of his Pope, Paul IV.[9] The ambassadors it mentions probably suggested their presence not

[1] Cf. Intro., p. xli.   [2] Cf. v. vi. 149 n.

[3] Cf. v. ii. 36–40 n., and v. iv. 66ff. n.   [4] Cf. v. iii. 157–8 n.

[5] Cf. v. iii. 135–46 n.   [6] Cf. II. i. 142–3 n. and III. ii. 235–6 n.

[7] Cf. J. R. Brown, *N. & Q.*, n.s., IV, xi (1957), 490–4.

[8] Viz. 'they searche', 'any letters', 'sollicitations', 'after they are entred', 'Princes Ambassadours' (twice), 'best ... affected', 'at a window'.

[9] I.e., 'giving over scrutiny' and 'falling to admiration' (IV. iii. 37–8); Florio's *A Letter* says that the election was 'by way of scrutinie' (B4ᵛ). By following Bignon, Webster also contradicted *A Letter* in the manner of announcing the new Pope's name: in *A Letter* it is first announced by servants and then one of the cardinals says, simply, '*Papam habemus*' (B3). Webster and Bignon also agree, against *A Letter*, in the manner of serving the cardinals' food.

only at the election but also at Vittoria's trial and marriage, and at the capture of Lodovico.

As Webster filled out the narrative he had heard or read, or had pieced together, about Vittoria, he must have relied upon his own inventiveness as well as upon his memory or notes of plays, *novelle*, histories, and pamphlets. This is the point at which a discussion of the accounts of the life and death of Vittoria Accoramboni leads to the threshold of the poet's imagination, and certain knowledge is no longer possible. Here it only remains to chart those areas of his play where Webster was least dependent on any known 'life' of Vittoria and to point out the major changes which he effected in the balance and emphasis of the narrative as it was probably known to him.

The relationship of Bracciano, Isabella, and Vittoria as presented in *The White Devil* could have been gathered in the merest outline—passion, murders of expediency, imprisonment, marriage, murders of revenge—from the two main accounts that have been examined here, the Fugger news-letter and Florio's *A Letter*. Webster's chief departures lay in making Vittoria more directly responsible for suggesting the murders of her husband and Isabella, and in developing the character of Vittoria's brother, Flamineo, so that he continually influences, comments upon, and forwards the main relationship. Furthermore, the young husband has been turned into the stock comic figure of an old cuckold, and Vittoria's mother and second brother turned into strongly disapproving critics of Bracciano, Flamineo, and Vittoria. A Moor, Zanche, has been provided as a waiting-maid; she is both lascivious and unfaithful, yet she is the maid who dies faithfully and bravely with her mistress. On Isabella's party, Monticelso is close to the Cardinal Montalto of *A Letter*, save only that Webster has made nothing of his peasant origins. Of Francisco de Medici, and of his vision of Isabella's ghost, his machiavellian plots, his following of Bracciano to Padua, his comments on court affairs when disguised as a Moor, and his entanglement with Zanche, Webster could have learnt almost nothing from his main sources; all that he may have gathered was that Francisco was Isabella's brother and concerned himself in protecting her son's right by instigating the murder of Vittoria.

Several accounts tell how Lodovico had been banished from Rome and most of them tell how he died bravely and scornfully, but his hidden passion for Isabella and his activities until the last scene of *The White Devil* are probably Webster's additions. The growing importance of Giovanni towards the end of the play and his meting out of justice are also without warrant in the extant versions of Vittoria's life.

As much of the characterization was independent of contemporary accounts of Vittoria, so the substance of the scenes in the first four acts of the play, up to the papal election, was probably wholly dependent on Webster's invention: there may have been suggestions for a meeting between Bracciano and Vittoria at Camillo's house, for a family council, a trial, and a scene in prison, but the management of the action and dialogue of those scenes probably derived solely from Webster. The deception of Camillo, the means of procuring Isabella's divorce and death, and the intrigue leading to Vittoria's escape from prison are all additions to any known contemporary account, and the manner of killing Camillo is different from that in every account which mentions it. Later in the play, Bracciano's marriage celebrations and his subsequent death involve rearrangements and amplifications of any known account, while Marcello's death, Bracciano's madness and that of Cornelia, the appearance of Bracciano's ghost and Flamineo's attempt to force money, or at least the truth, from Vittoria, all seem to be Webster's additions. The only scene in the whole play which bears any detailed resemblance to contemporary accounts of Vittoria is the last one of all, which depicts her facing death with religious-seeming boldness, and this has been largely transformed by the new importance of Flamineo and by the presentation of Lodovico's capture immediately afterwards. Most accounts continue to tell at some length of the retribution which befell Vittoria's murderers in the course of time; but Webster finished his play with attention focused on the inner thoughts and feelings of Flamineo and Vittoria, and then, very briefly, on the resolute Lodovico, and on the young prince pointing a general moral with innocent voice, and promising his 'justice' to evildoers, without a doubt of its efficacy or rectitude.

Similitudes and Sentences

Charles Crawford and other scholars in his train have been at pains to show that Webster borrowed many phrases, similes, and maxims (or 'sentences', as they were called) from other authors;[1] from some books he borrowed only a phrase or two (as from Stanyhurst's *Description of Ireland* or Jonson's *Masque of Queens*), from others he borrowed fifteen or twenty longish passages (as from Florio's translation of Montaigne or Pettie's translation of Guazzo's *Civil Conversation*). So far, more than a hundred imitative passages have been traced,[2] so that it almost looks as if

> This fellow pecks up wit as pigeons pease,
> And utters it again when God doth please.[3]

Webster's motives are most suspect when he has used a long string of passages from a single source; when he uses Guazzo nine times within a hundred-and-thirty lines or Alexander's *Monarchical Tragedies* nine times within a hundred-and-sixty lines, then it seems as if he has supplied his own lack of invention by the laziest of means.

In an age when a display of wit and learning was one way of selling books, there were many 'Word-pirates', as Thomas Dekker called them, fellows who made up their writings 'like a beggers cloake, . . . full of stolne patches'.[4] Thomas Lodge, for example, is known to have put together his pamphlets by 'conveying' passages that on one occasion covered 'twenty pages at a stretch'.[5] Many writers kept notebooks in which they jotted down passages for future use; such books were store-houses from which they might deck out their writings 'more artificially and masterly'.[6] And for

---

[1] R. W. Dent's *John Webster's Borrowing* (1960) is an account of verbal debts found by himself and earlier scholars. Annotations to this second edition of the Revels *W.D.* print the undoubted sources noted by Dent, except a series in de Serres' *General Inventory* (tr. 1607) discovered after the first edition was published; some other sources are printed that are not in Dent's book.

[2] App. IV to this edition is an index of Webster's borrowings.

[3] *LLL.*, v. ii. 315–16.

[4] *The Wonderful Year* (1603), Pref.

[5] Alice Walker, *R.E.S.*, viii (1932), 265.

[6] T. Nashe, *Lenten Stuff* (1599); *Wks*, III, 176.

this they had learned example: pedagogues taught their pupils to write in Latin and Greek by 'imitating' the phrases and similitudes of the ancients, while scholars, as Francis Bacon and Gabriel Harvey, kept notebooks of quotations for use in Latin and English compositions. Francis Meres, the compiler of a common-place book for other men's use, defended imitation soberly and pedantically by using a similitude from Seneca which others had used before him: 'Bees', he wrote, or rather re-wrote,

> out of diuers flowers draw diuers iuices, but they temper and digest them by their owne vertue, otherwise they would make no honny: so all authours are to be turned ouer, and what thou readest is to be transposed to thine own vse.[1]

The discovery that Webster freely borrowed from other authors proves, in itself, nothing; the quality of his indebtedness must be judged in its detail.

In fact Webster's 'imitation' was idiosyncratic, occasionally to a fault; he added further epithets, reversed the sense, particularized the general, altered the rhythm, transposed the key. So, for example, William Alexander's complacent:

> Ease comes with ease, where all by paine buy paine,
> Rest we in peace, by warre let others raigne.

becomes Webster's:

> This busy trade of life appears most vain,
> Since rest breeds rest, where all seek pain by pain.
>
> (v. vi. 273–4)

Besides altering the sense and tone, Webster has removed the jingling of 'by' and 'buy', simplified and intensified 'buy' as 'seek', and, one may guess, developed and clarified its commercial image in the phrase 'busy trade of life'. Webster did not borrow with a quiescent mind; rather, imitation quickened his own invention. A borrowed phrase was often a starting-off point only; so he borrowed Guazzo's 'The othes of lovers, carry as much credite as the vowes of Mariners', condensed it into 'Lovers' oaths are like mariners' prayers', and then his mind raced ahead, leaving Guazzo

---

[1] *Palladis Tamia* (1598), Mm 4ᵛ.

behind, with '. . . like mariners' prayers, uttered in extremity; but when the tempest is o'er, and that the vessel leaves tumbling . . .' and so on (v. i. 176ff.).[1] On occasion Webster so overlaid the phrasing of the original author that, were it not known that he was indebted to this particular author elsewhere in this particular scene, the imitation could not have been traced.[2]

Webster had a brooding, persistent, perhaps fretting mind; his imitation of other authors was but one manifestation of these qualities. He constantly imitated himself also, so that epithets and similes recur in different contexts or in different phrasings. He was fond of proverbs too, repeating common-places which he probably heard almost daily; and even these he changed, restlessly—so 'Fortune is fickle' became 'Fortune's a right whore' (I. i. 4), and Fortune's wheel was not merely a symbol of mutability, but became also a torturing wheel, an instrument of torture on which men hang 'manacled, Worse than strappado'd' (III. iii. 94–5). Webster was always rethinking what he had thought, heard or written; and so his work abounds, not only in imitations, but also in puns, ironic repetitions, and multiple meanings. For example, when he had told a story with an obvious application, he was pleased to apply it again in a second, unexpected way, even if the comparison did not hold 'in every particle'.[3] So also he returned to his central 'idea', or image, of the 'white devil' again and again in the course of the play; it recurs both in the management of action and in the detail of dialogue,[4] and ever in new or modified guise. The very structure of his play is an indication of this quality of his mind: it is full of repetitions—of several and varied intrigues, disguises, choric comments, death-beds, punishments; and in each repetition Webster was not so much developing the drama in a single direction, as retuning it, catching a new astringency, relaxation, particularity, complication. And when he came to write another play, he still imitated, repeating and modifying phrases, situations, and characters from his earlier ones; so the cardinal of *The White Devil* changed into the cardinal

[1] See also I. ii. 198–201 and IV. ii. 178-9.
[2] Cf. v. i. 168 and 205–7, and v. vi. 182.
[3] IV. ii. 240; see also I. ii. 243 and II. i. 327, and notes.
[4] Cf. pp. l–lvii below.

of *The Duchess of Malfi*, and Flamineo into Bosola, and later into Romelio of *The Devil's Law Case*. For Webster, to repeat, or to imitate, was to create.

3. THE TRAGEDY

'Willingly, and not ignorantly', Webster turned his back on classical example, and set before himself the achievements of poets of his own age: by the light of Chapman, Jonson, Beaumont and Fletcher, Shakespeare, Dekker, and Heywood he wished that what he wrote might be read. And, in making this request in the preface to *The White Devil*, he praised the classical drama in such repetitive and conventional terms that all his readers must instinctively be glad that he rid himself of any duty he might have felt to write in that manner. 'Willingly, and not ignorantly' let it be—but it is also necessary to observe for what he exchanged 'all the critical laws' of the ancients, their clear form and 'grave' and 'heightened' sentiments. It was not to one kind of drama that he committed himself; his avowed exemplars derived their craft from European and classical writings as well as English, from Christian and pagan religious rites as well as from secular entertainments; and they appealed not only to the audience of the Globe Theatre of London, but also to exclusive groups of the learned or the sophisticated, and to the pious, raucous, practical, or adventurous citizen audiences of the Red Bull or the Curtain. They were both experimental and old-fashioned, and they left no simple or single clue to those who might wish to follow them. Moreover, the dramatists whom Webster cited as his patterns make such a varied list that it looks as if he has simply put down the first names that came into his head, as a kind of general recommendation, or 'puff', for his book: if one name did not recommend itself to any particular reader, another probably would. But a careful perusal of his play silences this thought, or, rather, relegates such a motive to the casual and accidental. Mr T. S. Eliot has remarked that one of the characteristics of Webster's generation of playwrights was

> their artistic greediness, their desire for every sort of effect together, their unwillingness to accept any limitation and abide by it.[1]

[1] *Elizabethan Essays* (1934), p. 18.

This is especially true of Webster; the heterogeneous list of drama-tists in the preface to *The White Devil* is but a beginning of the list that might be made of those in whose footsteps he followed. To understand the nature of his art, it may be best to follow his own advice and read his work 'by their light', to try to appreciate his power of using this native and multifarious inheritance in his own greedy way.

In setting his play in Italy, with dukes, cardinals, and mistresses for its characters, with passionate love, ambition, jealousy, and revenge for its motives, and with machiavellian intrigues, poison-ings, stabbings, and court ceremonial for its action, Webster was following well-known examples: Shakespeare's Iago and Iachimo are Italian villains in this tradition; Marston's *Insatiate Countess* and Middleton's *Women Beware Women* are set within it. Some dramatists used this hot-house setting—a northerner's view of Italy in the fifteen-seventies and eighties—for its own sake, and to exploit its opportunities for eloquence, passion, and suspense. For others, it was a setting in which to cry aloud for 'Justice', the wild justice of revenge, or the more severe and personal justice of a northern, puritan conscience. For Webster, the Italian setting had both appeals: he rose fully to its eloquence, passion, and suspense, and throughout his play—not always loudly, but persistently—there is the cry for justice and revenge. To the last scene, both dramatic appeals are maintained; we are amazed and awed by the spectacle of Vittoria and Flamineo passionately and ambitiously dying, and we are also caught up in the meting out of justice, not only to them, but also, through Giovanni, to their persecutors. Webster seems to have exploited greedily all possibilities, but, on reflection, we must also own that his amalgam is dexterously consistent.

There are other modes of tragedy which Webster copied, as, for instance, the 'full and heightened style' of Chapman. His was a tragedy which took its form from a considered (if not very deep) view of court society and politics, and of stoical personal behaviour; basically its characters were examples of virtue and vice, and its climaxes were touched with sententious comment on human life in general. Webster praised Chapman and sometimes imitated him in his dialogue, and an even less 'popular' writer, William Alexander, he constantly used as a mine of sententious utterance for his own characters.[1] He followed both, certainly, in a tendency to generalize: the first 'sentence' is in the second line of *The White Devil*, and its last scene concludes with one. Webster's tragedy is not so obviously organized around a single theme as Chapman's, but its very title suggests that Vittoria is not only an individual but also a type; there is a general name which fits her, and which, it may sometimes seem, she is made to fit.

Webster's tragedy is also akin to various forms of narrative drama. Chronicle-plays are echoed in its episodes of the papal election and the wedding festivities, in its exploitation of supernumeraries such as lawyer, conjurer, courtier, or physician, and in its presentation of a sequence of events rather than a single crisis. And like the best history-plays—like Shakespeare's *Richard II*, *Henry IV*, or *King John*—it presents a series of related and contrasted figures, not a single hero, and is concerned with society as well as with individuals—although here it is an exclusively professional and court society. And, like Shakespeare in *Macbeth* or *Antony and Cleopatra*, Webster combined a chronicle-play technique with interests and devices derived from medieval narrative tragedy, and so presented the rise and fall of Fortune's wheel. Nor is that all, for when Flamineo turns to the audience and says:

> O men
> That lie upon your death-beds, and are haunted
> With howling wives, ne'er trust them, ...   (v. vi. 154–6)

Webster may have gone beyond Shakespeare's example and momentarily borrowed from plays like *Arden of Feversham* or Heywood's *A Woman Killed with Kindness*—domestic tragedies of exemplary narrative which were immediately relevant to the everyday life of their audiences.

By borrowing some structural devices from chronicle-plays, Webster was bound to lose something of the concentration which is often considered a hallmark of tragedy; but apparently this was

---

[1] For Webster's imitations, cf. App. IV; for his more general debt to Chapman, cf. T. Bogard, *The Tragic Satire of John Webster* (Berkeley, Cal., 1955).

not a fault in his eyes, for these devices are repeated in *The Duchess of Malfi*. Moreover, he went outside tragic example for other features of *The White Devil*. Possibly there is something of the sophisticated sensationalism of Beaumont and Fletcher's tragicomedies in some rapid changes in the attitudes of Monticelso, Vittoria, and Bracciano, and in Flamineo's feigned death. Certainly there is much of Marston's satiric mode in the comments of Flamineo, Lodovico, and Francisco, who are all, on occasion, satirical observers like the heroes of *The Malcontent*, *The Fawne*, or Sharpham's *The Fleire*.[1] Tourneur had also introduced a satirical observer into his tragedies, linking him, something in the manner of Hamlet, with the more old-fashioned revenger, and Jonson, while avoiding a single satirical mouthpiece, had chosen subjects for his tragedies which enabled satirical comments to accompany disaster. Webster may well have remembered all these examples, for the satire in *The White Devil* partakes of all these forms. Occasionally, when the relationship of Vittoria and Camillo, or even of Vittoria and Bracciano, is the object of the satire and Flamineo stands unengaged, manipulating the situation, it might even seem that Webster was indebted to the citizen comedies of cuckoldry which, earlier in his career, he had helped Dekker to write, and which—as his apparent borrowings from Sharpham's *Cupid's Whirligig* suggest[2]—he was probably still reading with pleasure and interest.

Webster wrote a mongrel drama—one hesitates to call it 'tragedy' after such a recital—and as far as we know he was only able to succeed in it twice. That, perhaps, is more than could be expected, for such cormorant tendencies would normally ensure a muddled failure. But he was a careful, painstaking writer, as we have already seen; he worked slowly and his restless mind was constantly leading him to repeat and modify what he had written. His compilations were not likely to be thoughtless; even if they were not perfect wholes, their various parts would be deeply and minutely considered. And two further points follow: his plays are highly individual, for, although he borrowed from others, few borrowed so

---

[1] For Webster's debt to Marston, cf. T. Bogard, *op. cit.*
[2] Cf. App. IV.

widely as he; and highly complex, for few borrowed so repeatedly as he.

Faced with such complexity, we should observe the effect of *The White Devil* as a whole and inquire what the critics have deduced about Webster's overall purpose in writing it. Lord David Cecil was convinced that it is a 'study of the working of sin in the world': 'His characters are ranged in moral divisions; there are the good and there are the bad'. In this view, even Webster's 'wickedest characters' are forced to recognize before they die 'the supremacy of that Divine Law, against which they have offended'.[1] But not all critics can discern this simple plan: their admiration is so drawn towards Vittoria and Flamineo that Lord David's 'good' characters can provide no effective contrast or criticism. Mr Ian Jack, for example, has claimed that the play's 'background of moral doctrine' has nothing to do with its action, 'having been superimposed by the poet in a cooler, less creative mood than that in which Flamineo had his birth'. Mr Jack believed that this 'dissociation' was a fundamental flaw in Webster, and that his play has no purpose beyond that of 'making our flesh creep'; in short, Webster was 'a decadent'.[2]

In recent years an attempt has been made to find a moral purpose in the play which could account for the bias that Mr Jack and others have observed. Professor Travis Bogard has judged that Vittoria and Flamineo, and other characters, are 'alive on the stage' because of their struggle to 'keep themselves as they are, essentially'; in his view, Webster was not concerned with 'traditional divisions of good and evil', but with 'integrity of life'; this is 'the sole standard of positive ethical judgement in the tragedies'.[3] Professor Clifford Leech had earlier seen something of the same purpose, but he did not think that Webster accepted the stoical conclusion so consciously, or so simply:

---

[1] *Poets and Story-Tellers* (1949), pp. 27–43. See also H. W. Wells, *Elizabethan and Jacobean Playwrights* (New York, 1939), p. 46, etc.

[2] *Scrutiny*, xvi (1949), 38–43. More recently Madeline Doran has accused Webster of an 'inveterate habit of emphasis on good theatre at the expense of artistic consistency, or on vivid sympathetic insights at the expense of ethical coherence' (*Endeavors of Art* (Madison, 1954), p. 355).

[3] *Op. cit.*, p. 40.

what comes after life may be uncertain, but there is a terrible certainty in the recognition of evil. That is the portion of Vittoria and Flamineo, and their power to stare it in the face gives them something of nobility. And that is worth ambition, though in hell.[1]

Dr Gunnar Boklund has suggested a further modification, for he has not felt sufficiently drawn by Vittoria and Flamineo to give them a central place in the drama; for him, Webster's purpose was to present 'a world without a centre':

> a world where mankind is abandoned, without foothold on an earth where the moral law does not apply, without real hope in a heaven that allows this predicament to prevail.[2]

It is small wonder that for critics less intent on defining Webster's purposes, there has always been something 'inexplicable' in his art, or some unresolved contradiction in their praise of it. Mr F. L. Lucas has claimed that 'it sometimes seems as if [Webster] felt courage to be the one vital thing in life', but, being astute and sensitive, he qualified this uneasy statement by adding elsewhere that 'if Vittoria were mean, and Bracciano cowardly, and Flamineo a fool, then we might turn away' from the sight of them.[3] Rupert Brooke, an earlier critic, seems to have anticipated Dr Boklund's description of a 'world without a centre', but he wrote of it with less satisfaction; he saw Webster's characters as 'writhing grubs in an immense night. And that night is without stars or moon'; then he qualified this with 'But it has sometimes a certain quietude in its darkness', and qualified even this with 'but not very much'. Rupert Brooke, like Mr Lucas, saw something he could not fully explain.

Critical opinion cannot speak with certain or united voice about Webster's purposes; it has proved possible to talk of him as an old-fashioned moralist, as a sensationalist, as a social dramatist, as an imagist or dramatic symphonist, as a man fascinated by death, or a man halting between his inherited and his individual values. Where an artist's purposes are thus uncertain, and where he follows no simple or single tradition, we may proceed towards an understanding of his art by another track, by trying to define more closely the nature of his individual style; for a dramatist this involves a study of

---

[1] *John Webster* (1951), p. 57.   [2] Boklund, pp. 179–80.
[3] Lucas, I, 39 and 95.

his use of language and his dramatic technique—a study of the kind of dramatic experience he communicates to an audience.

For a start we may say that the plot or structure of *The White Devil* is loose and rambling, a gothic aggregation rather than a steady exposition and development towards a single consummation. It has something of the width and range of a history-play. It could be called a revenge tragedy, yet there is no single revenger: Monticelso is at first ready to 'stake a brother's life' for the sake of revenge, but later he says ' 'tis damnable'; Francisco is a revenger who works mostly through other men and escapes scot-free at the end; Lodovico is a revenger who satisfies his own pride while working for Francisco, and finally loses his life; and Giovanni stands for justice in revenge, inexperienced but fully resolved. The play may also be called a tragedy of passion, or of great deeds overthrown, but there is no single disaster: Bracciano, Marcello, and Cornelia take their several exits, and only at the last do Vittoria and Flamineo die together. As a satirical drama, as we have already seen, it has three commentators instead of the more usual single one. (Notice that, when we begin to analyse the nature of Webster's dramatic style, his heterogeneous debts to other dramatists begin to make sense; at least they all seem to serve a consistent technical purpose.) Such multiplicity is not found in any of the contemporary accounts of Vittoria which may have been Webster's sources; it was he who introduced the death of Marcello and the madness of Cornelia in the last act, who developed Flamineo's role, brought Francisco to Padua to act as commentator, gave Lodovico a personal motive for revenge, and added to the importance of Giovanni at the close.

It is popularly supposed that *The White Devil* is contrived to present the maximum number of deaths and horrors; but this is true, if at all, of the last act only. In the earlier acts all seems to be contrived to allow the maximum variety of comment. The deaths of Isabella and Camillo are carefully presented in dumb show, so that they forward the narrative without engaging our interest too closely with their victims. Our interest is chiefly claimed, at this stage of the play, by arguments and direct comment: the first scene is an argument, the second and third present a series of them; when action is called for, Flamineo or some other is present to describe it and fill out our understanding. It might be said that Webster indulged an almost literary zeal for description, to a degree dangerous in a drama. The third act is chiefly occupied with a trial scene, worked up from the slightest of hints in his source, and used, as so often in other plays, for the exciting exploration of a single situation—and in this play, the situation remains almost the same at the end of it as it was at the beginning. It is only in the last act of all that action and horrors press upon us; and even there, a commentary is maintained throughout. Whatever action takes place, there is always some one observing and commenting upon it: Francisco watches Bracciano's helmet being sprinkled with poison, and Flamineo joins him to watch Bracciano die; Lodovico watches Zanche make love to Francisco; Francisco and Flamineo observe Cornelia's madness, and the very assassins are chorus to the stabbing of Zanche, Vittoria, and Flamineo; Flamineo describes Vittoria's death and then, uniquely, he alone describes his own.

Our attention has passed from the structure of the play to the handling of individual scenes; this was perhaps inevitable, for they show similar techniques. As a commentator is always provided for the action, so in the course of a scene the speeches are continually turning from the expression of individual feeling to the expression of generalities. The poisoning of Bracciano may be taken as an example: even as he is speaking of his own pain and helplessness, our attention is drawn aside to the disguised Francisco ironically commenting 'Sir be of comfort', and to the despairing Vittoria who cries 'I am lost for ever'; but more than this, Bracciano himself draws our attention away from himself, towards all physicians, to all soft, natural deaths and to howling women, and, as soon as he moves off-stage, Flamineo takes up his theme, speaking of the solitariness of all dying princes. In this play, intimate feeling for a single character is intermittent only: none of its characters draws attention wholly to himself for more than a few consecutive lines;[1] as we tend to identify ourselves with one character, we are forced

---

[1] It is noteworthy that the only two soliloquies of any length (at the ends of IV. i and V. iv) are sustained by making the soliloquizer address a vision or ghost of some other person.

back, not only to observe the other characters on the stage and their relationships, but also to contemplate the relevance of the action to mankind in general.

It is a restless technique; besides insisting on the general, Webster seems to have aimed at a continual series of shocks, not only large *coups de théâtre* (though the play has its share of them), but brief, stinging changes of direction. One might instance Cornelia trying to explain away the death of Marcello and so defend the life of her remaining son, Flamineo:

> . . . and so I know not how,
> For I was out of my wits, he fell with's head
> Just in my bosom.

There is a pause and she looks round for signs of belief, but a page speaks, 'This is not true madam'. 'I pray thee peace', flashes Cornelia, but at once she perceives that all is in vain, and she concludes in tame explanation (a third contrasted reaction):

> One arrow's graz'd already; it were vain
> T'lose this: for that will ne'er be found again.
>   (v. ii. 64–9)

More obviously theatrical are the changes of fortune in the last scene, where Webster, risking the serious reception of the play's last moments, introduced a bizarre, almost laughable, mock-suicide: Vittoria and Zanche think they are doomed, but then they see a chance of eliminating the newly dangerous Flamineo, and then are tricked into believing that they have succeeded, and then, finally, are shocked by Flamineo rising to his feet, having merely feigned death. (Webster was not like a photographer who composes a formal portrait or group, and carefully records it with a long exposure; he has recorded the movement of men rather than their composure, the strain as their wills conflict with their impulses, their reasons with their emotions.) And after so much excitement and movement, Flamineo draws our attention away again, to all men that lie upon their death-beds and to the cunning of all women. *The White Devil* presents its characters in flashlight moments, against a background as wide and general as continual choric comment can establish it.

Webster's use of language is in keeping with such techniques. Two characteristics stand out. First, the dialogue is often knotted and complex: in the more descriptive passages it sharpens towards the epigrammatic; its vocabulary and images are unexpected, various, punning, and sensuously evocative; the pulse of utterance alternately rushes, hesitates, tugs, and reiterates. Secondly, its fine passages—the poetic expressions which remain in the memory and have a winged validity both in and beyond their dramatic context— are for the most part extremely brief, a single image or phrase perhaps, or else are a little more extended, but nervously, almost hesitantly, expressed. There is, in short, little sustained poetic utterance; long speeches are either deliberate description (which is often in prose), or set-pieces like the telling of a dream or tale, or a considered statement in a law-court. The quarrel in Act IV, Scene ii may be taken as an example:

> Vittoria. '*Florence*'! This is some treacherous plot, my lord,—
> To me, he ne'er was lovely I protest,
> So much as in my sleep.
> Bracciano.   Right: they are plots.⁓
> Your beauty! O, ten thousand curses on't.
> How long have I beheld the devil in crystal?
> Thou hast led me, like an heathen sacrifice,
> With music, and with fatal yokes of flowers
> To my eternal ruin.⁓Woman to man
> Is either a god or a wolf.   (ll. 84–92)

There is an instantaneous change of thought at each dash marked in this passage; and within each train of thought there are progressions or minor changes of emphasis. The most extensive and powerful image is prepared for by another related to it (though more briefly expressed), and is itself presented, as it were, in two stages: 'With music, *and with* fatal yokes. . .' And immediately this statement has been attained, the pulse drops and Bracciano continues with a generalized aphorism. There follows, shortly, a more lengthy speech for Vittoria, but this is built up by a number of short questions, giving a breathless rather than a massive indictment. When Vittoria, like Bracciano, reaches a dominant image she expresses it in two, or possibly three, stages, and then changes the tone completely:

> I had a limb corrupted to an ulcer,
> But I have cut it off: and now I'll go
> Weeping to heaven on crutches.~For your gifts,
> I will return them all; and I . . .   (ll. 121-4)

An example of the complex descriptive passages is Flamineo's description of Camillo:

> a gilder that hath his brains perish'd with quick-silver is not more cold in the liver. The great barriers moulted not more feathers than he hath shed hairs, by the confession of his doctor. An Irish gamester that will play himself naked, and then wage all downward, at hazard, is not more venturous. So unable to please a woman that like a Dutch doublet all his back is shrunk into his breeches.
>
> (I. ii. 27-34)

There is a connection between all these details, yet the speaker is never at pains to make it fully explicit; his utterance is staccato and often grammatically incomplete or ironically casual; his images are unexpected and from widely differing sources, and his vocabulary is allusive ('all downward') and punning ('wage . . . hazard . . . venturous'). The effect of such a style is, as its nature, two-fold. First, it must be followed closely to be fully appreciated; being subtle and complex, it demands detailed attention—and this, of course, is in accordance with the multiplicity of the play's structure, for its audience must be ready to watch and hear many disparate yet related things. Secondly, our appreciation must be nervous, ready to respond to momentary stimulus.

A play's structure, scene-handling, and use of language all affect its characterization. In *The White Devil* this also is impressionistic or momentarily perceived, being repeatedly under the stress of conflict or surprise; and there are contrasts and relationships between many of the characters according to their roles of mistress, lover, machiavellian, revenger. Vittoria is one of the dominant characters (if not, as the title proclaims her, *the* dominant one), yet even she is presented fragmentarily; there are only four scenes of any length in which she appears and her mood, or tone, is very different in each of them. For an actress, this presents a great difficulty, for there is no build-up of presentation; each of Vittoria's scenes starts on a new note, with little or no preparation in earlier scenes.[1] Flamineo is the most consistent and continuously presented character, but his consistency lies in a mercurial nature; Webster made him draw attention to this:

> It may appear to some ridiculous
> Thus to talk knave and madman; and sometimes
> Come in with a dried sentence, stuff'd with sage.
> But this allows my varying of shapes,—
> Knaves do grow great by being great men's apes.[2]
>
> (IV. ii. 243-7)

So he varies shapes more quickly than other characters vary moods; the whole is fragmentary, subtle, intricate.

Such was Webster's dramatic style, the instrument he forged out of many elements. It is not the instrument to present, with massive assurance, types of good and evil; if a critic sees that in *The White Devil*, the assurance must come from him and not from the play. Nor is it an instrument for presenting a general society of men, or for varying the presentation of a number of general themes; if a critic sees only such things in the play, he must be insensitive to the immediacy of the dialogue which draws the audience momently towards individual characters. Yet there must have been some motive for creating so individual an instrument: it is good for variety, for shock and surprise; it is good for irony and detailed, critical humour; it is good for moments of poetic utterance and for the subtle, nervous presentation of human thought and feeling. Its disadvantages would seem to be—from the point of view of an easy success—its restlessness, its persistently small scale (in spite of presenting great events), and, finally, the demand it makes on its audience to pay attention minutely and unflaggingly. Since Webster created this dramatic style (and used it only slightly modified in his next play) we may suppose that he did not rate these disadvantages very highly; he may even have considered them to be advan-

---

[1] The actor of Francisco has the same problem in becoming, suddenly, a passive figure in Act V, the actor of Monticelso in the abrupt transition to Paul IV, and the actor of Lodovico on practically every appearance.

[2] See also III. i. 30-1.

tages. Let us examine what is, perhaps, the most dangerous of its shortcomings, the demands it makes on the audience's close attention. If we can see how this could have appeared as an advantage to Webster, we may come close to defining the nature of his artistic purposes, the bias of his dramatic vision.

The very title, *The White Devil*, offers an immediate clue, suggesting that this play presents some person or persons who are not what they seem, devils transformed into angels of light. In the play, this idea is repeated again and again: there are verbal echoes of it in 'We call the cruel fair' (I. ii. 213), 'If the devil Did ever take good shape' (III. ii. 216–17), and 'the devil in crystal' (IV. ii. 88). And the same idea is expressed in other images, in passages relating to other characters besides Vittoria:

> O the art,
> The modest form of greatness! that do sit
> Like brides at wedding dinners, with their looks turn'd
> From the least wanton jests, their puling stomach
> Sick of the modesty, when their thoughts are loose,
> Even acting of those hot and lustful sports
> Are to ensue about midnight . . .   (IV. iii. 143–9)

or again:

> O the rare tricks of a Machivillian!
> He doth not come like a gross plodding slave
> And buffet you to death: no, my quaint knave,
> He tickles you to death; makes you die laughing . . .
>   (V. iii. 193–6)

or more subtly and more comprehensively:

> I have liv'd
> Riotously ill, like some that live in court;
> And sometimes, when my face was full of smiles
> Have felt the maze of conscience in my breast.
> Oft gay and honour'd robes those tortures try,—
> We think cag'd birds sing, when indeed they cry.
>   (V. iv. 118–23)

Those that 'live in court'—that is, all the characters of this play—may be deceitful; as they smile they may be murdering, as they sing they may be weeping. To recognize their deceit a minute and determined scrutiny will be necessary. Webster's choice of images reinforces the same point. He used, for example, an extraordinary number of animal images—on one count, over a hundred[1]—so that, behind the human activity, sophisticated and courtly, the audience's attention is constantly drawn to an activity or habit which is animal. He also used many images associated with witchcraft, with illusions ('as men at sea think land and trees and ships go that way they go'), and with poisons ('the cantharides which are scarce seen to stick upon the flesh when they work to the heart'). And of course conjuring, poison, disguises and dissimulation are not only images, but recurrent episodes in the very action of the play.[2] With so much emphasis on deception in the action, images, and ideas of this play, an audience must watch closely and subtly if it is to see, hear, and understand aright; here lies a justification for the demands Webster's dramatic style makes upon an audience.

As soon as we begin to respond intently, subtleties open up before us: when Bracciano vows to protect Vittoria, we become aware that he is vowing to execute two murders; when Flamineo decries women, we become aware that he is encouraging Bracciano to be his sister's lover.[3] Some deceptions are made abundantly clear by subsequent action—as Francisco's pretence that he will not revenge[4]—but others are hidden or partly hidden so that we hardly know how to respond: when Flamineo explains that he has not asked Bracciano for reward, we cannot be sure that that is not precisely what he has done.[5] Our response becomes subtle and intricate, and also insecure. The comments which are so often made upon the action in the course of the play are no longer straightforward or reliable: all the time we question the true intention of the speaker, asking whether he is ironic or deceitful, or, for some ulterior purpose, bluntly honest; the comments do not simplify the play for us, they involve us in it, and make us question the implications

---

[1] So Muriel Bradbrook, *Themes and Conventions of Elizabethan Tragedy* (1935), p. 194.

[2] This relation between the play's images and action has been demonstrated in detail by H. T. Price (*P.M.L.A.*, lxx (1955), 717–39); he has claimed that such technique is uniquely elaborate in Webster.

[3] These are two of many examples in an admirable discussion of this aspect of Webster's style by J. Smith (*Scrutiny*, viii (1939), 265–80).

[4] Cf. iv. i. 3ff.   [5] Cf. iv. ii. 222–42.

of its action and dialogue. And the more intently we observe individual characters, the less simple they become: which of Flamineo's
many 'shapes' is his true one ? when Bracciano cries on his death-
bed 'Vittoria ? Vittoria!', is it in anger, or in love and faith ? Isabella
has often been called one of the very few simply 'good' characters in
the play; but such a view can scarcely survive a close scrutiny.
Arriving in Rome,[1] she goes first to her kinsmen and not to her husband (one might not censure her for this if later she herself did not
hotly deny that she had done, or ever would do, such a thing), and
her thoughts and hopes are all for herself, none for her husband:
the wrongs done to her are pardoned; her arms shall charm and
force him to obey her, and prevent him from straying from her. All
this is said in a quiet, lofty tone, without any criticism unless it be in
Francisco's brisk 'I wish it may. Be gone.' When Isabella comes, as
her kinsmen have arranged, face-to-face with Bracciano, neither he
nor she can speak peacefully: 'You are in health we see,' he tries
tentatively, but she answers with an innuendo, 'And above health
To see my lord well.' At one and the same time, Isabella presumes
the worst of him and presents herself as selflessly humble. Within
half-a-dozen lines, their incompatibility is manifest; while Bracciano is self-defensively angry, Isabella is always praising herself
and reminding him of his duties and shortcomings. Because she
appears as a defenceless woman speaking in a submissive tone, and
because he is openly angry, scornful, and brutal, the natural tendency is to side with Isabella. But on a closer, or more sensitive,
view, it is impossible to side with either. There is perhaps a further
subtlety: Isabella suggests laying the blame for their divorce on her
'supposed jealousy' and promises to deceive the others into believing this by playing her part with 'a piteous and rent heart', yet when
she does put the blame on herself, she does it with such abandoned
hatred towards Vittoria and in a manner so calculated to infuriate
Bracciano (who must now, of course, say nothing) that we may be
tempted to think she is indeed that which she seems, 'a foolish, mad,
And jealous woman', perhaps deceiving herself.

The other supposedly 'good' characters are likewise vulnerable.
Marcello says that his sister's chastity is dearer to him than her life,

[1] Cf. II. i. 1ff.

but, when Bracciano, by double murder, has made Vittoria his
duchess and promised to advance her kindred, he at once leaves
Francisco to follow Bracciano; there is indeed a touch of smugness
and self-pity in Marcello's avowals of honesty and poverty, and in
his question about his brother's misdeed when a child. Cornelia, so
powerful and peremptory in reproof of vice, also takes advantage of
Bracciano's fortunes; and in defeat she is deceitful, and in madness
concerned, not with honour or virtue,[1] but with the preservation of
her son's body; her regard for virtue has not been, we may suspect,
for its own sake. This may all seem *too* subtle and uncertain; and
one must grant that it would be hard to be conscious of all this
during a performance. Yet the play's title, its imagery and incidental comments, its dissimulating action, the complexity of its
plot and dialogue, all invite such a consciousness:

> Know many glorious women that are fam'd
> For masculine virtue, have been vicious ...
>
> (v. vi. 244–5)

May not Isabella or Cornelia be of this number?

One aspect of Webster's writing that was noticed earlier is the
manner in which disparate ideas are expressed in a single speech,
both in prose and verse, without any words bridging the gap between them. The only way to deliver such speeches satisfactorily in
the theatre is for the actor to be conscious of the unspoken connec-
tions; if this is not achieved—and a good actor delights to do it with
dialogue so nervously and richly alive as Webster's—the speeches
will remain a sequence of unrelated utterances and there can be no
dramatic development. The essential thing is for the actor to be
aware of the unspoken thoughts and feelings underneath, sustain-
ing the utterance, and so to find some expression of them. Members
of his audience may have very little conscious understanding of
such subtleties—they have no time to ask questions and make explicit judgements—but, nevertheless, as they respond to the actor's
total performance, they will, consciously or unconsciously, respond
to those elements of it. So Webster's very manner of writing makes

---

[1] As Ophelia is in her first mad-scene (the comparison is apposite, for
Webster was indebted to *Hamlet* here).

us aware, perhaps unconsciously, of that which is unspoken—and so why not of the hidden selfishness of Isabella or Cornelia ?

Webster's characterization of Vittoria uses a similar 'undertow' of thought and feeling. The dominant impression she gives is of a passionate, courageous woman, and one who suggests that her lover should kill his wife and her husband. But her reaction to Cornelia's rebuke and curse in the first act hints at something else, at a regard for conventional morality underneath; having protested that nothing 'but blood' could have 'allayed' Bracciano's suit to her, she cries 'O me accurst' and rushes from the stage alone, and perhaps frightened. Her attitude here is sharply contrasted to both Flamineo's and Bracciano's. In the trial scene, on the defensive, she gives no sign of a hidden conscience, save only that she counterfeits innocence with alarming exactitude, as if she knew what it might be like. In the scene in the house of convertites, she shows that she can, painfully for Bracciano, give herself over to expressions of repentance; again she may be acting a part, but certainly she acts it to the life. Later when she yields and so regains Bracciano, we can only guess at her thoughts and feelings, for she does not speak at all, perhaps guilefully, knowing this will whet his appetite, or perhaps shamefully, wishing to keep something to herself. At her wedding festivities she is silent also, but when she realizes that Bracciano is poisoned she is horror-struck and, between her cries of grief and attempts to comfort him, we hear only 'I am lost for ever' and 'O me, this place is hell'; then she leaves the stage alone, as she had done after her mother's curse. Such hints that Vittoria feels the 'maze of conscience' (and they include silences as well as words) might escape many people's notice—except, certainly, an actress trying faithfully to perform the part—or if noticed they might be considered of little account. But the intent, involved audience must surely take account of other passages in the last scene, which become, at last, not hints, but bare statement. At the beginning of this scene, Vittoria is 'at her prayers', but when Flamineo enters and threatens her life she is successively scornful, accusing, and pleading; it is Zanche who thinks of a way of escape, and then Vittoria is quickly deceitful, cruel, and exulting—so far, all is unlike her former behaviour. When Flamineo rises from his feigned death, she is at first silent and then cries for help. At this point her true assassins enter, masked. Now facing death for the second time, she tries asking for mercy, but she speaks now with more pride; then she tries flattery, and then a proud show of courage and womanliness. As she commands silence and respect, she rises to her part, and, at first trembling, overcomes her fear at the thought of death:

> I am too true a woman:
> Conceit can never kill me: I'll tell thee what,—
> I will not in my death shed one base tear,
> Or if look pale, for want of blood, not fear.

The stroke itself is felt:

> 'Twas a manly blow—
> The next thou giv'st, murder some sucking infant,
> And then thou wilt be famous.

And then, in the moment of her greatest courage, comes another thought, quite different, but one which has been heard before:

> O my greatest sin lay in my blood.
> Now my blood pays for't.

This implies no breakdown, for it is at this moment that Flamineo is drawn to her:

> Th'art a noble sister—
> I love thee now; if woman do breed man
> She ought to teach him manhood: . . .

Vittoria is silent for a time, and when she does speak it is clear that she has been thinking of life beyond death:

> My soul, like to a ship in a black storm,
> Is driven I know not whither.

And then, finally, her 'greatest sin' reminds her of other lives; after another long silence her last words are:

> O happy they that never saw the court,
> Nor ever knew great man but by report.

Taken by itself, this might be an expression of momentary weakness; but at such a moment, it may show courage, being the true expression of Vittoria's deepest thoughts. We may think, as Webster suggested at the beginning of this play, that:

> affliction
> Expresseth virtue, fully, whether true,
> Or else adulterate.　(I. i. 49–51)

Certainly Vittoria's acknowledgement of her 'greatest sin', and of the torment of her soul, expresses thoughts and feelings that have earlier been heard only momentarily; those brief statements and longer silences have all been sustained by a great undertow, and its force she has felt despite her outward committal to a life of passion, ambition, and cunning.

Isabella, Cornelia, and Marcello, hiding self-concern behind an appearance of goodness, Vittoria with a sense of sin behind her courage and passion, Bracciano at once weak and steadfast in his love, perhaps unable to reconcile all he knows within himself ('Where's this good woman? . . . Away, you have abus'd me'[1])— why was Webster so concerned with such characters, and why did he present them in this manner? Possibly Flamineo is there, at the end, to satisfy such a question. He too has had his moment of truth:

> I have a strange thing in me, to th'which
> I cannot give a name, without it be
> Compassion . . .[2]　(v. iv. 113–15)

and soon afterwards he has admitted that 'sometimes', when his face was 'full of smiles', he has 'felt the maze of conscience' in his breast. But he has put such thoughts behind him, and in the last scene he assumes more 'variety of shapes', to feed his own ambition and his appetite for ceaseless activity. When death comes to him, he tries to have done with all thought; he reiterates that he thinks of nothing:

> I remember nothing.
> There's nothing of so infinite vexation
> As man's own thoughts.

He tries to be concerned only with his immediate existence, for, in his state,

---

[1] v. iii. 17 and 82.
[2] For the powerful effect of these lines in the theatre, see pp. lx–lxi below.

> While we look up to heaven we confound
> Knowledge with knowledge. O I am in a mist.

Yet, as he assumes his last 'shape' of defiant villainy, his denial of conscience is a reality for him, and a pain; he knows:

> This busy trade of life appears most vain,
> Since rest breeds rest, where all seek pain by pain.

In *The White Devil*, Webster has presented a 'busy trade of life', where judgement seems inescapable, not judgement by death merely, but by pain. He shows human beings who are not what they seem: those 'famed for masculine virtue' are not necessarily at peace in their inner consciousness; those who seem careless of consequence may have felt compassion; and the white devil herself may know what sin is, and, in her ultimate access of courage, know what fear and honesty are too. Man lives in a net: if he sins, directly, or by using the outward show of a virtue he has no desire for, or by failing to face the full truth about himself, some retribution must follow; he cannot deceive without bearing the consequence. Man's judgement is within, perhaps unknown to others, perhaps unrecognized as such by himself.

This is the kind of world which Webster has presented in his tragedy, and for which his unique dramatic style seems to have been created; his use of language, the pulse of his verse and prose, his images, the continual choric comment, ironic, humorous, and straightforward, the sensational happenings and sudden changes in action and sentiment, all seem entirely appropriate to this purpose. The multiplicity and looseness of his dramatic structure give a width of presentation; besides the characters that have already been examined here, Monticelso, who veers so suddenly in his attitude towards revenge, and Francisco, who several times so curiously accepts the role of compassionate observer, seem to be caught in the same net, and motivated, on occasion, by some undertow of hidden, and perhaps unconscious, thought and feeling.

There is, possibly, a further purpose in the multiplicity of the play's structure, for the various characters are not merely in apposition and contrast to each other; their stories are inextricably bound together, one event causing others. So Webster showed, it would seem, that man's actions do not influence only himself, but other men also, and that one ill deed brings others with it. For this reason, perhaps, he made Vittoria think in her last moments of those who have not lived where she has lived: in the intensity of her suffering, she may presume that mankind misuses mankind only at the court, that the rest of the world cannot be so dangerous. And when she is dead we are shown the course of hatred and retribution continuing, first in Lodovico's defiant, yet belittling, stoicism, and then in Giovanni's promise that justice shall pursue all the murderers. As his youthful voice points the moral:

> Let guilty men remember their black deeds
> Do lean on crutches, made of slender reeds.

we must surely listen to his words carefully and scrutinize his face; does he really have 'his uncle's villainous look already' as Flamineo has suggested? or is there any hope in his self-reliant, innocent voice that the 'bed of snakes is broke', that will has become purified and that underneath there is now no pride, or greed, passion or selfishness? There is no answer; the play leaves us with a sense of insecurity. The predicament which Webster presented is continual.

In writing such a play Webster took great risks, for he made great demands upon his own craft and imagination, upon the dramatic form, upon his actors and his audience. But as we watch, awed and insecure, we will feel pity in our hearts for those who suffer, for those who by pain seek pain; with its horrors, its deadly laughter and its intricacies, the dramatic experience is humane, and in Vittoria's end ennobling.

4. THEATRE PRODUCTIONS

By 1631 *The White Devil* had been 'diuers times Acted, by the Queenes Maiesties seruants, at the Phoenix, in Drury Lane'; in 1665 it was being acted 'At this present (by His now Majesties) at the Theatre Royal', and, in 1672, it was still being performed there; and these few facts, recorded on the title-pages of the second, third, and fourth quartos, are almost all that is known about revivals of *The White Devil* on Caroline and Restoration stages. Samuel Pepys went to see it performed by the King's Company on 2 October 1661, but

> coming late, and sitting in an ill place, I never had so little pleasure in a play in my life.

He made another visit two days later but the laconic entry in his diary, 'saw a bit of "Victoria", which pleased me worse than it did the other day',[1] does not explain whether the play, the performance, or his own mood or inconvenience was to blame. John Downes, writing of the Drury Lane theatre in the years immediately following its opening in 1663, listed *The White Devil* among 'Old Plays ... Acted but now and then; yet being well Perform'd, were very Satisfactory to the Town';[2] he listed several of Jonson's comedies in the same category, and *The Merry Devil of Edmonton* and Shakespeare's *Merry Wives of Windsor* and *Titus Andronicus*. Gerald Langbaine in his *Account of the English Dramatic Poets* (1691) wrote that *The White Devil*, with *The Duchess of Malfi* and *Appius and Virginia*, had 'even in our Age gain'd Applause'—a hint that any failure to comprehend might be blamed upon Elizabethan barbarity and ignorance.

Nahum Tate was quite of this mind; he set about revising *The White Devil* for performance at the Theatre Royal, and his version was published in 1707 as *Injur'd Love: or, the Cruel Husband*. The prologue speaks confidently of 'our Reforming Play'; in it Vittoria has become a model of what Tate considered to be virtue and Bracciano's lust is the cause of all misfortune. Tate tried to simplify still further by reducing the number of scenes, being explicit where Webster had been suggestive, and eliminating subtleties, ironies, and comments. But the play could not be doctored so easily as he supposed; his version is confused in plotting and uncertain in tone, and, apparently, it was never performed.[3]

Without an acceptable modernized version, *The White Devil* dropped out of the repertories and the next professional performance was not given until the present century. Then two produc-

---

[1] *Diary*, ed. H. B. Wheatley, II (1918), 107 and 199.
[2] *Roscius Anglicanus* (1708), p. 9.
[3] Cf. H. Spencer, *E.L.H.*, i (1934), 235–49 and C. Leech, *John Webster* (1951), pp. 15–19.

tions followed each other in London within ten years, one on
11 October 1925, by the 'Renaissance Theatre' at the Scala, and
another on 17 March 1935, by the 'Phoenix Society' at St Martin's.
Reviews of these performances show that most critics were impressed, but were unable to accept the play as a whole. After the
1925 production, James Agate complained that 'Webster's lovers
do not work out their own damnation, and at no time are they conscious of it'.[1] This is a strange judgement in view of Agate's further
comments that Esmé Percy played Bracciano with 'all that show of
beauty and display of temperament which the portrayal . . .
demands', and that Cedric Hardwicke as Flamineo showed 'human'
feeling in his speech, 'I have a strange thing within me . . .' (v. iv.
113ff.). After the 1935 production, the critic of *The Times* praised
John Laurie's Flamineo for 'imaginative agony' in the same speech.
This critic thought that most performances were acceptable, noting
only that Oriel Ross's Vittoria lacked the 'rhetorical power' for the
trial scene. But the play as a whole still failed to commend itself; the
critic took no interest in the murders or disguises, reckoning them
only as 'the price one pays for the poetry'. Reviews of both productions suggest that Webster's words were often appreciated out of
context; his characters did not appear consistent human beings and
his violent action did not justify itself; in short, dramatic unity was
not achieved.

The next professional production, and until now the last to be
seen in London, did achieve a unity; and for this the producer, Mr
Michael Benthall, was given the credit. His production ran for
some months at the Duchess Theatre from 6 March 1947. For Mr
J. C. Trewin, 'the production as a whole excite[d] with its darting
lights, its alarums, and its quivering speed',[2] and for Mr Kenneth
Tynan, 'Mr Benthall achieved a cruel enthusiasm of production
which is exactly Webster's quality'.[3] Aided by Mr Paul Sheriff's
sets and Miss Audrey Cruddas' costumes, the producer ensured
that violent action and sensational spectacle were the dominating
and unifying impressions. Miss Margaret Rawlings' Vittoria was

---

[1] *Brief Chronicles* (1943), pp. 144–6.
[2] *We'll Hear a Play* (1949), p. 215.
[3] *He that Plays the King* (1950), pp. 69–71.

praised for being 'convincingly voluptuous' and Mr Robert Help-
mann's Flamineo for being 'vivid' and 'sinister',[1] yet little subtlety
or psychological tension seems to have been communicated.
Critics were not much impressed with this 'busy trade of life'
where 'rest breeds rest, [and] all seek pain by pain' (v. vi. 273-4); as
Mr Tynan put it, none of the characters seemed to feel 'tenderness,
or regret, or nostalgia'. Interestingly, the only exception was
Flamineo's speech about compassion; this was again picked out by
the critics[2] as an irrelevant, yet touching, moment. But many spec-
tators have agreed that they left the theatre thinking, chiefly, that
the worst of horrors had been imaged, that death had been sated.

Tastes have changed within thirty years: in 1925 and 1935, *The
White Devil* was heard for its occasional poetry, in 1947 it was seen
and heard for its compelling picture of violence and death, and then
on Monday evening, 14 March 1955, at the Phoenix Theater, New
York, there was yet another kind of acceptance. On this occasion,
Mr Jack Landau produced the play in modern dress and with no
more scenery than those few pieces which could be utilized from a
full-scale production of Ibsen's *Master Builder*, the current attrac-
tion at the theatre on other evenings of the week. Mr Landau saw
The White Devil as 'an Elizabethan Mickey Spillane world',[3] and so
was unconcerned with the panoply of Renaissance Italy; *The New
York Times* reported that he placed 'all the emphasis on the turbu-
lence of the script'. Mr Fritz Weaver's Flamineo was especially
praised, and all the actors were said to have played 'with speed,
force and intelligence'. It would seem that this first New York production lacked splendour but presented both Webster's violence
and his subtlety, together with clear characterization. It had another
quality too, for the critic of *The New York Times* concluded with
the assurance that 'Webster's melodrama' had proved to be 'a lot of
fun'; without having seen the production, one cannot say whether
this is just another critical misunderstanding or another theatrical
gaffe, or whether this is the critic's attempt to say that Webster's

[1] Other admired performances were Miss Martita Hunt's Cornelia, Mr
Andrew Cruickshank's Francisco, and Mr Hugh Griffith's Monticelso.
[2] Cf. K. Tynan, *ibid.*, and Audrey Williamson, *Theatre of Two Decades*
(1951), p. 284.
[3] J. Landau, *Theatre Arts*, xxxix (Aug. 1955), pp. 25 and 87.

cold, alert, and sometimes complicated humour was also communicated on this occasion.

Besides these professional productions, the last few decades have seen many revivals of *The White Devil* by amateur drama groups, especially those connected with universities in the United Kingdom and the United States; within two years the present writer has seen three such productions at the Universities of Oxford, London, and Birmingham. Clearly, the audience for Webster is growing once more; it may not be long before another professional production can be attempted.

5. THE TEXT

The Quarto of 1612

The title-page of the first edition of *The White Devil* reads as follows:

THE / WHITE DIVEL, / OR, / The Tragedy of *Paulo Giordano* / *Vrsini*, Duke of *Brachiano*, / With / The Life and Death of Vittoria / Corombona the famous / Venetian Curtizan. / *Acted by the Queenes Maiesties Seruants.* / Written by IOHN WEBSTER. / *Non inferiora secutus.* // *LONDON*, / Printed by *N.O.* for *Thomas Archer*, and are to be sold / at his Shop in Popes head Pallace, neere the / Royall Exchange. 1612.

It is a quarto (the usual format for single plays at this time) and contains forty-four unnumbered leaves, viz. A^2 B–L^4 M^2. Page AI is the title-page and AI^v is blank. The author's preface 'To the Reader' is printed on A2 and 2^v, and the text itself begins on BI, under a head-title reading:

THE TRAGEDY / OF PAVLO GIORDANO / Vrsini Duke of Brachiano, and Vittoria / Corombona.

The running-title throughout the rest of the book is 'Vittoria Corombona'. The miscellaneous sub-titles may be quite without authority; Nicholas Okes (the printer referred to on the title-page as '*N.O.*') was given to furnishing such variations, while, in the dedication to *The Devil's Law Case*, Webster himself was content to call this play '*The white Deuill*'.

Webster's preface, 'To the Reader', and his note on the first performance which is printed at the end of the book show that this first edition was published on his own initiative: 'In publishing this tragedy', he wrote, 'I do but challenge to myself that liberty, which other men have ta'en before me . . .' Such was a recently established procedure, but his references to 'so open and black a theatre' and to the 'ignorant asses' in his audience strike a truculent note which is not echoed in the preface or dedication of any other play emanating from the repertory of the Queen's Men at this time.[1] They suggest that Webster was more than usually independent in these matters as in so much else, and that his play was sent to the printer with little, if any, help from the players; the manuscript was probably one of his own, not one copied in the theatre nor one stored or used there. In order to support these inferences it is necessary to consider the actual printing of the first edition.

Nicholas Okes was in a small way of business[2] and it has proved possible to identify two compositors who were responsible for many of the books that came from his printing-shop within a few years of *The White Devil*. They were first identified by the late Philip Williams, who called them A and B;[3] A was distinguished by his preference for the forms 'I'le', 'do', and final '-y', and B by his preference for 'Ile', 'doe', and final '-ie'. On these grounds Williams showed that B set the whole of *King Lear* (1608) and that A and B shared the work for *The Maids of Moreclack* (1609) and *The White Devil* (1612). Further research has added to the differentiating spellings; the most consistent of them are A's 'we', 'me', 'here', and initial 'en-', where B preferred 'wee', 'mee', 'heere', and initial 'in-'. All this confirms Williams' division of the three books that he investigated, and shows, in addition, that A was probably responsible for the whole of Jonson's *Masque of Queens* (1609), Heywood's *Golden Age* (1611), Dekker's *Troia-Noua Triumphans* (1612), Webster's *Monumental Column* (1613), and R. Coverte's *True and almost Incredible Report* (a reprint of 1614). A survey of Okes' books of this period suggests that B was the more experienced workman

---

[1] For a fuller account of this and consequent matters, see J. R. Brown, *S.B.*, vi (1954), 117–28 and viii (1956), 113–17.

[2] Cf. *Records . . . of the Stationers' Company*, ed. W. A. Jackson (1957), p. 75.

[3] Cf. *S.B.*, i (1948), 61–8.

and that A was a younger man, taking an increasing share in the work. *The White Devil* was set between them in this manner: Compositor A: B1–1^v, C1–F2^v, G1–2^v, H2, 2^v, 4, 4^v, I3, 3^v, 4^v, K1, 3^v–4^v, L3–M2^v, A1–2^v; Compositor B: B2–4^v, F3–4^v, G3–H1^v, 3, 3^v, I1–2^v, 4, K1^v–3, L1–2^v.[1]

It has long been recognized that the dialogue of *The White Devil* is free from any major textual obscurity; the main problem has been the number of minor errors, such as come from careless printing rather than from difficult copy. Because of these obvious errors, an editor must constantly be suspicious of unusual brevity or roughness of phrasing, peculiar syntax, and, more difficult to identify, unnecessary glibness or repetition. It is here that a knowledge of the compositors is of help, for, when the text is divided between them, it is obvious that Compositor A was the chief offender. If we consider the errors which two modern and independent editors, Lucas and Harrison, have concurred in correcting, A was responsible for fifteen omissions of single letters from the middle of words, B for only one; A added final letters (as 'leaves' for 'leave' and 'your' for 'you') six times, and B not once; he omitted a final letter (as 'the' for 'they' and 'bring' for 'brings') eight times for B's four, and left out a small word six times for B's twice; as for mis-reading copy, he appears to have done this nine times for B's four. The dialogue of *The White Devil* was sent to the printer in a reasonably clear and clean copy; A's part was somewhat carelessly set, B's part carefully set.[2]

Stage-directions and speech-prefixes present a more complex problem. Both compositors set their material within as few pages as possible, and in consequence both sometimes misplaced a direction in order to fit it within the text-space to the right of the dialogue and so avoid using an extra line or so of type.[3] Possibly A was a little freer in these matters (he misplaced one direction where plenty of text-space was available)[4], but both must be held suspect. Where

---

[1] B's takes were: I. i. 57 to I. ii. 223, III. ii. 328 to III. iii. 133, IV. ii. 0 to 220, IV. iii. 46 to 118, v. i. 42 to 190, v. ii. 33 ('rear up's head; . . .') to 71, v. iii. 60 to 202, v. iv. 39–40 ('in all . . .') to v. vi. 21.

[2] Especially when he had become accustomed to the handwriting; cf. I. ii. 22 n.

[3] Cf. II. i. 146.1–2 for A, and I. ii. 204.1–3 and note for B.

[4] Cf. IV i. 122.

they differ significantly is in placing directions outside the text-space, in the outer margins of the quarto page. This was not a common practice (no other play printed by Okes before 1616 has more than two or three marginal notes), and it involved the compositors in considerable extra trouble. It is therefore hard to see why they both adopted it for this play, and why they chose some directions for this treatment and rejected others. One cannot say that the compositors chose a few of the longer descriptive directions for placing in the margin; they include a brief exit and four entries. Nor did they choose those which would not fit into the text-space; at least six of them would do so easily. Nor did they adopt the practice completely for a few selected formes; with the exception of the inner forme of F, each forme which has marginal directions has normally placed ones as well. The issue is clarified only when it is seen that at first Compositor B alone set marginal directions, but for sheet L, at the end of the book, A followed his example. It may be supposed that in the manuscript sent to the printer some directions were marked in a distinctive manner—perhaps marked off by rules, or written in the left margin, or in an italic hand—and that, therefore, one of the compositors—the more careful of the two—might safely leave these directions to be added to the type when each forme was ready for imposition; so he would represent the distinction in his copy by printing in the outer margin of the quarto page; when his task was done, he probably saw to it that his fellow adopted the same practice for the remaining pages. The directions which were thus printed were obviously written by the author himself, and some of them suggest that they were written with publication in book-form in his mind; such are '*The Conspirators here imbrace*' and '*Brachiano seemes heare neare his end* . . .'[1]

Many of the other, normally placed stage-directions and some of the speech-prefixes of the quarto have characteristics which Sir Walter Greg has adduced as signs that a printer's copy was the author's 'foul papers', that is a 'copy representing the play more or less as the author intended it to stand, but not itself clear or tidy enough to serve as a prompt-book'.[2] In both speech-prefixes and

---

[1] v. i. 63–4 and v. iii. 129.1–5.
[2] W. W. Greg, *The Shakespeare First Folio* (1955), p. 106.

stage-directions the names by which the characters are designated change in a way that would have confused a prompter but would have satisfied an author: 'Zanche' alternates with 'Moor', 'Francisco' with 'Florence', 'Vittoria' (or 'Victoria') with 'Corombona', and 'Doctor' changes to 'Julio'; these variations occur within the work of each compositor, and often a change was made where the dialogue could have given no suggestion of the new name. *The White Devil*'s stage-directions also include the 'ghost' characters '*little* Iaques *the Moore*', Christophero, Guid-antonio, and Farnese,[1] characters which have no lines to speak and no individualized action to perform; if the original manuscript had been used in a theatre a prompter could have removed such sources of confusion with simple strokes of the pen, and so it may be argued, with Sir Walter Greg,[2] that the names in the quarto are relics of undeveloped or discarded ideas reproduced from a manuscript close to the author's 'foul papers'. Several entries are omitted in the printed text and two marked for 'others' where specific characters are required;[3] again an author might not be worried by such imprecisions, but a prompter would be particularly careful to avoid them.

Against these signs of 'foul papers', there are no clear signs that the manuscript sent to the printer had been altered or added to in the theatre. Every surviving seventeenth-century playhouse manuscript has some sort of division into acts or scenes,[4] yet this text has none at all. It is also quite without a prompter's note of actors playing minor parts, or of properties or characters which have to be in readiness for later entry. The entries which are marked prematurely need not reflect the copy itself, but, like those which are marked too late, have probably been misplaced by the compositors for their own convenience.[5]

This textual evidence agrees with and amplifies the inferences made from the conditions of publication: the printer's copy was a clean text, such as an author interested in publication might himself have provided, and it was closer to his 'foul papers' than to any manuscript that might have been used, annotated, or copied in a

---

[1] II. i. 0, II. ii. 1st *D.S.*, and v. i. 43.3.   [2] *Op. cit.*, p. 112.
[3] Cf. II. i. 144, III. iii. 83.1, v. ii. 44.2–3, and v. iii. 0.3–5 and 81.1–2.
[4] Cf. Greg, *op. cit.*, pp. 142–5.   [5] Cf. p. lxiv, above.

theatre. There are, however, some curious errors among the stage-directions which have yet to be accounted for. These are four duplicate entries,[1] an entry for Isabella when she has been killed in the previous act,[2] an exit for Monticelso when he has been rightly directed to leave some seventy lines earlier,[3] and, probably, an entry marked for Antonelli thirteen lines too late.[4] Duplicate entries are sometimes found in printed texts of this period because compositors have reproduced a prompter's anticipatory note, but this explanation will not hold for at least two of these duplications; one is an erroneous addition to a correctly timed group entry, another a supplement to an incorrect entry four lines later. There is no doubt at all that the other errors must have been made by some one other than a prompter. It is at this point that the marginal directions must be remembered; they might well have been marked in a distinctive way in the manuscript because they were late additions to it, and, since some of them are especially literary in tone, they may have been added by Webster when he was preparing that manuscript for the printer. The errors just considered could originate from just such a correction,[5] not being marked in any distinctive way because the manuscript had sufficient space for them without recourse to such aids to clarity. It is not fair to judge the quality of this process of correction by the errors it left; there might be many true corrections and additions which will pass unnoticed in the printed book.

This theory will fit all the facts: Webster supplied a manuscript for the printer which was accurate and complete as far as the dialogue was concerned, but incomplete and inaccurate in its preparation for use in a theatre. Such a manuscript might well have been in his possession, for he was a consciously literary writer who prided himself on his work; it might well have been in his own hand-

---

[1] II. i. 225 and 278; IV. iii. 0.1 and 2; IV. iii. 79 and 83–4; and v. i. 33 and 43.1.

[2] III. ii. 0.3.   [3] IV. i. 139.   [4] III. iii. 96.

[5] The entry for Isabella at the beginning of III. ii must have been an irrational slip; anyone familiar with the *dramatis personae* might have made it, but it is easier to imagine the author doing so (correcting his manuscript confidently and, perhaps, in haste), than an 'editor' (reconstructing the action as he worked from scene to scene).

writing. But before despatching this manuscript Webster found that it needed amplification and correction if its action was to be understood by a reader, so, with all possible speed, he attempted to supply this lack; having no theatre manuscript to help him, he made some slips and left some errors, redundancies, and omissions.

Webster was not finished with his play once the manuscript had reached the printer. Variants between different copies of the quarto show that press-corrections were made during the printing of some of the sheets.[1] These corrections are not of equal authority. In most formes the errors could have been identified and corrected by a proof-reader without consulting any authority beyond his own wits. But for a few formes, the outer formes of D and H and the inner formes of G and K, either the manuscript copy or Webster himself must have been consulted; for instance, mere reading of proof could not have shown that 'come' of II. i. 161 should have been 'am', nor that the omitted speech at II. i. 314 was the doctor's 'Sir I shall'. The variants which suggest that Webster was involved are restricted to G inner and H outer; they are the change of 'Looke' to 'Call' and 'thought on' to 'louely', and the additions of a Latin benediction and an entry for Monticelso with consequent changes of speech-prefixes; in each of these cases, if the printer's manuscript copy had had the correct reading, the incorrect reading would never have been set.

The introduction of these authorial corrections coincided with some interruption in the regular working of the printing-shop. Usually a large majority of the copies are found in the corrected state, but for H outer and I outer, only three or four copies out of fifteen are corrected; this suggests that for these formes the press was stopped unusually late in the printing-off. Moreover it is precisely at this point that the alternation of the two compositors became strangely muddled. It would seem that after sheet E they were meant to alternate regularly, each in turn setting four consecutive pages; for sheets F, G, L, and M this worked smoothly, but apparently A was delayed over G1–2^v and so the pattern was broken by B setting H1–1^v; the pattern was almost restored for sheet I, but K is again muddled until K3^v.

[1] They are listed in *S.B.*, viii (1956), 113–17.

The first edition of *The White Devil* was followed by three more quarto editions, dated 1631, 1665, and 1672. All these were straight reprints, clearing up some obvious errors and introducing some new ones. Thereafter the play appeared in Dodsley's collection, and was edited, together with Webster's other plays, by Alexander Dyce, W. C. Hazlitt, and F. L. Lucas. There have been many other editions of this play alone, but most of them appeared in textbooks and are without much editorial value.

This edition

The present text is that of the first quarto (which I shall call Q), modernized in spelling and, where desirable, emended.

In accordance with what has been deduced about the nature of the printer's copy, I have been more conservative in emending the dialogue than the stage-directions; most changes in the dialogue are rectifications of careless printing. I have also been guided by the differing abilities and predilections of the two workmen who set the type; sometimes this has affected my decision to emend, sometimes it has led me to accept one modernization rather than another. All emendations are noted in a collation, and, where there is any reasonable doubt about the appropriate modern form, Q's spelling is also there noted.

Since Q has no act or scene divisions, my text is printed continuously, with the customary divisions marked at the left of the page for ease of reference. Q's stage-directions are reproduced, emended where necessary, and supplemented by additional directions which are printed within square brackets. Speech-prefixes are regularized silently unless Q's form represents an alternative name (as '*Florence*' for '*Francisco*'); in such cases the change is noted in the collation.

Both compositors used italic type, more or less regularly, for stage-directions, and for proper names, Latin words and some quotations in the main text. This usage does not add to the meaning of the text, so I have followed normal modern practice in these matters, collating Q's italics only when they indicate quotation.[1] The use of italics and inverted commas to mark sententious pas-

---

[1] I have collated one exceptional use of italic type at I. ii. 233ff.

sages is, however, a special case. Dr G. K. Hunter has surveyed occurrences of such gnomic pointing in both printed and manuscript dramatic texts of the period,[1] and he found that it was 'not normally a part of the working text but [was] added to presentation [manuscript] copies as to "definitive" editions to give an impression of scholarship and moral weight'. Since the present text reproduces stage-directions which were probably added by Webster for literary rather than dramatic reasons, it would seem consistent to reproduce the literary gnomic pointing as well. But there is another fact to take into account: while both compositors set passages of dialogue abounding in sententious utterance, with only two exceptions, all the marked passages are in the work of Compositor A. Even if Webster was responsible for gnomic pointing in the manuscript copy,[2] the pointing of Q is unlikely to represent fully his selection of passages for this distinction. In view of this, I have regularized my text by omitting all Q's gnomic pointing, but have always recorded it in the collation.

Q's lining presents special difficulties. Some of these are due to the occasional freedom of Webster's versification, and to his habits of intermingling very short passages of prose,[3] and of using short, 'uncompleted' lines of verse as a means of dramatic emphasis.[4] But the difficulties inherent in these practices were greatly heightened by the printer's attempt to save paper and compress the long play within as short a compass as possible. Almost invariably, if there was space, the first line (or part line) of a new speech was printed in the same line of type as the last line (or part line) of the preceding one, regardless of whether, metrically, they were one, one-and-a-half, or two lines. Often, in the course of a speech, two lines, or one-and-a-half, were set together as one.[5] Occasionally the lining was altered to accommodate a stage-direction at approximately the cor-

---

[1] Cf. *Libr.*, 5th ser., vi (1951), 171–88.

[2] A printing-house 'editor' might have been responsible.

[3] See, for example, IV. ii. 37–205.

[4] On several occasions a stage-direction shows that the short line indicates a pause for special business (e.g. IV. i. 122 and V. iv. 135): on other occasions a change of thought or person addressed shows the need for a pause at a short line (e.g. III. ii. 251 and V. iii. 205).

[5] I haye not found any pages where inaccurate casting-off has obviously affected the line-arrangement.

rect place.[1] To cope with these various difficulties, I decided to pay very little regard to whether Q printed the last and first lines of two consecutive speeches in one or two lines of type;[2] I have not noted its arrangement in the collation unless there seemed special reason to do so. For the rest, vigilance is the only remedy, and I have collated all changes from Q. In general, I have tried to counteract the compositors' manifest tendencies by preferring to open out rather than compress the text.

Q's punctuation, despite some anomalies, seems to be more faithful to copy than either its capitals, italics, or lining. This is shown by the good 'dramatic' sense which its pointing usually gives and by a comparison of the practice of the two compositors in this and other texts. I have therefore tried to preserve as much as possible of Q's punctuation, noting all changes which affect the sense or dramatic force. There are, however, a few general points of procedure that need explaining. First, all single, short dashes are my own additions, unless the collation notes otherwise. I have introduced this form of punctuation because Q, in the work of both compositors, sometimes has only a comma, or no stop at all, between the expression of two different ideas.[3] If, in accordance with modern usage, I had introduced a colon or full stop at such places, the balance of the pointing as a whole would have been disturbed; a dash, marking a change of sense but not a pause in delivery, seemed the best way of retaining the pulse of the original. I have also added short, single dashes wherever one speaker is interrupted by another and Q has only a comma, colon, or no punctuation at all. Secondly, Compositor A had a tendency, more pronounced at the beginning of his work but continuing throughout, of ending a line of verse with an unnecessary comma, or with a colon or full stop where a comma is required;[4] in view of this I have, in doubtful cases, been more than usually ready to lighten his punctuation at the ends of

---

[1] As at II. i. 19 (Compositor A) and IV. ii. 128 (Compositor B).

[2] In MSS. of the period each speech usually begins on a new line, so that Q's arrangement almost certainly has no authority.

[3] After III. ii, both compositors used this form of punctuation less frequently, but it is once more common in the last scene of all.

[4] A's work in Heywood's *Golden Age* and Webster's *Monumental Column* also shows this characteristic.

lines. Thirdly, Q sometimes has a comma where 'that' is to be understood; this is grammatical rather than dramatic usage, and so, where the sense is clear and no pause is required, I have occasionally omitted these commas in accordance with the predominantly dramatic pointing of the text as a whole. Fourthly, all inverted commas have been introduced by me.

The various elided forms in Q are fairly evenly distributed among the work of its two compositors,[1] and usually seem to be in accordance with metrical requirements; I have therefore reproduced Q in this respect, noting all changes in the collation. I have added apostrophes to clarify some of Q's forms without notification in the collation. Where there is any doubt whether elision is intended (as in 'Like' for 'Alike', or 'Faith' for 'In faith'), the apostrophe is printed only if it appears in Q. I have followed modern usage in printing compound words (including such common ones as 'myself', 'thyself', etc.) and in introducing or deleting hyphens; this is because I have not found that Q varies such matters significantly.[2] I have also expanded all contractions. These changes are not recorded in the collation unless sense or metre seems to be significantly affected. A few old-fashioned spellings have been retained in the text itself, where a pun, quibble, or rhyme would be lost if the corresponding modern forms were used; such are 'travailing' (I. ii. 52), 'abhominable' (II. i. 310), 'Machivillian' (v. iii. 193), 'tallants' (v. iv. 8), and 'bin' in rhyme with 'sin' (v. iv. 22).

The collation records all substantive readings from subsequent editions which I consider might be correct, or which are of special textual interest. I have normally given only the first known authority for each reading. I have not recorded the correction of obvious technical slips, such as turned letters, where there is no doubt of the required reading. This present text is quoted in the collation in the same type as the text and is followed by its authority. Other readings are quoted in their original spelling but in the same type as the

---

[1] In Coverte's *Report* I have noticed only three occasions (at G1, G3, and K2) when Compositor A introduced an elision into the text; I noticed one when he omitted to mark one (at D3).

[2] It is sometimes impossible to decide whether a compound is printed as one or two words. In the Coverte reprint, Compositor A both added and deleted hyphens quite frequently.

relevant quotation from this text; where more than one authority is given for such a reading, the spelling is that of the first authority quoted. For collating the 1631, 1665, and 1672 quartos I have used the copies in the Folger Shakespeare Library. The following is a list of editions collated and of the symbols used to refer to them:

Q	First Quarto of 1612; variant readings due to proof-correction during printing are distinguished by 'Q^a' for the uncorrected state, 'Q^b' for the corrected; doubtful readings due to imperfect printing are designated as 'Q ?'.
Q2	Second Quarto of 1631.
Q3	Third Quarto of 1665.
Q4	Fourth Quarto of 1672.
Dod i	R. Dodsley, *A Select Collection of Old Plays* (1744), III.
Dod ii	R. Dodsley, *A Select Collection of Old Plays* (1780), VI.
Scott	Walter Scott, *Ancient British Drama* (1810), III.
Dod iii	R. Dodsley, I. Reed, O. Gilchrist, and J. P. Collier, *A Select Collection of Old Plays* (1825), VI.
Dyce i	A. Dyce, *The Works of John Webster* (1830), I.
Dyce ii	A. Dyce, *The Works of John Webster* (1857).
Haz	W. Hazlitt, *The Dramatic Works of John Webster* (1857), II.
Sym	J. A. Symonds, *The Best Plays of Webster & Tourneur* (1888).
Samp	M. W. Sampson, *The White Devil and The Duchess of Malfi* (Boston and London, 1904).
Thorn	A. H. Thorndike, *Webster and Tourneur* (New York, 1912).
Wheel	C. B. Wheeler, *Six Plays by Contemporaries of Shakespeare* (1915).
Luc	F. L. Lucas, *The Complete Works of John Webster* (1927), I.
Ol	E. H. C. Oliphant, *Shakespeare & His Fellow Dramatists* (New York, 1929).
Wal	H. R. Walley and J. H. Wilson, *Early Seventeenth-Century Plays* (New York, 1930).
Har	G. B. Harrison, *The White Devil* (1933).
Sp	H. Spencer, *Elizabethan Plays* (Boston, 1933).
Par	E. W. Parks and R. C. Beatty, *The English Drama* (New York, 1935).

THE WHITE DEVIL

In publishing this tragedy, I do but challenge to myself that
liberty, which other men have ta'en before me; not that I
affect praise by it, for, *nos hæc novimus esse nihil*, only since it
was acted, in so dull a time of winter, presented in so open and
black a theatre, that it wanted (that which is the only grace and   5
setting out of a tragedy) a full and understanding auditory: and
that since that time I have noted, most of the people that come
to that playhouse, resemble those ignorant asses (who visiting
stationers' shops their use is not to inquire for good books, but
new books) I present it to the general view with this confidence: 10

     Nec rhoncos metues, maligniorum,
     Nec scombris tunicas, dabis molestas.

If it be objected this is no true dramatic poem, I shall easily

5. black] *Q;* blank *conj. Steevens;* bleak *conj. Malone (ap. Dyce i).*

---

   1. *challenge*] claim.
   3. nos ... nihil] i.e., 'we know these things are nothing' (Martial, XIII, 2);
Webster could have found this quotation together with that of ll. 14–15 in
either Dekker's preface to *Satiromastix* (1602) or Florio, II, xvii (p. 335ᵃ).
   3–6. it ... auditory] Cf. Intro., pp. xx–xxii.
   4. *open*] The central yards of 'public' theatres were open to the sky; only
the smaller and more expensive 'private' theatres were fully indoors (cf.
Intro., pp. xxii–xxiii).
   11–12. Nec ... molestas] i.e., 'you [the poet's book] will not fear the
sneers of the malicious, nor be used for wrapping mackerel' (Martial, IV,
86).
   13–24. *If it* ...] Cf. Jonson's preface to *Sejanus* (1605): 'if it be obiected,
that what I publish is no true *Poëme;* in the strict Lawes of *Time.* I confesse
it: as also in the want of a proper *Chorus,* whose Habite, and Moodes are
such, and so difficult, as not any, whome I haue seene since the *Auntients,*
(no, not they who haue most presently affected Lawes) haue yet come in the
way off. Nor is it needful, or almost possible, in these our Times, and to
such Auditors, as commonly Things are presented, to obserue the ould
state, and splendour of *Drammatick Poëmes,* with preseruation of any popular delight. . . In the meane time, if in truth of Argument, dignity of Persons, grauity and height of Elocution, fulnesse and frequencie of Sentence,
I haue discharg'd the other offices of a *Tragick* writer, let not the absence of
these *Formes* be imputed to me, wherein I shall giue you occasion hereafter
(and without my boast) to thinke I could better prescribe, then omit the
due use, for want of a conuenient knowledge'. Cf. also, Marston's preface

confess it,—*non potes in nugas dicere plura meas: ipse ego quam dixi,*—willingly, and not ignorantly, in this kind have I faulted: 15
for should a man present to such an auditory, the most senten-
tious tragedy that ever was written, observing all the critical
laws, as height of style, and gravity of person, enrich it with the
sententious *Chorus*, and as it were lifen death, in the passionate
and weighty *Nuntius*: yet after all this divine rapture, *O dura* 20
messorum ilia, the breath that comes from the uncapable multitude is able to poison it, and ere it be acted, let the author
resolve to fix to every scene, this of Horace,

    – – – – *Haec hodie porcis comedenda relinques.*

To those who report I was a long time in finishing this tragedy, 25
I confess I do not write with a goose-quill, winged with two
feathers, and if they will needs make it my fault, I must answer them with that of Euripides to Alcestides, a tragic writer:
Alcestides objecting that Euripides had only in three days

---

19. lifen] *Q* (life'n)*; enliven *Q3*; liven *Dyce i.*

---

to *Malcontent* (1604): 'In plainenesse therefore understand, that in some
things I have willingly erred, ...'

14–15. non ... dixi] i.e., 'you cannot say more against my trifles than I
have said myself' (Martial, XIII, 2). See l. 3 n. above.

19–20. lifen . . . Nuntius] i.e., 'make death seem a living reality by means
of the passionate and forcible (or serious) report of a messenger'. O.E.D.,
lifen, only quotes Marston, *Antonio's Revenge* (1602), II. v.: 'and with such
sighs, / Laments and applications lyfen it, / As if ...' For *weighty* (and 'uncapable' of l. 21) cf. Marston, *ibid.*, Prol.: 'If any spirit breathes within
this round, / Uncapable of waightie passion ...'

20–1. O ... ilia] i.e., 'O strong stomachs of harvesters' (Horace, *Epod.*,
III, 4; alluding to the yokels' love of garlic).

24. Haec ... relinques] i.e., 'What you leave will be for the pigs to eat
today' (Horace, *Epist.*, I, vii, 19).

28–33. Euripides ...] The story is from Valerius Maximus, III, vii, 11. It
is found in L. Lloyd, *Linceus Spectacles* (1607), F1: 'As *Alcestides* a Tragi-
call Poet taunted Euripides, for that he was three dayes in making three
verses, sithence my selfe (said *Alcestides*) haue made three hundred Verses
in three dayes, *Euripides* answered him, and said, *Tui tantum in triduum
sunt mei autem in omne tempus*, Thy three hundred Verses are but for three
dayes, mine are for all times'. In Valerius, the poet's name is 'Alcestis', but
it occurs only in the dative 'Alcestidi', whence Lloyd's error has arisen.
Jonson repeats the story in *Discoveries* (*Wks*, VIII, 638) where, as in Valerius,
Alcestis boasts of only one hundred lines. No poet Alcestis is known; Lucas
suggested that Valerius meant Acestor, a butt of Aristophanes.

composed three verses, whereas himself had written three 30
hundred: 'Thou tell'st truth,' (quoth he) 'but here's the difference,—thine shall only be read for three days, whereas mine
shall continue three ages.'

Detraction is the sworn friend to ignorance: for mine own
part I have ever truly cherish'd my good opinion of other 35
men's worthy labours, especially of that full and height'ned
style of Master Chapman, the labour'd and understanding
works of Master Jonson: the no less worthy composures of the
both worthily excellent Master Beaumont, and Master Fletcher: and lastly (without wrong last to be named) the right 40
happy and copious industry of Master Shakespeare, Master
Dekker, and Master Heywood, wishing what I write may be
read by their light: protesting, that, in the strength of mine
own judgement, I know them so worthy, that though I rest
silent in my own work, yet to most of theirs I dare (without 45
flattery) fix that of Martial:

> – – – *non norunt, hæc monumenta mori.*

---

37. *understanding*] possibly 'displaying intelligence'; *O.E.D.* first records
this use (s.v., 2b) in J. Taylor, the water poet, in 1635.

42–3. *wishing . . . light*] Stoll compared Jonson, *Catiline*, Dedic.: 'In so
thick, and darke an ignorance, as now almost couers the age, I craue leaue
to stand neare your light: and, by that, bee read'.

47. non . . . mori] i.e., 'These monuments do not know how to die'
(Martial, x, ii, 12; comparing literature with ruined tombs).

[DRAMATIS PERSONAE

MONTICELSO, *a Cardinal, later Pope* PAUL IV.

FRANCISCO de MEDICI, *Duke of Florence; in the last Act, disguised as* MULINASSAR, *a Moor.*

The Duke of BRACCIANO, *otherwise, Paulo Giordano Orsini; husband first of Isabella, and later of Vittoria.*

GIOVANNI, *his son by Isabella.*

Count LODOVICO, *sometimes known as Lodowick; in love with Isabella; later a conspirator in the pay of Francisco.*

CAMILLO, *first husband of Vittoria; cousin to Monticelso.*

ANTONELLI ⎱ *friends to Lodovico; later conspirators in the pay of*
GASPARO ⎰ *Francisco.*

CARLO ⎱ *of Bracciano's household; in secret league with Francisco.*
PEDRO ⎰

HORTENSIO, *of Bracciano's household.*

FLAMINEO, *secretary to Bracciano; brother to Vittoria.*

MARCELLO, *his younger brother; of Francisco's household.*

ARRAGON, *a Cardinal.*

JULIO, *a doctor.*

ISABELLA, *first wife of Bracciano; sister to Francisco.*

VITTORIA COROMBONA, *a Venetian lady; wife first of Camillo, and later of Bracciano.*

CORNELIA, *mother to Vittoria, Marcello, and Flamineo.*

ZANCHE, *a Moor; servant to Vittoria; in love first with Flamineo, and later with Francisco.*

Ambassadors; Courtiers; Officers and Guards; Attendants. Conjuror; Chancellor, Register and Lawyers; Conclavist; Armourer; Physicians; Page.

Matron of the House of Convertites; Ladies.

SCENE: *Rome for the first four acts, Padua for the fifth.*]

Monticelso] The variant form 'Montcelso' occurs in some stage-directions.

Bracciano] Q's 'Brachiano' is probably an attempt to represent the Italian pronunciation of the name; but it is confusing, especially since the 'ch' in 'Zanche' is clearly meant to be pronounced as in Italian (cf. the form 'Zanke' in the marginal stage direction at v. vi. o.1).

secretary to Bracciano] an office of some influence; cf. E. Sharpham, *The Fleire* (1607), F2: '—. . . if I were a great man thou shouldst be my Secretarie.—And I hope I should discharge the place sufficiently: for I haue learning enough to take a bribe, and witte enough to be prowd . . .'

The White Devil

[I. i]

Enter Count LODOVICO, ANTONELLI *and* GASPARO.

Lod. Banish'd?

Ant.　　　　　It griev'd me much to hear the sentence.

Lod. Ha, ha, O Democritus thy gods
　　　That govern the whole world!—Courtly reward,
　　　And punishment! Fortune's a right whore.
　　　If she give aught, she deals it in small parcels,　　　　5

I. i] *Q4; not in Q; Act.* I. *Q3.*　　1–5.] *so Q3; as prose Q.*　　1. Banish'd?]
Q; Banish'd! *Dod ii.*

White Devil] The phrase was proverbial; cf. Tilley D310: 'The white
devil is worse than the black' (*c.* 1598).

L. Andrewes (*The Wonderful Combat* (1592), G6), describing Christ's
temptation in the wilderness, wrote that Satan 'commeth here lyke a white
diuell, or like a Diuine . . . with a Psalter in his hand'; he also quoted
2 Corinthians, xi. 14 in this connection: 'Satan himself is transformed into
an angel of light' (another proverbial phrase; cf. Tilley D231).

These usages were adapted in *The Revenger's Tragedy* (*c.* 1606), where
Vindice denounces the duke as 'Royall villaine, white diuill' (III. iv).

'White devil' sometimes meant, simply, 'hypocrite'; cf. T. Adams, *The
White Devil, or the Hypocrite Uncased* (1613).

I. i.] The general location of Acts I to IV is Rome.

1–5.] printed as prose in Q to make room for an ornamental capital for
'Banish'd'.

1. *Banish'd?*] In Jacobean texts '?' was often used where, today, we
would use '!', but in Compositor A's work in Q's first four sheets there is not
a single '?' which should certainly be modernized as '!'; moreover '!'
occurs six times as in modern usage.

2–4. *Democritus* . . .] Dent compared Guevara, *Dial of Princes*, tr. North
(1557), III. i (F4ᵛ): 'Democritus affirmed, there were 2. gods, whiche
gouerned the uniuersal world: yᵗ is to wete, reward, & punishment.' Cf. W.
Baldwin, *Moral Philosophy* (ed. 1584), D7: Democritus 'gaue his possessions & riches innumerable vnto the weale publike, onely reseruing to himselfe a little garden, wherein hee might . . . search out the secretes of nature'.

4. *Fortune's . . . whore*] intensifying the common proverb, 'Fortune is
fickle' (Tilley F606).

5. *parcels*] portions, instalments.

That she may take away all at one swoop.
This 'tis to have great enemies, God quite them:
Your wolf no longer seems to be a wolf
Than when she's hungry.

Gasp.   You term those enemies
Are men of princely rank.

Lod.   O I pray for them.   10
The violent thunder is adored by those
Are pash'd in pieces by it.

Ant.   Come my lord,
You are justly doom'd; look but a little back
Into your former life: you have in three years
Ruin'd the noblest earldom—

Gasp.   Your followers   15
Have swallowed you like mummia, and being sick
With such unnatural and horrid physic
Vomit you up i'th'kennel—

Ant.   All the damnable degrees
Of drinkings have you stagger'd through—one citizen
Is lord of two fair manors, call'd you master   20
Only for caviare.

Gasp.   Those noblemen
Which were invited to your prodigal feasts,

---

13. You are] *Q;* You're *Q3.*   19. drinkings] *Q;* drinking *Haz.*   you]
Q2 (you,); you, you *Q.*

---

6. *swoop*] *O.E.D.* (s.v., 3b) cites this passage for the meaning 'sudden descent, as of a bird of prey', quoting *Mac.,* IV. iii. 219. But this is unlikely to be Webster's sense here, for there is no reference to birds of prey. Rather the meaning 'blow, stroke' is required which *O.E.D.* (s.v., 1) cites in commercial usage in keeping with 'deals' and 'parcels' of l. 5.

7. *quite*] reward, requite.

8–9. *wolf . . . hungry*] i.e., a wolf only shows its true nature when it is hungry; so a needy man may appear wolfish, but a prosperous 'great man' who is equally destructive may appear friendly.

11–12.] Cf. v. vi. 276.

16. *mummia*] a pitch used for embalming, and, hence, embalmed flesh; both the pitch and the mummied flesh were recommended medicines.

18., *kennel*] gutter.

21. *caviare*] This delicacy was particularly rare in Webster's time, *O.E.D.* first recording it in 1591.

Wherein the phoenix scarce could scape your throats,
Laugh at your misery, as fore-deeming you
An idle meteor which drawn forth the earth   25
Would be soon lost i'th'air.

Ant.   Jest upon you,
And say you were begotten in an earthquake,
You have ruin'd such fair lordships.

Lod.   Very good,—
This well goes with two buckets, I must tend
The pouring out of either.

Gasp.   Worse than these,   30
You have acted certain murders here in Rome,
Bloody and full of horror.

Lod.   'Las they were flea-bitings:
Why took they not my head then?

Gasp.   O my lord
The law doth sometimes mediate, thinks it good
Not ever to steep violent sins in blood,—   35
This gentle penance may both end your crimes,
And in the example better these bad times.

Lod. So,—but I wonder then some great men scape
This banishment,—there's Paulo Giordano Orsini,
The Duke of Bracciano, now lives in Rome,   40

---

23. *the phoenix*] the rarest of dishes, for it was said that only one phoenix was alive at any one time and that each new bird rose from the bones or ashes of its predecessor; Dent compared Du Bartas, *Judith* (tr. Hudson, 1608), VI. 7–16: 'O glutton throtes, . . . the Phoenix sole can skarse escape your iawes.'

25. *meteor*] The word could be used for practically any atmospheric phenomenon. It was thought that the sun drew forth impurities from garbage and dead bodies in the form of vaporous exhalations, or meteors.

29–30. *well . . . either*] Cf. J. Heywood, *Epigrams* (1562): 'As fast as one goth, an other cumth in vre [i.e., use] / Twoo buckets in a well, come and go so sure' (quoted, Tilley B695). Webster often used this kind of dialogue; cf. *D.M.*, I. i. 292ff., *D.L.C.*, II. i. 176ff., and *A.V.*, IV. i. 216ff.

29. *tend*] attend to.

31. *acted*] brought about, or carried out (from L. *agere*; cf. *O.E.D.*, s.v., 2 and 3).

34. *mediate*] avoid extremes (so *O.E.D.*, s.v., 2b, for which this is the only citation); or, possibly, 'settle by mediation'.

37. *in the example*] i.e., by force of its example.

And by close pandarism seeks to prostitute
The honour of Vittoria Corombona,—
Vittoria, she that might have got my pardon
For one kiss to the duke.

Ant. Have a full man within you,—   45
We see that trees bear no such pleasant fruit
There where they grew first, as where they are new set.
Perfumes the more they are chaf'd the more they render
Their pleasing scents, and so affliction
Expresseth virtue, fully, whether true,   50
Or else adulterate.

Lod.   Leave your painted comforts,—
I'll make Italian cut-works in their guts
If ever I return.

Gasp.   O sir.

Lod.   I am patient,—
I have seen some ready to be executed
Give pleasant looks, and money, and grown familiar   55
With the knave hangman, so do I,—I thank them,
And would account them nobly merciful
Would they dispatch me quickly,—

Ant.   Fare you well,
We shall find time I doubt not to repeal   59
Your banishment.

Lod.   I am ever bound to you: *A sennet*
This is the world's alms;—pray make use of it,—   *sounds.*

---

46. such] *Q*b*;* sweet *Q*a.   47. they are] *Q2;* the are *Q.*   55. grown] *Q*
(growne)*;* grow *Dod i.*   60–1. *A . . . sounds.*] *This ed.; Enter | Senate Q;*
Sennet. (*at beginning of 0.1 below*) *Dyce i.*

45.] be the complete, the fully fortified and resolved man.

46–9. *We see . . . scents*] Dent compared Guevara, *Dial of Princes,* tr.
North (1557), III. xli (R2v): 'the tree beareth not so muche fruite, where it
first grewe, as there where it is againe planted: and the sauors are more
odiferous, when they are most chafed.' See also Tilley S746.

51. *painted comforts*] i.e., false comforts (a Jacobean set phrase).

52. *cut-works*] openwork embroidery, considered to be a particularly
Italian fashion.

60–1. A sennet sounds] A sennet was a flourish of trumpets accompany-
ing (rather than announcing) a ceremonial entrance (cf. J. S. Manifold,
Music in English Drama (1956), pp. 28–30). A *sennet* may 'sound', but not

Great men sell sheep, thus to be cut in pieces,
When first they have shorn them bare and sold their fleeces.

Exeunt.

[I. ii]

    Enter BRACCIANO, CAMILLO, FLAMINEO, VITTORIA
        COROMBONA [, *and Attendants*].

Brac. Your best of rest.
Vit.   Unto my lord the duke,
    The best of welcome. More lights, attend the duke.

[*Exeunt* CAMILLO *and* VITTORIA.]

Brac. Flamineo.
Flam.   My lord.
Brac.   Quite lost Flamineo.
Flam. Pursue your noble wishes, I am prompt
    As lightning to your service,—O my lord!   5
    (*whispers*) The fair Vittoria, my happy sister
    Shall give you present audience,—gentlemen
    Let the caroche go on, and 'tis his pleasure
    You put out all your torches and depart. [*Exeunt Attendants.*]
Brac. Are we so happy?
Flam.   Can't be otherwise?   10

62. sheep, thus] *Q;* sheep thus, *Luc.*

1. ii] *Q4; not in Q.*   0.2. *Corombona . . . Attendants*] *Dyce i; Corombona Q.*
2.1.] *Dod ii; not in Q; Exit Vit Q4.*   6. (*whispers*)] *Wheel;* (*whisper* (*after*
l. 7) *Q,* (*after l. 6*) *Dyce i.*   9. S.D.] *Dyce i; not in Q.*

'Enter'; possibly the phrasing of Q's direction implies that the trumpeters
appear on stage. But, more probably, the copy read simply 'Senate'
(a 17th-century spelling) and so gave rise to Q's literally impossible
note.

    The position of the direction in Q is probably correct, for there would
have been plenty of space to print it with the following entry had it
been so placed in the copy. By placing it early, Webster has emphasized the
clandestine nature of Lodovico's conference (it is broken off at the approach of other persons), and has built up expectancy for the first entrance
of Vittoria. The sennet also gives force to Monticelso's charge that Vittoria
'did counterfeit a prince's court' (III. ii. 75–6).

    61. *This*] i.e., the following maxim (cf. IV. ii. 246).
    make . . . it] profit by the knowledge.

    1. ii.] The location of this scene is Camillo's house.
    8. *caroche*] a stately kind of coach.

> Observ'd you not tonight my honour'd lord
> Which way soe'er you went she threw her eyes?
> I have dealt already with her chamber-maid
> Zanche the Moor, and she is wondrous proud
> To be the agent for so high a spirit.   15

Brac. We are happy above thought, because 'bove merit.

Flam. 'Bove merit! we may now talk freely: 'bove merit; what
is't you doubt? her coyness? that's but the superficies of
lust most women have; yet why should ladies blush to
hear that nam'd, which they do not fear to handle? O they   20
are politic, they know our desire is increas'd by the difficulty of enjoying; whereas satiety is a blunt, weary and
drowsy passion,—if the buttery-hatch at court stood continually open there would be nothing so passionate
crowding, nor hot suit after the beverage,—   25

Brac. O but her jealous husband.

Flam. Hang him, a gilder that hath his brains perish'd with
quick-silver is not more cold in the liver. The great bar-

---

14. Zanche] *Q*b; Zawche *Q*a.   22. whereas] *Dod i;* where a *Q.*   satiety]
*Q*b; sotiety *Q*a.

19–20. *why . . . handle*] Cf. Florio, II, xvii (p. 324ª): 'Wee have taught
ladies to blush, onely by hearing that named which they nothing feare to
doe'. In Webster there is a quibble on *handle*: (1) 'to touch' (cf. Florio's
'doe'), and (2) 'to talk of' (cf. *hear . . . named* and *Tit.*, III. ii. 29).

21–3. *desire . . . passion*] Cf. Florio, II, xv (p. 315ᵇ): 'discontent and
vexation . . . sharpen love and set it afire. Whereas satiety begets distaste: it
is a dull, blunt, weary, and drouzy passion'. As Dyce noted, the second part
of this quotation was used by Marston in *Fawn* (1606), IV. i: 'fie on this
satiety, tis a dul, blunt . . .'

22. *whereas*] Q's 'where' can mean 'whereas', but *whereas* occurs in
Florio and seems to be Webster's normal usage. Compositor B seldom
omitted final letters, but two of the three certain instances of it are in this,
his first, section of the book.

23. *buttery*] store-room for drinks and for provisions generally.

27–8. *gilder . . .*] In gilding an amalgam of gold and mercury was applied
to the object and then the mercury abstracted as a vapour by the application
of heat; through inhaling this poisonous vapour, gilders were prone to
tremors and insanity.

28. *liver*] the supposed seat of the passions.

28–9. *barriers*] For entertainment and display of prowess, duels were
fought on foot across a waist-high barrier; the usual weapons were pike
and sword.

riers moulted not more feathers than he hath shed hairs,
by the confession of his doctor. An Irish gamester that   30
will play himself naked, and then wage all downward, at
hazard, is not more venturous. So unable to please a
woman that like a Dutch doublet all his back is shrunk
into his breeches.
Shroud you within this closet, good my lord,—   35
Some trick now must be thought on to divide
My brother-in-law from his fair bed-fellow,—
Brac. O should she fail to come,—
Flam. I must not have your lordship thus unwisely amorous,
—I myself have loved a lady and pursued her with a great 40
deal of under-age protestation, whom some three or four
gallants that have enjoyed would with all their hearts have
been glad to have been rid of: 'tis just like a summer bird-
cage in a garden,—the birds that are without, despair to
get in, and the birds that are within despair and are in a 45

---

35. Shroud . . .] *indented Q.*

---

29. *feathers*] plumes struck from the combatants' helmets (so Steevens).
shed hairs] implying that he has undergone treatment for venereal disease; a common imputation (so Lucas). But possibly it here merely implies lack of virility.
30-2. *An . . . hazard*] From R. Stanyhurst's 'Description of Ireland' (viii) in Holinshed's *Chronicles* (ed. 1577): 'There is among them [i.e., the 'Wild Irish'] a brotherhood of Karrowes, that profer to play at chartes all ye yere long, and make it their onely occupation. They play away mantle and all to the bare skin, and then trusse themselues in strawe or in leaues, . . . For default of other stuffe, they paune theyr glibs [i.e., locks of hair on their foreheads], the nailes of their fingers and toes, their dimissaries [i.e., testicles], which they leese or redeeme at the curtesie of the wynner' (quoted H. D. Sykes, *N. & Q.*, xi ser., vii (1913), 342-3). Camillo would be ready to risk his dimissaries ('all downward'), for his virility was as nothing.
33. *Dutch doublet*] Lucas quoted Moryson, *Itinerary*, IV, 213: 'Their [i.e., the Netherlanders'] doublets are made close to the body, their breeches large'.
back] a weak back is another sign of impotency; a similar jest is made at the expense of Castruchio, in *D.M.*, II. iv. 54.
41. *under-age protestation*] youthful, inexperienced wooing.
43-6. *summer . . . out*] Cf. Florio, III, v (p. 433^a): 'It [marriage] may be compared to a cage, the birds without dispaire to get in, and those within dispaire to get out'.

consumption for fear they shall never get out: away away
my lord,—   [*Exit* BRACCIANO.]

Enter CAMILLO.

[*aside*] See here he comes, this fellow by his apparel
Some men would judge a politician,
But call his wit in question you shall find it   50
Merely an ass in's foot-cloth,—[*to Camillo*] how now brother—
What travailing to bed to your kind wife ?
Cam. I assure you brother no. My voyage lies
More northerly, in a far colder clime,—
I do not well remember I protest   55
When I last lay with her.
Flam. Strange you should lose your count.
Cam. We never lay together but ere morning
There grew a flaw between us.
Flam.   'Thad been your part
To have made up that flaw.
Cam.   True, but she loathes   60
I should be seen in't.
Flam.   Why sir, what's the matter ?
Cam. The duke your master visits me—I thank him,
And I perceive how like an earnest bowler
He very passionately leans that way
He should have his bowl run—

---

47. S.D.] *Dyce i; not in* Q.   48. *aside*] *This ed.; not in* Q.   51–2. Merely
. . . wife] *so Dod iii;* . . . cloath, / How . . . Q.   51. *to Camillo*] *This ed.; not
in* Q.   52. travailing] Q; travelling *Q3*.   55–6. I do . . . her] *so Dod ii;
one line* Q.   57. lose] *Q4;* loose Q.   60–1. True . . . in't] *so Dod iii; one
line* Q.   65. should] Q; would *Q3*.

---

51. *foot-cloth*] a rich cloth laid over the back of a horse to protect the
rider from mud and dust; it was a mark of dignity and rank (cf. *D.M.*, II. i.
41–3). Camillo's clothes are rich, but underneath he has the mind of an ass.

52. *travailing*] Q's spelling may be retained to indicate the quibble on (1)
'to journey', and (2) 'to work'; this was a common quibble.

57. *count*] a bawdy pun; cf. *H8*, II. iii. 41.

59, 60. *flaw*] part of a sequence of word-play; from *travailing* and *voyage*
grows the idea of two ships which *lay* together, and then of a *flaw*, or squall,
which parted them; Flamineo then turns the sense by using *flaw* as 'crack'
or 'breach'.

Flam.   I hope you do not think— 65
Cam. That noblemen bowl booty ? Faith his cheek
        Hath a most excellent bias, it would fain
        Jump with my mistress.
Flam.   Will you be an ass,
        Despite your Aristotle or a cuckold
        Contrary to your ephemerides   70
        Which shows you under what a smiling planet
        You were first swaddled ?
Cam.   Pew wew, sir tell not me
        Of planets nor of ephemerides—
        A man may be made cuckold in the day-time
        When the stars' eyes are out.
Flam.   Sir God boy you,   75
        I do commit you to your pitiful pillow
        Stuff'd with horn-shavings.

67–8. Hath . . . mistress] *so Dod iii; one line Q.*   69. your] *Q3;* you *Q*
75. God boy] *Q;* good-bye t' *Dod ii;* God b'wi' *Dyce i.*

---

66. *booty*] the 'greatest and grossest' cozenage in bowls (so Dekker, *Bel-man* (1608), quoted *O.E.D.*, s.v., 4b); two players combine together to the disadvantage of a third (*booty* originally meant, 'plunder, spoil').

For Camillo's usage, cf. Overbury, *Characters* (1615), 'A Chamber-Maide': 'only the knave *Sumner* makes her bowle booty, & over-reach the Maister'.

66–8. *cheek . . . mistress*] a sequence of bowling terms: Bracciano's *cheek* has a *bias* (or inclination), like that of the *bias* (or weight) in the *cheek* (or side) of a bowl, to come together with Vittoria's, as a bowl will *jump with* (or run up against) the *mistress* (or 'jack', the small white ball at which the bowls are aimed).

There is also a quibble on *jump* meaning 'to lie with' (cf. *Wint.*, IV. iv. 194–6).

Webster's contemporaries often wrote of love-making in metaphors derived from the game of bowls; they are elaborately worked out in Quarles, *Emblems* (1635), I, x. See also *Troil.*, III. ii. 50: 'So, so; rub on and kiss the mistress'.

69. *Despite your Aristotle*] 'illogically' (so Sampson), or 'despite your philosophical learning' (so Lucas).

70. *ephemerides*] astronomical almanacs.

75. *boy you*] a contracted form of 'be with you'; more often 'buy you'.

77. *horn-shavings*] Horns were said to grow on cuckolds' foreheads (cf. ll. 92–4 below). Flamineo may be grotesquely suggesting that the shavings

Cam.   Brother.

Flam.   God refuse me,
    Might I advise you now your only course
    Were to lock up your wife.

Cam.   'Twere very good.

Flam. Bar her the sight of revels.

Cam.   Excellent.   80

Flam. Let her not go to church, but like a hound
    In leon at your heels.

Cam.   'Twere for her honour—

Flam. And so you should be certain in one fortnight,
    Despite her chastity or innocence
    To be cuckolded, which yet is in suspense: 85
    This is my counsel and I ask no fee for't.

Cam. Come you know not where my night-cap wrings me.

Flam. Wear it a' th' old fashion, let your large ears come
    through, it will be more easy,—nay I will be bitter,—bar
    your wife of her entertainment: women are more willingly 90

---

82. leon] *Q;* leam *conj. Steevens, Haz;* lyam *Dyce i.*   90. entertainment:]
Q; entertainment ? *Wheel.*

---

came from this cuckold's attempt to cut away his horn, so hiding his shame.
    78–92. *Might I . . .*] Sampson suggested that Webster was here indebted
to R. Tofte's translation of Ariosto, *Satires* (1608), 14–4ᵛ: 'To go to feasts
and weddings mongst the best, / Is not amisse: for there suspect is least. /
Nor is it meet, that she the Church refraine, / Sith there is vertue, and her
noble traine. / . . . When shee's abroad, thy feare is of small worth, / The
danger's in the house when thou art forth.' Webster was certainly indebted
to this translation for *D.M.*, II. i. 34–7 (see Sampson).
    81. *but*] unless, except.
    82. *leon*] leash (probably a form of 'lyam').
    87.] a variation of the common proverb, 'Every man knows best where
the shoe pinches' (Tilley M129); Camillo means that there is not room in
his cap for his cuckold's horn. Flamineo mockingly takes him to mean that
there is not room for his long ears, the tokens that he is an ass. Both ideas
occur in *W.Ho,* I. i. 213–15.
    90. *entertainment:*] Wheeler's ' ?' may be right, for in his first section of
the book (B2–4ᵛ), Compositor B omitted about ten queries, while marking
ten correctly. However, Flamineo may sound more 'bitter' (l. 89) without
marking an ironic question here.
    90–1. *more . . . chaste*] Cf. Florio, II, viii (p. 198ᵇ): '[Women are] more
willingly and gloriously chaste, by how much fairer they are'.

and more gloriously chaste, when they are least restrain-
ed of their liberty. It seems you would be a fine capricious
mathematically jealous coxcomb, take the height of your
own horns with a Jacob's staff afore they are up. These
politic enclosures for paltry mutton makes more rebellion   95
in the flesh than all the provocative electuaries doctors
have uttered since last Jubilee.

Cam. This doth not physic me.

Flam. It seems you are jealous,—I'll show you the error of it
by a familiar example,—I have seen a pair of spectacles   100
fashion'd with such perspective art, that lay down but
one twelvepence a' th' board 'twill appear as if there
were twenty,—now should you wear a pair of these
spectacles, and see your wife tying her shoe, you would
imagine twenty hands were taking up of your wife's   105
clothes, and this would put you into a horrible cause-
less fury,—

95. mutton] mutton, *Q.*   makes] *Q;* make *Q4.*

---

92. *capricious*] There may be a pun on L. *caper*, the horned goat; cf.
AYL., III. iii. 8.

93. *mathematically*] with scientific accuracy.

94. *Jacob's staff*] an instrument for measuring altitudes.

95. *mutton*] slang for loose women; cf. *Meas.*, III. ii. 192–6. Flamineo
quibblingly alludes to the enclosures for sheep farming that were causing
hardship in country districts in England at this time.

mutton makes] Since the plural subject is separated from the verb
by a singular noun (cf. W. Franz, *Sprache Shakespeares*, p. 570), and
since Compositor B does not elsewhere add unwanted letters to the
ends of words, *Q*'s *makes* may be retained. For *Q*'s punctuation, see v. i.
125 n.

96. *provocative*] exciting to lust (the earliest sense; *O.E.D.* first records
as an adjective in 1621).

electuaries] medicinal conserves; here, specifically, aphrodisiacs.

97. *uttered*] put on sale.

Jubilee] This may be a specific reference to the year of jubilee instituted
by Pope Boniface VIII in 1300 as a time for obtaining indulgence by acts of
piety; the year recurred at intervals, first of a hundred years, then of fifty or
twenty-five years; for Webster, the 'last' would be 1600.

100–1. *spectacles . . . art*] Sampson quoted R. Scot, *Discovery of Witchcraft* (1584), XIII, xix, which refers to glasses cut by 'art perspective' so that
'one image shall seeme to be one hundred'. *perspective* = 'optical'.

102. *board*] card, or gaming, table.

Cam. The fault there sir is not in the eye-sight—

Flam. True, but they that have the yellow jaundice, think all
objects they look on to be yellow. Jealousy is worser, her   110
fits present to a man, like so many bubbles in a basin of
water, twenty several crabbed faces,—many times makes
his own shadow his cuckold-maker.

Enter [VITTORIA] COROMBONA.

See she comes,—what reason have you to be jealous of
this creature? what an ignorant ass or flattering knave   115
might he be counted, that should write sonnets to her
eyes, or call her brow the snow of Ida, or ivory of
Corinth, or compare her hair to the blackbird's bill,
when 'tis liker the blackbird's feather. This is all: be
wise, I will make you friends and you shall go to bed to-   120
gether,—marry look you, it shall not be your seeking, do
you stand upon that by any means,—walk you aloof, I
would not have you seen in't,—sister (my lord attends

---

110. worser] *Q; worse Q2.*   113–14. -maker. / See] *so Dod i; as continuous
prose Q.*   113.1.] *so Dod i; outer margin, small type, to left of line, with
asterisk after* -maker. *Q.*

109–10. *they . . . be yellow*] Cf. Florio, II, xii (p. 307ᵃ): 'Such as are
troubled with the yellow jandise deeme all things they looke upon to be
yellowish, . . .'

112. *makes*] Since Compositor B was not prone to add erroneous final
letters, it is preferable to retain Q and consider 'Jealousy' (l. 110), rather
than 'fits' (l. 111), as subject of this verb.

117. *Ida*] a range of mountains near Troy; the reference may be ironic for
Ida was usually associated with the green groves in which Paris lived as a
shepherd. Or, possibly, *Ida* is the mountain in Crete.

118. *Corinth*] The town seems to have had no particular connection with
'ivory'; it was renowned as a market for rich goods, and for its marble and
the beauty and number of its prostitutes (this last may provide an ironic
undertone, as with 'Ida' in previous line).

compare . . . bill] an ironically mundane allusion to the conventional
praise of a 'fair' beauty.

122. *stand*] insist.

123–44.] Compositor B was unable to clarify Flamineo's cross-talk;
for this passage it seems preferable to use brackets to mark asides to
Vittoria.

you in the banqueting-house), your husband is won-
drous discontented.   125

Vit. I did nothing to displease him, I carved to him at supper-
time—

Flam. (You need not have carved him in faith, they say he is a
capon already,—I must now seemingly fall out with
you.) Shall a gentleman so well descended as Camillo (a   130
lousy slave that within this twenty years rode with the
black guard in the duke's carriage 'mongst spits and
dripping-pans)—

Cam. Now he begins to tickle her.

Flam. An excellent scholar, (one that hath a head fill'd with   135
calves' brains without any sage in them), come crouching
in the hams to you for a night's lodging ?—(that hath an
itch in's hams, which like the fire at the glass-house hath
not gone out this seven years)—is he not a courtly
gentleman ? (when he wears white satin one would take   140
him by his black muzzle to be no other creature than a
maggot),—~~you are a goodly foil, I confess, well set out~~

128–30. (You ... you.)] You ... you. *Q;* You ... (They ... *Samp.*   133.
-pans] -pannes. *Q.*   135–6. (one ... them), come] one ... them,—come
Q; (one ... them, come *Thorn.*   137–9. (that ... years)]—that ...
yeares— *Q;* that ... years) *Thorn.*

126. *carved*] quibblingly used: (1) 'to serve' (at table), and (2) 'to show
courtesy', or 'to make advances' (cf. *Wiv.*, I. iii. 49).

128. *carved*] i.e., castrated.

129. *capon*] castrated cock, and, hence, eunuch (cf. *O.E.D.*, s.v., 2).

132. *black guard*] a common term for the lowest menials of a noble
household.

134. *tickle*] arouse, provoke.

136. *sage*] a quibble (as at IV. ii. 245), on (1) the herb used in cooking, and
(2) sagacity; 'calf' was a synonym for a young fool.

138. *glass-house*] glass-factory; Lucas noted that there was one near the
Blackfriars theatre. Webster again alludes to it in *D.M.*, II. ii. 7, *W.Ho*, II.
i. 215, and *A.Q.L.*, I. i. 323.

140–2. *when ... maggot*] Cf. Middleton, *Michaelmas Term* (1607), II. iii.
13: 'how does he appear to me when his white satin suit's on, but like a
maggot crept out of a nutshell—a fair body and a foul neck ?' (quoted by
Lucas).

142. *foil*] setting for a jewel, or, more precisely, a leaf of metal placed
under a transparent gem to enhance its brilliance.

~~(but cover'd with a false stone—yon counterfeit diamond).~~

Cam. He will make her know what is in me.   145

Flam. [*aside to Vittoria*] Come, my lord attends you, thou
    shalt go to bed to my lord.

Cam. Now he comes to't.

Flam. With a relish as curious as a vintner going to taste new
    wine,—[*to Camillo*] I am opening your case hard.   150

Cam. A virtuous brother a'my credit.

Flam. He will give thee a ring with a philosopher's stone in it.

Cam. Indeed I am studying alchemy.

Flam. Thou shalt lie in a bed stuff'd with turtles' feathers,
    swoon in perfumed linen like the fellow was smothered   155
    in roses,—so perfect shall be thy happiness, that as men
    at sea think land and trees and ships go that way they go,

143. cover'd] Q^b (couerd); couer Q^a.   yon] Q^b; your Q^a; you Q_2.
146. S.D.] *Haz subs.; not in Q, Samp.*   146–7. thou . . . lord] *Q; as aside
Samp.*   149–50. With . . . wine] *Q; as aside to Vittoria Haz.*   150. *to
Camillo*] *Wheel; not in Q; at end of speech Dod i, Haz; as aside to Vit. Samp.*
154–60. Thou . . . necessity] *Q; as aside Dod i.*

---

143. *cover'd . . . stone*] with a *double entendre*; for *cover'd*, cf. quotation at
ll. 342–4 n. below.

146–7. *Come, . . .*] Some editors have not marked an aside; so Vittoria
would understand Bracciano by *my lord*, and Camillo would understand
himself. But Camillo is only a gentleman (cf. ll. 130–3 above). Camillo's
next speech can be occasioned by observation, not by overhearing.

150. *I . . . hard*] with a *double entendre*; cf. *D.L.C.*, IV. ii. 255–6 and *Wiv.*,
IV. i. 64–70.

152–60.] Flamineo now speaks freely: to Vittoria he speaks of Bracciano,
while Camillo believes that all is said on his behalf.

152. *philosopher's stone*] the object of alchemists' search; it was reputed
to turn base metals into gold, to prolong life, and to cure diseases. For the
double entendre Lucas compared Lyly, *Gallathea*, v. i. 24–6.

155–6. *fellow . . . roses*] Sykes (quoted by Lucas) suggested two possible
origins for this: (1) Goulart, *Histoires Admirables* (tr. 1607), p. 458: 'a
Bishop of *Breslawe*, named *Lawrence*, was smothered with the smell of
Roses', and (2) Nashe, *Unfortunate Traveller* (1594), *Wks*, II, 243: 'Those
who were condemned to be smothered to death by sincking downe into the
softe bottome of an high built bedde of Roses, neuer dide so sweet a
death. . .'

156–8. *men . . . voyage*] Cf. Florio, II, xiii (pp. 310–11): 'As they who
travell by sea, to whom mountaines, fields, townes, heaven and earth,
seeme to goe the same motion, and keepe the same course they doe'.

so both heaven and earth shall seem to go your voyage.
Shalt meet him, 'tis fix'd, with nails of diamonds to inevitable necessity.   160

Vit. [*aside to Flamineo*] How shall's rid him hence ?

Flam. [*aside to Vittoria*] I will put breese in's tail, set him
          gadding presently,—[*to Camillo*] I have almost wrought
          her to it,—I find her coming, but—might I advise you
          now—for this night I would not lie with her, I would   165
          cross her humour to make her more humble.

Cam. Shall I, shall I ?

Flam. It will show in you a supremacy of judgement.

Cam. True, and a mind differing from the tumultuary opi-
          nion, for *quæ negata grata*.   170

Flam. Right—you are the adamant shall draw her to you,
          though you keep distance off:—

Cam. A philosophical reason.

Flam. Walk by her a'the nobleman's fashion, and tell her
          you will lie with her at the end of the progress—   175

Cam. Vittoria, I cannot be induc'd, or as a man would say
          incited ...

Vit. To do what sir ?

---

159. Shalt] Shal't *Q*; Shall't *Dod i*.   161. S.D.] *Q4 subs.; not in Q.*
162. S.D.] *Haz subs; not in Q.*   163. S.D.] *Dyce ii; not in Q; to right of
text Q4.*   177. incited ...] incited. *Q.*

---

159. *Shalt*] For Q's 'Shal't', see v. i. 44 n.

159–60. *fix'd . . . necessity*] Dent compared de Serres' Supplement to
Matthieu, *General Inventory*, tr. Grimeston (1607), p. 936 : '. . . that which
was yesterday voluntarie, is this day fastened with nayles of Diamonds to
an ineuitable necessity.'

162. *breese*] gadflies (*breese* has the same form, sing. and plural).

163. *presently*] immediately, at once.

164. *coming*] complaisant, forward; cf. Jonson, *Epicoene* (pf. 1609), v. i.
77–8 : 'is shee comming, and open, free ?'

169. *tumultuary*] irregular, haphazard.

170. *quæ negata grata*] i.e., what is denied is desired; cf. Tilley F585.

171. *adamant*] an alleged mineral of great hardness, sometimes identified
with the loadstone or magnet (by false derivation from L. *ad-amare*).

173. *philosophical*] probably a quibble: (1) 'wise', and (2) 'scientific' (i.e.,
of natural philosophy).

175. *progress*] state visit or journey; cf. v. i. 208–9 n.

176. *man*] Lucas suggested that the unmanly Camillo is being unconsciously ironic.

Cam. To lie with you tonight; your silkworm useth to fast
    every third day, and the next following spins the better.   180
    Tomorrow at night I am for you.

Vit. You'll spin a fair thread, trust to't.

Flam. But do you hear—I shall have you steal to her chamber
    about midnight.

Cam. Do you think so? why look you brother, because you   185
    shall not think I'll gull you, take the key, lock me into the
    chamber, and say you shall be sure of me.

Flam. In troth I will, I'll be your gaoler once,—
    But have you ne'er a false door?

Cam. A pox on't, as I am a Christian—tell me tomorrow how   190
    scurvily she takes my unkind parting—

Flam. I will.

Cam. Didst thou not mark the jest of the silkworm? good-
    night—in faith I will use this trick often,—

Flam. Do, do, do.   *Exit* CAMILLO.   195
    So now you are safe. Ha ha ha, thou entanglest thyself in
    thine own work like a silkworm—

Enter BRACCIANO.

187. say] *Q; so Q4.*   188–9. In . . . door] *so Q; as prose Dyce ii.*   193–4.
Didst . . . often] *so Q; . . . silkworm? / Good-. . . Dod i.*   193. mark] *Q4;*
make *Q.*   197. silkworm] *Q;* silk-worm. Act I. Scen. 3 *Q4.*   197.1.] *so*
Q; after l. 201 Q4.

179–80. *your . . . better*] In fact silkworms fast two days before they spin,
and then spin for not more than nine days consecutively without food (cf.
T. Moffett, *Silkworms* (1599), 12ᵛ–3—one of the current publications
urging the culture of silkworms in England).

182.] In capping Camillo's simile, Vittoria uses a very common ironic
phrase; cf. Sharpham, *Cupid's Whirligig* (1607), ed. 1926, p. 28: 'haue not
I spun a faire thred . . . to be a verry Baude, and arrant wittall', and Tilley
T252.

191. *scurvily*] sourly, rudely (cf. *O.E.D.*, s.v., 1b, 1607).

unkind] possibly with two shades of meaning: (1) 'unnatural', and (2)
'ungentle'.

196–7. *entanglest . . . silkworm*] Cf. Florio, III, xiii (p. 547ᵇ): 'She [the
mind] . . . uncessantly goeth turning, winding, building, and entangling
her selfe in hir owne worke, as doe our silke-wormes, and therein stifle hir
selfe.'

197.1.] Compositor B has interrupted the consecutive prose for this

Come sister, darkness hides your blush,—women are
like curst dogs, civility keeps them tied all daytime, but
they are let loose at midnight, then they do most good or   200
most mischief,—my lord, my lord—
Brac. Give credit: I could wish time would stand still
And never end this interview, this hour,
But all delight doth itself soon'st devour.

>   ZANCHE *brings out a carpet, spreads it and*
>   *lays on it two fair cushions. Enter* CORNELIA
>   [*listening, behind.*]

Let me into your bosom happy lady,   205
Pour out instead of eloquence my vows,—
Loose me not madam, for if you forego me
I am lost eternally.

---

199. civility] *Q;* cruelty *Q2.*   204.1–3.] *so this ed.; to right of ll. 203–6 Q;*
Zanche . . . cushions. (after l. 201) | Enter . . . listening (after l. 204) Dod i.
204.3. *listening, behind.*] *Dyce i subs.; not in Q; listening MS. correction,*
Garrick copy Q, Dod i.   207. Loose] *Q;* Lose *conj. this ed.*   207–8.
Loose . . . eternally] *so Dod ii; one line Q.*

---

direction (as at l. 195 above), so he almost certainly is following copy in so
placing it here, rather than at l. 202.

198–201. *women . . . mischief*] Cf. Florio, III, v (p. 450[a]): 'they [women]
will have fire: . . . Luxurie is like a wild beast, first made fiercer with tying,
and then let loose'. Webster repeats the idea in *D.M.*, IV. i. 12–15.

199. *curst*] savage, vicious; but the word was often used in weakened
senses, as 'shrewish'.

civility] good polity or social behaviour.

202. *Give credit*] i.e., believe me.

204.1–3.] Compositor B fitted this direction into the only available space
in the text-space in the vicinity; its position in Q cannot therefore be taken
as representing its exact position in the copy (cf. v. i. 62.1–2 n.).

If the copy had directed either Zanche or Cornelia to enter immediately
after l. 201 above, there would have been space for a brief direction; we
may therefore presume that they enter *after* that point.

The fact that Zanche '*brings out*' a carpet and cushions suggests that
Bracciano and Vittoria do not remain in some sort of 'inner' stage (as Lucas
suggested); such properties could have been 'discovered' (cf. v. iv. 64) if the
action was meant to take place there. The lovers probably play this scene
centre-stage.

207. *Loose*] 'To loose' and 'to lose' were not distinguished in spelling;
cf., for example, Compositor B's setting at v. ii. 40. Both verbs may be,

Vit.   Sir in the way of pity
   I wish you heart-whole.

Brac.   You are a sweet physician.

Vit. Sure sir a loathed cruelty in ladies   210
   Is as to doctors many funerals:
   It takes away their credit.

Brac.   Excellent creature.
   We call the cruel fair, what name for you
   That are so merciful?

Zan.   See now they close.

Flam. Most happy union.   215

Cor. [*aside*] My fears are fall'n upon me, O my heart!
   My son the pandar: now I find our house
   Sinking to ruin. Earthquakes leave behind,
   Where they have tyrannized, iron, or lead, or stone,
   But—woe to ruin—violent lust leaves none.   220

Brac. What value is this jewel?

Vit.   'Tis the ornament
   Of a weak fortune.

Brac. In sooth I'll have it; nay I will but change
   My jewel for your jewel.

Flam.   Excellent,
   His jewel for her jewel,—well put in duke.   225

Brac. Nay let me see you wear it.

Vit.   Here sir.

Brac. Nay lower, you shall wear my jewel lower.

Flam. That's better—she must wear his jewel lower.

208–9. Sir . . . -whole] *so Dod ii; one line Q.*   211–12. Is . . . credit] *so
Dod ii; . . . funeralls: It . . . (one line) Q.*   216. aside] *Haz subs.; not in Q.*
219. or lead] *Q;* lead *Q2.*   221–2. 'Tis . . . fortune] *so Q; one line Q2.*
226. sir.] *Q;* sir? *Dyce i.*

---

quibblingly, implied here: (1) *Loose* = 'to release, withdraw hold over',
and (2) 'Lose' in modern senses and, possibly, = 'to ruin, destroy'. The
quibble would be continued by 'forego', meaning 'to forsake, neglect' or,
perhaps, 'to lose' (cf. *O.E.D.*, s.v., 7b), and clinched by 'lost' of l. 208.
   221. *jewel*] For the *doubles entendres*, cf. *Per.*, IV. vi. 164–5 and *Lucr.*,
l. 1191, where *jewel* stands for virginity and married chastity respective-
ly.

Vit. To pass away the time I'll tell your grace,
     A dream I had last night.
Brac.   Most wishedly.   230
Vit. A foolish idle dream,—
     Methought I walk'd about the mid of night,
     Into a church-yard, where a goodly yew-tree
     Spread her large root in ground,—under that yew,
     As I sat sadly leaning on a grave,   235
     Chequered with cross-sticks, there came stealing in
     Your duchess and my husband, one of them
     A pick-axe bore, th'other a rusty spade,
     And in rough terms they gan to challenge me,
     About this yew.
Brac.   That tree.
Vit.   This harmless yew.   240
     They told me my intent was to root up
     That well-grown yew, and plant i'th'stead of it
     A withered blackthorn, and for that they vow'd

233, 234, 240 (*bis*), 242, 254. yew] *italicized Q* (Eu).   240. tree.] *Q*;
tree ? *Dod i.*

233, etc. *yew*] Italics in Q point the pun of l. 240; cf. IV. iii. 120 where the
same compositor did not italicize the same word.
    Lucas noted that the pun is found in Lyly, *Sapho*, III. iv. 75–9, where it is
shortly followed by an allegorical dream about a 'tall Caedar'.
    236. *cross-sticks*] This has not been satisfactorily explained. Sampson,
followed by Lucas, suggested 'patterned with crosses stuck in graves'; but
cross-sticks has not been found in this sense and it is, perhaps, simpler to
suppose that, by the light of the night sky, the overhanging and inter-
twined branches of the yew tree threw a chequered pattern of light and
shade on the grave. Dent suggested some allusion to witchcraft, for *cross-
sticks* were used to raise storms (cf. 'whirlwind', l. 252). In his second edition, Lucas suggested that *cross-sticks* refers to the criss-crossed osiers protecting or binding together the grave (he compared Broad, *Pop. Antiq.*,
p. 485, and Gay, *Fifth Pastoral*, 145–6.
    243. *blackthorn*] The dream is obscurely allusive: Vittoria represents
Isabella and Camillo as saying that she (Vittoria) intends to displace the
worthy, and therefore noble, Camillo (the 'yew') with a shameful, and
therefore ignoble, Bracciano (the 'blackthorn'); this, of course, is not
Vittoria's own view and so she continues representing Bracciano (and not
Camillo) as the 'yew' that strikes on her behalf. She gives, in fact, two
opposing interpretations of the dream.

To bury me alive: my husband straight
With pick-axe gan to dig, and your fell duchess   245
With shovel, like a Fury, voided out
The earth and scattered bones,—Lord how methought
I trembled, and yet for all this terror
I could not pray.

Flam. No the devil was in your dream.   250

Vit. When to my rescue there arose methought
A whirlwind, which let fall a massy arm
From that strong plant,
And both were struck dead by that sacred yew
In that base shallow grave that was their due.   255

Flam. Excellent devil.
She hath taught him in a dream
To make away his duchess and her husband.

Brac. Sweetly shall I interpret this your dream,—
You are lodged within his arms who shall protect you,   260
From all the fevers of a jealous husband,
From the poor envy of our phlegmatic duchess,—
I'll seat you above law and above scandal,
Give to your thoughts the invention of delight
And the fruition,—nor shall government   265
Divide me from you longer than a care
To keep you great: you shall to me at once
Be dukedom, health, wife, children, friends and all.

Cor. [*coming forward*] Woe to light hearts—they still forerun
our fall.

Flam. What Fury rais'd thee up? away, away! *Exit* ZANCHE. 270

247. earth] *Q; earth, Q2.*   256–7. Excellent ... dream] *so Q; one line
Dyce i.*   263. scandal,] *Q; scandal. Q4.*   269. S.D.] *Dyce ii; not in
Q; at end of line Dod i subs.*

262. *envy*] The modern sense is required here, but probably with some
trace of the original one of 'ill-will, malice' (cf. L. *invidia*).

phlegmatic] A person's 'temperament' was thought to be governed by the
proportions of their bodily 'humours'; an excess of phlegm, the watery
humour, was manifested in a cold, dull temper.

265–7. *shall ... great*] i.e., 'I shall only spend such time on affairs of
government as is required to maintain your state'.

Cor. What make you here my lord this dead of night ?
      Never dropt mildew on a flower here,
      Till now.
Flam.   I pray will you go to bed then,
      Lest you be blasted ?
Cor.   O that this fair garden
      Had with all poisoned herbs of Thessaly   275
      At first been planted, made a nursery
      For witchcraft; rather than a burial plot,
      For both your honours.
Vit.   Dearest mother hear me.
Cor. O thou dost make my brow bend to the earth,
      Sooner than nature,—see the curse of children!   280
      In life they keep us frequently in tears,
      And in the cold grave leave us in pale fears.
Brac. Come, come, I will not hear you.
Vit.   Dear my lord.
Cor. Where is thy duchess now adulterous duke ?
      Thou little dream'd'st this night she is come to Rome. 285
Flam. How ? come to Rome,—
Vit.   The duchess,—
Brac.   She had been better,—
Cor. The lives of princes should like dials move,
      Whose regular example is so strong,

272–3. Never . . . now] *so Dyce i; one line Q.*   273. pray] *Q;* pray you *conj. this ed.*   275. with all] *Q3;* all *Q;* all with *MS. correction, Garrick copy Q, Dod i.*   277. than] *Q3* (then); *not in Q.*   282. leave] *Q4;* leaues *Q.*   284. adulterous] *Q;* adult'rous *Dod i.*   285. dream'd'st] *Q;* dream'st *Q3.*   she is] *Q;* she's *Q4.*

---

273. *pray*] Compositor A may have omitted a following 'you'; cf. his errors at ll. 275 and 277 below, and II. i. 108, II. ii. 23.7, etc.

275. *Thessaly*] a district in ancient Greece, famous for witchcraft and poisonous drugs and herbs.

281. *frequently*] incessantly.

282. *leave*] Q *might* be right (cf. I. ii. 95 n.), but Compositor A elsewhere adds erroneous final letters (as at III. ii. 193, 276, and 286 and v. ii. 2, etc.), and 'keep' and 'us' of l. 281 make emendation desirable.

287. *dials*] sundials, clocks. Lucas suggested an allusion to Guevara's *Dial of Princes* (tr. 1557); it listed the attributes of a perfect prince.

They make the times by them go right or wrong.
Flam. So, have you done ?
Cor.   Unfortunate Camillo.   290
Vit. I do protest if any chaste denial,
    If anything but blood could have allayed
    His long suit to me,—
Cor.   I will join with thee,
    To the most woeful end e'er mother kneel'd,—
    If thou dishonour thus thy husband's bed,   295
    Be thy life short as are the funeral tears
    In great men's,—
Brac.   Fie, fie, the woman's mad.
Cor. Be thy act Judas-like—betray in kissing,
    May'st thou be envied during his short breath,
    And pitied like a wretch after his death.   300
Vit. O me accurst.   *Exit* VITTORIA.
Flam. [*to Cornelia*] Are you out of your wits ? My lord,
    I'll fetch her back again.
Brac.   No I'll to bed.
    Send Doctor Julio to me presently,—
    Uncharitable woman thy rash tongue   305
    Hath rais'd a fearful and prodigious storm,—

293. me,] me. *Q.*   297. men's] *This ed.;* mens. *Q;* men's deaths *Dod i;*
men's— *Dod ii;* mens eyes *conj. Luc.*   299. May'st] *Q4;* Maiest *Q.*
300. his] *Q2;* this *Q.*   301. *Vittoria*] *Victoria Q.*   302. S.D.] *Freeman.*
302. wits ? My lord,] *Haz. subs.;* wits, my Lord *Q;* wits, my lord ? *Q4.*
303. again.] againe ? *Q.*

289. *times*] a quibble: (1) particular periods of time, and (2) state of
affairs at a particular period.
    292. *blood*] ambiguous: (1) 'life-blood', and (2) 'passion' or, as often in
Shakespeare, 'sensual appetite' (cf. *Mer.V.*, III. i. 36). Vittoria clearly puns
on the two senses in v. vi. 240–1.
    293. *I ... thee*] Presumably Vittoria is already kneeling.
    297. *men's,*—] Elsewhere in this play, sentences are interrupted by other
speakers but not so that a possessive, or an adjective, is left without its noun
(save, possibly, at III. ii. 59); 'lives' should be inferred from 'life' of the
preceding line.
    299. *envied*] Cf. l. 262 n. above.
    302. S.D.] Suggested by A. Freeman, *N. & Q.*, n.s., 10 (1963), 101–2.
    306. *prodigious*] ominous, portentous.

Be thou the cause of all ensuing harm. 　　*Exit* BRACCIANO.

Flam. Now, you that stand so much upon your honour,
　　Is this a fitting time a'night think you,
　　To send a duke home without e'er a man ? 　　　　　310
　　I would fain know where lies the mass of wealth
　　Which you have hoarded for my maintenance,
　　That I may bear my beard out of the level
　　Of my lord's stirrup.

Cor. 　　　　　　　　What ? because we are poor,
　　Shall we be vicious ?

Flam. 　　　　　　　　Pray what means have you 　　　315
　　To keep me from the galleys, or the gallows ?
　　My father prov'd himself a gentleman,
　　Sold all's land, and like a fortunate fellow,
　　Died ere the money was spent. You brought me up
　　At Padua I confess, where I protest 　　　　　320
　　For want of means,—the university judge me,—
　　I have been fain to heel my tutor's stockings
　　At least seven years: conspiring with a beard ꭰ oᴦ
　　Made me a graduate,—then to this duke's service:
　　I visited the court, whence I return'd, 　　　　　325
　　More courteous, more lecherous by far,
　　But not a suit the richer,—and shall I,
　　Having a path so open and so free
　　To my preferment, still retain your milk

324. service:] seruice, *Q.*

313–14. *bear . . . stirrup*] i.e., cease to walk beside my lord's horse, on a level with his stirrup; cf. *D.M.*, III. ii. 228–31.

322–3. *heel . . . years.*] Poor scholars often kept themselves at a university by performing menial tasks for their college or for richer students or tutors; cf. J. B. Mullinger, *The University of Cambridge*, II (1884), 397–400, which instances such tasks as rousing one's master for morning chapel, cleaning his boots, and dressing his hair.

323–4. *conspiring . . . graduate*] The exact sense is doubtful; possibly Flamineo merely means that he had grown up and so completed the residence requirements (so that mere years, rather than wisdom or scholastic knowledge, had made him a graduate), or that he had graduated through the connivance of some very senior man for whom he had done some service.

In my pale forehead ? no this face of mine   330
I'll arm and fortify with lusty wine
'Gainst shame and blushing.
Cor. O that I ne'er had borne thee,—
Flam.   So would I.
I would the common'st courtezan in Rome
Had been my mother rather than thyself.   335
Nature is very pitiful to whores
To give them but few children, yet those children
Plurality of fathers,—they are sure
They shall not want. Go, go,
Complain unto my great lord cardinal,   340
Yet may be he will justify the act.
Lycurgus wond'red much men would provide
Good stallions for their mares, and yet would suffer
Their fair wives to be barren.
Cor. Misery of miseries.   *Exit* CORNELIA. 345
Flam. The duchess come to court, I like not that,—
We are engag'd to mischief and must on:
As rivers to find out the ocean
Flow with crook bendings beneath forced banks,
Or as we see, to aspire some mountain's top,   350
The way ascends not straight, but imitates

---

336. pitiful] *Q2* (pittifull)*;* pittfull *Q.*   341. Yet] *Q;* It *Q2.*   349.
crook] *Q* (crooke)*;* crookt *Q3.*

342–4.] Cf. Plutarch, 'Lycurgus', *Lives* (ed. 1898), I, 188: 'Lycurgus
thought also there were many foolish vain joys and fancies, in . . . other
nations, touching marriage: seeing they caused their bitches and mares to
be lined and covered with the fairest dogs and goodliest stalons that might
be gotten, . . . and kept their wives notwithstanding shut up safe under lock
and key, for fear lest other than themselves might get them with child, although they were sickly, feeble brained, and extreme old.'

347–54.] G. K. Hunter (*N. & Q.*, n.s., iv (1957), 53) compared Chapman, *Byron's Conspiracy* (1608), III. i. 68ff.: '. . . wind about them like a
subtle River / That . . . still finds out / The easiest parts of entry to the
shore'.

349. *crook*] crooked (cf. 'crook-back').
forced] fabricated, artificial (cf. *O.E.D.*, s.v., 4 & 6, 1612).
350. *aspire*] mount up to, attain.

The subtle foldings of a winter's snake,
So who knows policy and her true aspect,
Shall find her ways winding and indirect.   *Exit.*

[II. i]

Enter FRANCISCO DE MEDICI, *Cardinal* MONTICELSO, MARCELLO,
ISABELLA, *young* GIOVANNI, *with*
Attendants.

Fran. Have you not seen your husband since you arrived ?
Isa. Not yet sir.
Fran.   Surely he is wondrous kind,—
If I had such a dove-house as Camillo's
I would set fire on't, were't but to destroy

352. winter's] Q (Winters); Winter Q2.

II. i] *Q4; not in Q; Act. 2. Q3.*   0.1. *Monticelso] Mountcelso Q.*   0.3.
Attendants] This ed.; little Iaques the Moore Q.   3. such a] *Q2;* a
such *Q.*

---

352. *winter's snake*] Q2 may be right in view of Compositor A's characteristics (cf. I. ii. 282 n.) and 'winter plums' of v. vi. 65.
    Topsell (*History* (1607–8), B2ᵛ) notes that 'Serpents in the Winter time,
. . . growe dead and stiffe through cold' and moving with difficulty may
more easily be caught. Webster may, however, be alluding to the mythical
amphisbaena, an adder with two heads; Batman's version of Bartholomaeus (ed. 1582, Mmm6ᵛ) notes that it 'runneth and glideth and wrigleth
with wrinkles, corcels, & draughts of the body after either head: and among
Serpents, onelye this . . . putteth out himselfe in cold'.

    II. i. 0.3. Attendants] Q's 'little Iaques the Moore' is only a name; he says
and does nothing. Since the printer's copy came from Webster and not
from the theatre (cf. Intro., p. lxvi), we may suppose that either Webster
thought of writing a part for Jaques and then did not do so, or else that he
had written one and then excised it; in either case Webster's second
thoughts (as represented by the extant dialogue) are best served by omitting
Jaques' name from the stage-direction. There are similar 'ghost' characters
in II. ii and v. i, and in *D.M.* and *D.L.C.*
    Precedent for excising his name may be found in the practice of excising
the 'good' quarto's Innogen from *Ado*, I. i.
    3. *dove-house*] ironic; doves were proverbially innocent, loving, and
tame (cf. Tilley D572–4).

The pole-cats that haunt to't, – – – my sweet cousin.   5
Giov. Lord uncle you did promise me a horse
        And armour.
Fran.   That I did my pretty cousin,—
        Marcello see it fitted.
Mar. My lord—the duke is here.
Fran.   Sister away—
        You must not yet be seen.
Isa.   I do beseech you   10
        Entreat him mildly, let not your rough tongue
        Set us at louder variance,—all my wrongs
        Are freely pardoned, and I do not doubt
        As men to try the precious unicorn's horn
        Make of the powder a preservative circle   15
        And in it put a spider, so these arms
        Shall charm his poison, force it to obeying
        And keep him chaste from an infected straying.
Fran. I wish it may. Be gone.   *Exit* [ISABELLA].

9–10. Sister . . . seen] *so Samp; one line Q.*   10–11. I . . . tongue] *so Dod ii;*
. . . mildely, / Let . . . Q.   19. I . . . chamber] *so Dyce i; . . . gone. /*
Void . . . Q.   19. S.D.] *Luc; Exit Q; not in Dyce i; Exeunt Isabella, and*
Giovanni (to right of ll. 18–19) Q4, (. . . Giovanni, &c) Dod ii.

5. *pole-cats*] often used abusively; they are destructive, ferret-like
animals, with a fetid smell.
        haunt] have resort.
14–18.] Reputed specimens of *unicorn's horn* were indeed *precious* and
commanded great prices; Topsell (*History* (1607–8), Sss4ᵛ) believed there
were only twenty whole horns in Europe.
        Isabella describes (ll. 14–16) a test which was supposed to prove whether
a sample was true unicorn's horn. Birch's *History of the Royal Society*, i
(1756), tells how on 24 July 1661, 'A circle was made with powder
of unicorn's horn, and a spider set in the middle of it'; it was said that
if the horn were genuine, the spider would remain inside the circle of
powder.
        Isabella then alludes (l. 17) to the horn's supposed power as a charm
against poison; Topsell described this power and Sir T. Browne (*Vulgar
Errors* (1646), III, xxiii) investigated it.
18. *infected*] probably in a double sense: (1) 'tainted' (with poison), and
(2) 'depraved, immoral' (cf. *O.E.D.*, s.v., 2).

Enter BRACCIANO, *and* FLAMINEO.

Void the chamber,—
[*Exeunt* FLAMINEO, MARCELLO,
GIOVANNI, *and Attendants.*]
You are welcome, will you sit ? I pray my lord   20
Be you my orator, my heart's too full,—
I'll second you anon.
Mont.   Ere I begin
Let me entreat your grace forego all passion
Which may be raised by my free discourse.
Brac. As silent as i'th'church—you may proceed.   25
Mont. It is a wonder to your noble friends,
That you that have as 'twere ent'red the world
With a free sceptre in your able hand,
And have to th' use of nature well applied
High gifts of learning, should in your prime age   30
Neglect your awful throne, for the soft down
Of an insatiate bed. O my lord,
The drunkard after all his lavish cups,
Is dry, and then is sober, so at length,
When you awake from this lascivious dream,   35
Repentance then will follow; like the sting

19.1.] *so Q; at end of line Dyce i.*   19.2–3.] *This ed.; not in Q, Q4, Dod ii;*
Exeunt . . . , *and Jaques Luc.*   27. that have] *Luc;* haue *Q;* hauing *Q2,*
Dyce i, Haz; who have *Wheel.*   29. have] *Q, Wheel, Luc; not in Dyce i;*
having *Haz.*

---

19. S.D's.] The comings and goings are awkward, perhaps intentionally
so, to stress the contrived nature of the occasion.
27. *that*] Lucas' emendation is to be preferred because, (1) 'That' at the
beginning of the line could have confused the compositor, and (2) Compositor A has omitted single short words elsewhere in this section of the
book (cf. I. ii. 275 and 277, and II. ii. 23.7). It might be argued that *that*
was left to be implied (as, for example, at I. i. 10 and 12), but in this context
the usage would be confusing (and Monticelso's is a considered speech)
and the metre seems to require an extra syllable.
29. *use of nature*] i.e., profit, or advantage (cf. *O.E.D.*, s.v., 20), of natural
disposition, or capacity.
36–7. *sting . . . tail*] Lucas compared J. Maplet, *Green Forest* (1567), K5:

Plac'd in the adder's tail: wretched are princes
When fortune blasteth but a petty flower
Of their unwieldy crowns; or ravisheth
But one pearl from their sceptre: but alas!   40
When they to wilful shipwreck loose good fame
All princely titles perish with their name.
Brac. You have said my lord,—
Mont.   Enough to give you taste
How far I am from flattering your greatness?
Brac. Now you that are his second, what say you?   45
Do not like young hawks fetch a course about—
Your game flies fair and for you,—
Fran.   Do not fear it:
I'll answer you in your own hawking phrase,—
Some eagles that should gaze upon the sun
Seldom soar high, but take their lustful ease,   50
Since they from dunghill birds their prey can seize,—
You know Vittoria,—

40. sceptre] *Q; Scepters Q2.   41. to] Q;* thro' *Dod i.   loose] Q;* lose
Dod i.   44. greatness?] Q; greatness. *Q4.   52. Vittoria,] Q;* Vittoria?
Dod i.

'It [the adder] loueth . . . to hurt both with tooth and mouth, and also with
his hinder part or taile'.

38–9. *flower . . . crowns*] The word-play is two-fold: *flower* can mean
'jewel, precious thing' (cf. *O.E.D.*, s.v., 6) and so is appropriate to *crowns*,
but *crown* can also mean 'garland of flowers' and so is appropriate to
flower (cf. *R3*, III. ii. 41).

41. *loose*] See I. ii. 207 n.; again both words might be implied, but 'to . . .
shipwreck' suggests that *loose* is dominant here.

42. *titles*] a quibble: (1) 'appellation of rank' (cf. 'name', following), and
(2) 'rights, possessions' (cf. *Mac.*, IV. ii. 7).

name] good name, honour (cf. l. 389 below).

46.] Lucas quoted Turberville, *Falconry* (ed. 1611), H7ᵛ: 'For most
commonly if a yong hawke bee let flee at olde game, shee will turne tayle,
and cowardly giue it ouer'.

49–51.] Cf. Intro., p. xxi. It was said that an eagle was the only bird that
could gaze at the sun (cf. *3H6*, II. i. 91).

For *ease*, cf. Turberville, *ibid.*, FIᵛ: 'if after your Hawke haue flowen the
Hearon, you should let her flee any other sleighter fowle or prey, Shee will
. . . become a slugge and take disdaine, . . . and will turn to her owne ease
. . . shee will giue herselfe to prey vpon fowle, that is more easie to reach,

Brac.   Yes.

Fran.   You shift your shirt there
    When you retire from tennis.

Brac.   Happily.

Fran. Her husband is lord of a poor fortune
    Yet she wears cloth of tissue,—

Brac.   What of this?   55
    Will you urge that my good lord cardinal
    As part of her confession at next shrift,
    And know from whence it sails?

Fran.   She is your strumpet,—

Brac. Uncivil sir there's hemlock in thy breath
    And that black slander,—were she a whore of mine   60
    All thy loud cannons, and thy borrowed Switzers,
    Thy galleys, nor thy sworn confederates,
    Durst not supplant her.

Fran.   Let's not talk on thunder,—
    Thou hast a wife, our sister,—would I had given
    Both her white hands to death, bound and lock'd fast   65
    In her last winding-sheet, when I gave thee
    But one.

Brac.   Thou hadst given a soul to God then.

Fran.   True.
    Thy ghostly father with all's absolution,
    Shall ne'er do so by thee.

Brac.   Spit thy poison,—

---

53. tennis.] *Q;* tennis? *Dod i.*   Happily] *Q3;* Happely *Q;* Haply *Q4.*
54. lord] *Q;* the Lord *MS. correction, Garrick copy Q, Dod i.*   63. on] *Q;*
of *Q4.*

---

and will forget or foreslow her valiant hardinesse' (quoted by Lucas).
   53. *Happily*] commonly used as 'haply' (cf. IV. iii. 133).
   55. *cloth of tissue*] rich cloth (often interwoven with gold or silver).
   61. *Switzers*] Swiss mercenaries were frequently used in feuds between
Italian noblemen.
   63. *supplant*] overthrow, dispossess.
   67. *Thou . . . God*] Lucas suggested that this was a sneer at Isabella's
saintliness and compared *R3*, I. ii. 104–5: '—O, he was . . . virtuous. / —
The fitter for the King of heaven, that hath him'.

Fran. I shall not need, lust carries her sharp whip   70
          At her own girdle,—look to't for our anger
          Is making thunder-bolts.
Brac.   Thunder ? in faith,
          They are but crackers.
Fran.   We'll end this with the cannon.
Brac. Thou'lt get nought by it but iron in thy wounds,
          And gunpowder in thy nostrils.
Fran.   Better that   75
          Than change perfumes for plasters,—
Brac.   Pity on thee,
          'Twere good you'd show your slaves or men condemn'd
          Your new-plough'd forehead—Defiance!—and I'll meet
              thee,
          Even in a thicket of thy ablest men.
Mont. My lords, you shall not word it any further   80
          Without a milder limit.
Fran.   Willingly.
Brac. Have you proclaimed a triumph that you bait
          A lion thus ?
Mont.   My lord.

78. new-plough'd] *Q* (new plow'd)*; new plum'd *conj. Dyce i.*   forehead
. . . and] fore-head defiance, and *Q; forehead-defiance. *Dod i;* forehead-
defiance; and *Dod iii;* fore-head. Defiance!—and *Luc.*   82–3. Have . . .
thus] *so Dod i; . . . baite a / *Lyon . . . Q

---

73. *crackers*] then, as now, a kind of firework, but since the word was used
of boasters and braggarts, it may here also mean 'boasts' or 'lies' (the latter
sense is first recorded in *O.E.D.* (s.v., 3) in 1625).

75. *gunpowder . . . nostrils*] i.e., your own cannon will do no harm to me,
they will only annoy you.

76. *change . . . plasters*] i.e., after indulgence, reap venereal disease.

78. *new-plough'd*] i.e., newly furrowed with anger. Lucas compared
Cæs., IV. iii. 43–4: 'Go show your slaves how choleric you are, / And make
your bondmen tremble.'

Defiance!] Some drastic repunctuation is necessary. Dodsley's solution
is metrically difficult and the compound hard to parallel elsewhere in Webster. An abrupt change of mood and address, as implied by the punctuation
of this edition, is paralleled in other speeches by Bracciano (cf. l. 181 below,
and III. ii. 178).

82. *bait*] i.e., enrage as if for a fight in a Roman spectacle.

Brac.   I am tame, I am tame sir.

Fran. We send unto the duke for conference
　　　'Bout levies 'gainst the pirates, my lord duke   85
　　　Is not at home,—we come ourself in person,
　　　Still my lord duke is busied,—but we fear
　　　When Tiber to each prowling passenger
　　　Discovers flocks of wild ducks, then my lord—
　　　'Bout moulting time I mean,—we shall be certain   90
　　　To find you sure enough and speak with you.

Brac.   Ha?

Fran. A mere tale of a tub, my words are idle,—
　　　But to express the sonnet by natural reason,

Enter GIOVANNI.

　　　When stags grow melancholic you'll find the season—
Mont. No more my lord, here comes a champion   95

---

83 (*bis*). I am] *Q;* I'm *Dod i.*   84, 92. *Fran.*] *Flan. Q.*   88. prowling]
Dod iii; proling *Q.*   93.1.] so *Q;* to right of l. 95 *Q4;* after l. *94 Dod i.*

---

89. *wild ducks*] i.e., prostitutes (so Lucas who quoted *Troil.*, III. ii. 56).
See also *N.Ho*, v. i. 249–50: 'I am a Cockold . . .: who lay ith segges with
you to night wild-ducke[?]'

90. *moulting time*] i.e., end of the mating season (cf. l. 94 and note
below). Lucas pointed out that there was also an allusion to loss of hair
through venereal disease (cf. notes at I. ii. 29 and l. 92 below).

92. *tale of a tub*] i.e., cock-and-bull story. There is also an allusion to the
sweating-tub used as a cure for venereal disease.

93. *express . . . reason*] i.e., put it simply, or, possibly, explain this simple
matter scientifically (cf. B. Rich, *Faults* (1606), E4: 'One will prooue by
naturall reason, that fire is hote: . . .'). *sonnet* = 'short poem or verse' (not
necessarily of regular form, but usually amatory).

93.1.] The position of this direction is suspect for it is as near to l. 95 as
the text-space in Q permitted (cf. Intro., p. lxiv).

94. *When . . . melancholic*] Cf. Topsell, *History* (1607–8), M5: 'When one
month or sixe Weekes of their rutting is past, they [stags] grow tame againe,
. . . and returne to their solitary places, digging euery one of them by himselfe a seuerall hole or Ditch, wherein they lie, to aswage the stronge
sauour of their lust, for they stinke like Goates, . . .'

season] Spencer suggested that this was an allusion to the salt, or pickle,
of the powdering tub (cf. l. 92 n. above).

95. *champion*] Giovanni enters wearing the armour he was promised in
l. 7 above.

Shall end the difference between you both,
Your son the prince Giovanni,—see my lords
What hopes you store in him, this is a casket
For both your crowns, and should be held like dear:
Now is he apt for knowledge, therefore know   100
It is a more direct and even way
To train to virtue those of princely blood,
By examples than by precepts: if by examples
Whom should he rather strive to imitate
Than his own father? be his pattern then,   105
Leave him a stock of virtue that may last,
Should fortune rend his sails, and split his mast.

Brac. Your hand boy—growing to a soldier?
Giov. Give me a pike.
Fran. What practising your pike so young, fair coz?   110
Giov. Suppose me one of Homer's frogs, my lord,

108. to a] *Q2;* to *Q.*

101–5.] Cf. Pettie, III, 54–5: 'the Mayster doeth them not so much good by his good instructions, as the Father doeth them harme by his evill Example, for that they are by nature lead rather to followe his steppes, then the maysters precepts . . .'—this is a version which Webster certainly came across (cf. App. IV) of a commonplace theme (cf., for example, Tilley E213). *even* (l. 101) = 'straightforward', or 'just'.

106. *stock*] (1) 'line of ancestors', and (2) 'store, fund'.

108. *to a soldier*] As Greg pointed out (*R.E.S.*, iv (1928), 454), the noun does not necessarily require an article; but the run of the line seems to require it and Compositor A's certain errors in omitting short words (cf. l. 27 n. above) makes this easy slip the more likely.

Stoll compared the martial ambitions of the boys in *R3, 3H6, Mac.,* and *Cor.,* but Lucas suggested that Giovanni might owe something to Prince Henry of England who died on 6 Nov. 1612 and for whom Webster wrote an elegy; it was widely known that Prince Henry wished to emulate his namesake's deeds at Agincourt (cf. Webster's *Monumental Column,* ll. 66–98, and 'French foe' of l. 122 below) and, at an early age, practised martial arms.

111–12. *Homer's . . . bulrush*] from *The Battle of Frogs and Mice,* a burlesque epic, attributed to Homer; Webster seems to have used W. Fowldes' translation of 1603: '. . . all the *Frogs,* from greatest to the least, / For these ensuing warres their studies bend / To get such weapons as befit them best: . . . / In their left hands these water-souldiers bare / A leafe of Colewort for a trusty shield, / And in their right (for all parts armed were) / They tosse a bulrush for a pike or speare' (F1ᵛ).

Tossing my bulrush thus,—pray sir tell me
Might not a child of good discretion
Be leader to an army?

Fran.　　　　　　　Yes cousin a young prince
Of good discretion might.

Giov.　　　　　　Say you so,—　　　　115
Indeed I have heard 'tis fit a general
Should not endanger his own person oft,
So that he make a noise, when he's a'horseback
Like a Dansk drummer,—O 'tis excellent!
He need not fight, methinks his horse as well　　120
Might lead an army for him; if I live
I'll charge the French foe, in the very front
Of all my troops, the foremost man.

Fran.　　　　　　　What, what,—

Giov. And will not bid my soldiers up and follow
But bid them follow me.

Brac.　　　　　　Forward lapwing.　　125
He flies with the shell on's head.

Fran.　　　　　　Pretty cousin,—

Giov. The first year uncle that I go to war,
All prisoners that I take I will set free
Without their ransom.

Fran.　　　　　Ha, without their ransom,—

115. so,] *Q; so? Q4.*　　118. make] *Q;* makes *Q3.*　　129. ransom,] *Q;*
ransome? *Q4.*

---

115. *discretion*] Giovanni's answer suggests that Francisco is mocking
him by taking his *discretion* of l. 113 in the Falstaffian sense of 'prudence'
(i.e., knowing when to hang back), not as he had used it, in the sense of
'discernment, mature judgement'; cf. *1H4*, v. iv. 121 where Falstaff mis-
applies an old maxim about the better part of valour. The Falstaffian sense
is found in *King and no King* (pf. 1611), IV. iii. 62.

116–23.] Cf. *D.M.*, I. i. 93–104. A similar discussion is in Florio, II. xxi.

119. *Dansk*] Danish; cf. Sharpham, *Cupid's Whirligig* (1607), ed. 1926,
p. 23: '—doe you not perceiue his heart beate hither?—I, for all the world
like a Denmarke Drummer'.

125. *lapwing*] a type of precocity; Sampson quoted Meres, *Wit's
Treasury* (1598), G4: 'the Lapwing runneth away with the shell on her
head, as soone as she is hatched'.

	How then will you reward your soldiers	130

How then will you reward your soldiers   130
That took those prisoners for you?

Giov.   Thus my lord,
I'll marry them to all the wealthy widows
That fall that year.

Fran.   Why then the next year following
You'll have no men to go with you to war.

Giov. Why then I'll press the women to the war,   135
And then the men will follow.

Mont.   Witty prince.

Fran. See a good habit makes a child a man,
Whereas a bad one makes a man a beast:
Come you and I are friends.

Brac.   Most wishedly,
Like bones which broke in sunder and well set   140
Knit the more strongly.

Fran. [*to Attendant off-stage*] Call Camillo hither—
You have received the rumour, how Count Lodowick
Is turn'd a pirate.

Brac.   Yes.

Fran.   We are now preparing
Some ships to fetch him in:

[*Enter* ISABELLA.]

133. fall] *Q4;* fals *Q.*   141. S.D.] *conj. Luc, this ed.; not in Q; Exit
Marcello (at end of line) Dyce i; Exit Servant (at end of line) Samp.*   141.
Camillo] *Q;* Isabella *Q4.*   142. Lodowick] *Q (Lodowicke);* Lodovico
Q4.   143. pirate.] *Q;* pirate? *Dyce i.*   144.1.] *Wheel subs.; not in Q;
to right of l. 147 Q4; after* entreaty *(l. 146) Dod ii; after l. 146 Dyce i.*

---

133. *fall*] Q might be right (cf. Franz, *Sprache Shakespeares*, p. 574), but
Compositor A was prone to add erroneous final letters; cf. I. ii. 282 n.

141. *Camillo*] There is no need to emend; Isabella can enter of her own
accord (we may imagine that she has been overhearing); moreover, the
following dialogue concerns the pirates against whom Camillo is to have a
commission. Camillo enters later (l. 278).

142–3. *Count . . . pirate*] Pirates did indeed maraud along the coasts of
Italy at the time portrayed in this play, but there is no reference to them in
contemporary accounts of Vittoria; some accounts say Lodovico was a
bandito, but not a pirate (so Boklund).

behold your duchess,—

We now will leave you and expect from you   145
Nothing but kind entreaty.

Brac.   You have charm'd me.

Exeunt FRANCISCO, MONTICELSO,
GIOVANNI.

You are in health we see.

Isa.   And above health
To see my lord well,—

Brac.   So—I wonder much
What amorous whirlwind hurried you to Rome—

Isa. Devotion my lord.

Brac.   Devotion?   150
Is your soul charg'd with any grievous sin?

Isa. 'Tis burdened with too many, and I think
The oft'ner that we cast our reckonings up,
Our sleeps will be the sounder.

Brac.   Take your chamber.

Isa. Nay my dear lord I will not have you angry,—   155
Doth not my absence from you two months
Merit one kiss?

Brac.   I do not use to kiss,—
If that will dispossess your jealousy,
I'll swear it to you.

Isa.   O my loved lord,
I do not come to chide; my jealousy?   160
I am to learn what that Italian means,—

146.1–2.] *so Dyce i subs.; to right of ll. 144–5 Q; to right of ll. 145–6 Q4; after*
entreaty (*l. 146*) *Dod i, Dod ii.*   148. So] *Q;* So, *Q4;* So: *Dod iii.*
153. reckonings] *Q;* reck'nings *Q4.*   156. two] *Q;* now two *Q3;* these
two *MS. correction, Garrick copy Q, Samp.*   161. am] *Q*b*;* come *Q*a*.

146.1–2.] misplaced in Q for lack of text-space.

150. *Devotion*] Isabella means devotion to her husband; Bracciano mis-
interprets.

156. *two*] Some word may have been omitted (cf. A's errors elsewhere),
but it would be hard to say which. The stress which the irregular metre
seems to give to *two* strengthens Q's reading a little.

161. *am to learn*] i.e., am ignorant of (a common phrase).

          You are as welcome to these longing arms
          As I to you a virgin.

Brac.   O your breath!
    Out upon sweet meats, and continued physic!
    The plague is in them.

Isa.   You have oft for these two lips   165
    Neglected cassia or the natural sweets
    Of the spring violet,—they are not yet much withered,—
    My lord I should be merry,—these your frowns
    Show in a helmet lovely, but on me,
    In such a peaceful interview methinks   170
    They are too too roughly knit.

Brac.   O dissemblance!
    Do you bandy factions 'gainst me ? have you learnt
    The trick of impudent baseness to complain
    Unto your kindred ?

Isa.   Never my dear lord.

Brac. Must I be haunted out, or was't your trick   175
    To meet some amorous gallant here in Rome
    That must supply our discontinuance ?

Isa. I pray sir burst my heart, and in my death
    Turn to your ancient pity, though not love.

---

163. virgin] *Q;* virgin. *Kisses him Ol.*   171. too too] to too *Q;* too *Dod i.*
173–4. The . . . kindred] *so Q*ᵇ; . . . vnto / Your . . . *Q*ᵃ.   175. haunted] *Q;*
hunted *Q4.*

Italian] Italians were proverbially jealous; cf. *C.C.,* v. i. 259: 'the
Italian Plague . . . , Jealousie', and *W.Ho,* III. iii. 82–5: 'why your Italians
in general are so Sun-burnt with these Dog-daies, that your great Lady
there thinkes her husband loues her not, if hee bee not Iealious'.
    166. *cassia*] properly a kind of cinnamon, but also, in poetic usage (deriv-
ed in part from Psalms, xlv. 8), a fragrant shrub or plant (so *O.E.D.*); it is
referred to as a most expensive and luxurious perfume in *D.M.,* IV. ii. 217.
    172. *bandy*] band together, league (cf. F. *se bander;* so *O.E.D.*).
    175. *haunted*] The word appears apt but, while 'to haunt' could mean
'to frequent' or 'to visit', *O.E.D.* gives no closer or earlier parallel to this
usage than Lord Orrery (s.v., 5, *c.* 1679): 'My ghost shall haunt thee out in
every place'. Perhaps 'hunted' should be read (but nowhere else in this
text has a 'u' been misread as an 'a'). Or, possibly, Webster intended to
combine the meanings of both verbs.

Brac. Because your brother is the corpulent duke,   180
          That is the great duke,—'Sdeath I shall not shortly
          Racket away five hundred crowns at tennis,
          But it shall rest upon record: I scorn him
          Like a shav'd Polack,—all his reverend wit
          Lies in his wardrobe, he's a discreet fellow   185
          When he's made up in his robes of state,—
          Your brother the great duke, because h'as galleys,
          And now and then ransacks a Turkish fly-boat,
          (Now all the hellish Furies take his soul,)
          First made this match,—accursed be the priest   190
          That sang the wedding mass, and even my issue.
Isa. O too too far you have curs'd.
Brac.   Your hand I'll kiss,—
          This is the latest ceremony of my love,
          Henceforth I'll never lie with thee, by this,
          This wedding-ring: I'll ne'er more lie with thee.   195
          And this divorce shall be as truly kept,
          As if the judge had doom'd it: fare you well,
          Our sleeps are sever'd.
Isa.   Forbid it the sweet union
          Of all things blessed; why the saints in heaven
          Will knit their brows at that.
Brac.   Let not thy love   200
          Make thee an unbeliever,—this my vow
          Shall never, on my soul, be satisfied

186. he's] *Q;* he is *Dyce i.*   192. too too] to too *Q.*

180–1. *corpulent . . . great*] Cf. Intro., p. xxix, n.
    182. *Racket . . . tennis*] For the popularity of tennis among courtiers in
the reign of James I, cf. *Shakespeare's England*, II, 459–62. See also *D.M.*,
I. i. 154–6.
    183–4. *scorn . . . Polack*] i.e., as of no account: Fynes Moryson reported
that 'the Germans say, that in Poland they care no more to kill a man then
a dogg' (*Shakespeare's Europe*, ed. Hughes (1903), p. 390). For *shav'd*,
Reed quoted Moryson, *Itinerary* (1617), III, iv: 'The Polonians shave all
their heads close, excepting the haire of the forehead, which they nourish
very long, . . .'
    188. *fly-boat*] small, fast sailing boat, or pinnace.
    202. *satisfied*] fulfilled, discharged fully.

With my repentance : let thy brother rage
Beyond a horrid tempest or sea-fight,
My vow is fixed.

Isa.   O my winding-sheet,   205
Now shall I need thee shortly! dear my lord,
Let me hear once more, what I would not hear,—
Never ?

Brac. Never.

Isa. O my unkind lord may your sins find mercy,   210
As I upon a woeful widowed bed
Shall pray for you, if not to turn your eyes
Upon your wretched wife, and hopeful son,
Yet that in time you'll fix them upon heaven.

Brac. No more,—go, go, complain to the great duke.   215

Isa. No my dear lord, you shall have present witness
How I'll work peace between you,—I will make
Myself the author of your cursed vow—
I have some cause to do it, you have none,—
Conceal it I beseech you, for the weal   220
Of both your dukedoms, that you wrought the means
Of such a separation, let the fault
Remain with my supposed jealousy,—
And think with what a piteous and rent heart,
I shall perform this sad ensuing part.   225

Enter FRANCISCO, FLAMINEO, MONTICELSO, MARCELLO.

Brac. Well, take your course—my honourable brother!

Fran. Sister,—this is not well my lord,—why sister!—
She merits not this welcome.

Brac.   Welcome say ?
She hath given a sharp welcome.

208. Never ?] Neuer. *Q.*   209. Never.] Neuer ? *Q.*   225. part.] *Q;*
part. / Act. 2. Scen. 2 *Q4.*   225.1. *Monticelso*] Montcelso *Q.*   *Marcello*]
Samp; Marcello, Camillo Q; not in Dyce i.   226. course] *Q;* course; *Q4.*
227. sister !] sister, *Q.*

204. *horrid*] dreadful.
219.] Leęch compares *Lr.,* IV. vii. 75.

Fran.   Are you foolish ?
        Come dry your tears,—is this a modest course,   230
        To better what is nought, to rail and weep ?
        Grow to a reconcilement, or by heaven,
        I'll ne'er more deal between you.
Isa.   Sir you shall not,
        No though Vittoria upon that condition
        Would become honest.
Fran.   Was your husband loud,   235
        Since we departed ?
Isa.   By my life sir no,—
        I swear by that I do not care to lose.
        Are all these ruins of my former beauty
        Laid out for a whore's triumph ?
Fran.   Do you hear ?—
        Look upon other women, with what patience   240
        They suffer these slight wrongs, with what justice
        They study to requite them,—take that course.
Isa. O that I were a man, or that I had power
        To execute my apprehended wishes,
        I would whip some with scorpions.
Fran.   What ? turn'd Fury ? 245
Isa. To dig the strumpet's eyes out, let her lie
        Some twenty months a-dying, to cut off
        Her nose and lips, pull out her rotten teeth,
        Preserve her flesh like mummia, for trophies

---

230. course,] *Dod i;* course. *Q;* course ? *Q2;* course *Luc.*   231. weep ?]
weepe, *Q;* weepe: *Q2.*   234. No] *Q;* Not *conj. Luc.*   237. lose] *Q4;*
loose *Q.*   241. with] *Q;* and with *MS. correction, Garrick copy Q,
Dod i.*

---

231. *nought*] probably a quibble: (1) 'of little or no account', and (2)
'wicked' or 'worthless'.
235. *honest*] chaste (cf. *Oth.,* III. iii. 384).
244. *apprehended*] conscious, fully understood.
245. *whip . . . scorpions*] Cf. *D.M.,* II. v. 78: 'find scorpions to string
my whips'. The idea derives from I Kings, xii. 11: 'my father hath chas-
tised you with whips, but I will chastise you with scorpions'—where
'scorpions' is thought to mean knotted or barbed scourges (so *O.E.D.*).
249. *mummia*] Cf. I. i. 16 n.

Of my just anger: hell to my affliction   250
Is mere snow-water: by your favour sir,—
Brother draw near, and my lord cardinal,—
Sir let me borrow of you but one kiss,
Henceforth I'll never lie with you, by this,
This wedding-ring.

Fran.   How? ne'er more lie with him?—   255

Isa. And this divorce shall be as truly kept,
As if in thronged court, a thousand ears
Had heard it, and a thousand lawyers' hands
Seal'd to the separation.

Brac. Ne'er lie with me?

Isa.   Let not my former dotage   260
Make thee an unbeliever,—this my vow
Shall never, on my soul, be satisfied
With my repentance,—*manet alta mente repostum.*

Fran. Now by my birth you are a foolish, mad,
And jealous woman.

Brac.   You see 'tis not my seeking.   265

Fran. Was this your circle of pure unicorn's horn
You said should charm your lord? now horns upon thee,
For jealousy deserves them,—keep your vow,
And take your chamber.

Isa. No sir I'll presently to Padua,   270
I will not stay a minute.

Mont.   O good madam.

Brac. 'Twere best to let her have her humour,
Some half day's journey will bring down her stomach,
And then she'll turn in post.

Fran.   To see her come
To my lord cardinal for a dispensation   275
Of her rash vow will beget excellent laughter.

---

263. manet . . . repostum] i.e., 'It shall be treasured up in the depths of
my mind' (Virgil, *Aeneid*, 1, 26). Cf. Intro., p. xxxi.

267. *horns upon thee*] i.e., may your husband be unfaithful; a transposed
reference to the cuckold's horns (cf. I. ii. 77).

274. *turn in post*] i.e., return post-haste.

Isa. Unkindness do thy office, poor heart break,—
　　Those are the killing griefs which dare not speak.   *Exit.*

　　　　　　　　　Enter CAMILLO.

Mar. Camillo's come my lord.
Fran. Where's the commission ?   280
Mar. 'Tis here.
Fran. Give me the signet.
Flam. [*to Bracciano*] My lord, do you mark their whispering ?
　　I will compound a medicine out of their two heads,
　　stronger than garlic, deadlier than stibium,—the can-   285
　　tharides which are scarce seen to stick upon the flesh
　　when they work to the heart, shall not do it with more
　　silence or invisible cunning.

　　　　　　　　Enter Doctor [JULIO].

277. *Isa.*] „*Isa. Q.*   278. Those] „Those *Q.*   speak.] *Q*b*; speake, *Q*a.
278.1. *Enter Camillo*] so Dod i; to right of l. 279 Q; to right of l. 281 Q4;
Enter Marcello and Camillo Dyce i.   283. S.D.] *Luc subs.; not in Q.*
288.1.] *so Q; after* Candy (*l. 291*) *Dyce ii.*

───────────────────────────────

278.] a common proverb (Tilley G449); cf. *Mac.,* IV. iii. 209. Leech
(*John Webster* (1951), p. 54, n.) compared Seneca, *Phaedra*: 'Curae leves
loquuntur, ingentes stupent'.
　278.1.] There was no space for Compositor A to print Camillo's entry on
the same line as Isabella's exit (cf. l. 93.1 n. above).
　283. to Bracciano] Flamineo and Bracciano walk forward, the others
retiring to the back of the stage until l. 323 below.
　285. *stibium*] metallic antimony (used as a poison).
　285–6. *cantharides*] *cantharis vesicatoria,* or Spanish fly. They were used
medicinally, applied externally to raise blisters as a counter-irritant, and
taken internally. But they were dangerous if taken unadvisedly: so Topsell
(*History* (1607–8), K2v), having spoken of their medicinal properties, proceeds: 'They are . . . in the number of most deadly and hurtfull poysons,
not onely because they cause erosion and inflammation, but more in regard
of their putrifactiue quality and making rotten, wherein they exceede.
Their iuyce beeing . . . layd vppon the skinne outwardly so long till it hath
entred the veines, is a most strong poyson, . . .' Webster has invented their
secret working; perhaps this was suggested by the fact that they were both
medicinal *and* poisonous.
　288.1.] There was room for this entry later in the text-space, so we may
presume that Compositor A placed it here in accordance with his copy
(see l. 93.1 n. above).

Brac. About the murder.

Flam. They are sending him to Naples, but I'll send him to   290
~~Candy,~~—here's another property too.

[margin note: Cede]

Brac. O the doctor,—

Flam. A poor quack-salving knave, my lord, one that should
have been lash'd for's lechery, but that he confess'd
~~a judgement, had an execution laid upon him, and so put~~   295
~~the whip to a *non plus*.~~

[margin note: nolo contendere]

Jul. And was cozen'd, my lord, by an arranter knave than
myself~~, and made pay all the colourable execution.~~

Flam. He will shoot pills into a man's guts, shall make them
have more ventages than a cornet or a lamprey,—he will   300
poison a kiss, and was once minded, for his master-piece,

---

289. murder.] *Q;* murder ? *Dod i.*   297, 306, 314, and 318. *Jul.*] Doct.
Q subs.

290–1. *to Candy*] i.e., to death; cf. Beaumont and Fletcher, *Double
Marriage* (pf. *c.* 1621), II. iii: 'Her men are gone to Candia, they are
pepper'd'. Sampson suggested there may be word-play on 'candied' (i.e.,
preserved, mummified). Lucas suggested that the point of the phrase was
that the Candians were believed to live on poisonous snakes (cf. Nashe,
Unfortunate Traveller (1594), *Wks*, II, 299: 'He is not fit to trauel, that
cannot, with the *Candians* liue on serpents, make nourishing food euen of
poison'). *Candy* = Crete.

291. *property*] instrument (cf. *O.E.D.*, s.v., 4).

293. *quack-salving*] acting like a quack doctor.

293–8. *should . . . execution*] i.e., when he was convicted of lechery, he
pretended that he had previously been convicted and sentenced for debt,
and so he was taken into custody and thus escaped whipping; in the end,
however, he was cheated by another rogue who announced that he was the
creditor and so received payment according to the supposed judgement.
colourable = plausible.

Cf. *Eastward Ho* (1605), v. iii. 64ff.: 'Say he should be condemned to be
carted, or whipt, for a *Bawde*, or so, why Ile lay an Execution on him o'two
hundred pound, let him acknowledge a Iudgement, he shal do it in halfe an
howre, they shal not all fetch him out without paying the Execution, o'my
word'.

300. *cornet*] in the 17th century, a simple musical instrument of the oboe
class.

lamprey] Cf. Sir T. Browne, *Vulgar Errors* (1646), III, xix: the notion
that 'Lampries have nine eyes . . . [was] deduced from the appearance of
diverse cavities or holes on either side, which some call eyes that carelesly
behold them'; the 'holes' are for conveying water to and from the gills.

because Ireland breeds no poison, to have prepared a
deadly vapour in a Spaniard's fart that should have
poison'd all Dublin.

Brac. O Saint Anthony's fire!   305

Jul. Your secretary is merry my lord.

Flam. O thou cursed antipathy to nature,—look his eye's
bloodshed like a needle a chirurgeon stitcheth a wound
with,—let me embrace thee toad, and love thee O thou
abhominable loathsome gargarism, that will fetch up   310
lungs, lights, heart, and liver by scruples.

305. Anthony's] *Q2* (Anthonies); Anthony *Q*.   310. abhominable] *Q*;
abominable *Q3*.   loathsome] *Q*ᵇ (loth-/some); le-/than *Q*ᵃ; lethal *conj.*
Sym.

---

302. *Ireland . . . poison*] Cf. Stanyhurst's 'Description of Ireland' (which
Webster must have read; cf. I. ii. 30–2 n.), A4ᵛ–5: 'No venemous creeping
beaste is brought forth, or nourished, or can liue in Irelande, being brought
or sent. . . There be some, that mooue question, whither [this] . . . be to be
imputed to the propertie of the soyle, or to be ascribed to the prayers of
S. Patricke, who conuerted that Islande. The greater parte father it on
S. Patricke, especially such as wryte hys lyfe.'

303–4. *vapour . . . Dublin*] an allusion to the Spaniard, Don Diego, who
made himself offensive in St Paul's before 1598; cf. *Wyatt*, E2ᵛ: 'There
came but one Dundego into England, & hee made all Paules stinke agen'.
    The doctor probably thought this device was particularly apt for use
among Irishmen: cf. Nashe, *Pierce Penniless* (1592), *Wks*, I, 188: 'The
Irishman will drawe his dagger, and bee ready to kill and slay, if one breake
winde in his company'.

305. *Saint . . . fire*] i.e., erysipelas (a local febrile disease causing inflammation of the skin); it was said that prayers to St Anthony saved many
lives in an epidemic of it in 1089 (so *O.E.D.*).
    The emendation *Anthony's* seems warranted because (1) Q's is an
irregular, rare form, (2) Compositor A is prone to omit a final letter (cf.
ll. 312 and 322), and (3) the phrase occurs thus in Webster's *N.Ho*, III. i.
122: 'Saint *Antonies* fire light in your Spanish slops' (note, incidentally, the
repeated connection with Spaniards).

308. *bloodshed*] bloodshot (this adjectival form is first quoted in *O.E.D.*
in 1658).

chirurgeon] surgeon.

310. *abhominable*] Q's spelling suggests that Webster may have remembered the absurd etymology, *ab homine* (cf. *LLL.*, v. i. 26–7).

loathsome] The proof-corrector may have consulted the manuscript copy
for some of his press-corrections to this forme (cf. Intro., p. lxviii), so *loathsome* may be accepted from Q*ᵇ*. But it is hard to see how *loathsome* in
the copy could have been misread as 'lethan'; if Q*ᵇ* is not authoritative,

Brac. No more,—I must employ thee honest doctor,
     You must to Padua and by the way,
     Use some of your skill for us.
Jul.   Sir I shall.
Brac. But for Camillo ?   315
Flam. He dies this night by such a politic strain,
     Men shall suppose him by's own engine slain.
     But for your duchess' death ?
Jul.   I'll make her sure—
Brac. Small mischiefs are by greater made secure.
Flam. Remember this you slave,—when knaves come to   320
     preferment they rise as gallowses are raised i'th'Low
     Countries, one upon another's shoulders.

                         Exeunt [BRACCIANO, FLAM-
                         INEO, *and Doctor* JULIO].

Mont. Here is an emblem nephew—pray peruse it.
     'Twas thrown in at your window,—
Cam.   At my window ?
     Here is a stag my lord hath shed his horns,   325
     And for the loss of them the poor beast weeps—

---

312. thee] *Q*^b*; the *Q*^a*.   313–14. You . . . us] *so Dod ii; one line Q.*
314. *Jul.* Sir I shall] *Q*^b (*Doc.* Sir . . .); *not in *Q*^a*.   315. Camillo ?] *Q*^b*;
Camillo, *Q*^a*.   322. another's] *Q3* (anothers); *another *Q.   322.1–2.
Exeunt . . . Julio] *Dyce i subs.; *Exeunt *Q; . . . Doctor. | Scene ii *Sym.*

Symonds' conjecture 'lethal' (i.e., 'deadly') is very attractive (for the usage,
cf. Florio, II, ii (p. 316^a): 'lethall security').
  gargarism] gargle.
  311. *scruples*] very small quantities or portions.
  316. *strain*] force, compulsion.
  317. *engine*] means, contrivance.
  319.] a common proverb (Tilley C826).
  321. *gallowses*] gallows-birds, those deserving the gallows (for pl. form,
cf. *Cym.*, v. iv. 214).
  321–2. *rise . . . shoulders*] The reference is to improvised gallows, where
the condemned man is placed on the shoulders of another who then steps
aside, leaving the prisoner hanging (so Sampson).
  324.] Cf. *Cæs.*, I. iii. 144–5 (so Lucas).
  325–6.] Cf. Topsell, *History* (1607–8), M2^v: 'Every yeare in the month
of Aprill they [Stags] loose their hornes, and so hauing lost them, they hide
themselues in the day time, inhabiting the shadowy places, . . .'

The word '*Inopem me copia fecit*'.

Mont. That is,
Plenty of horns hath made him poor of horns.

Cam. What should this mean?

Mont.   I'll tell you,—'tis given out   330
You are a cuckold.

Cam.   Is it given out so?
I had rather such report as that, my lord,
Should keep within doors.

Fran.   Have you any children?

Cam. None my lord.

Fran.   You are the happier—
I'll tell you a tale.

Cam.   Pray my lord.

Fran.   An old tale.   335
Upon a time Phoebus the god of light
(Or him we call the sun) would need be married.
The gods gave their consent, and Mercury
Was sent to voice it to the general world.
But what a piteous cry there straight arose   340
Amongst smiths, and felt-makers, brewers and cooks,
Reapers and butter-women, amongst fishmongers
And thousand other trades, which are annoyed

---

328. is,] is. *Q.*   337. need] *Q* (neede); needs *Q2.*

---

327. *word*] motto, device.

Inopem . . . fecit] i.e., 'Abundance has made me destitute' (Ovid, *Metam.*, III, 466; Narcissus complaining to his reflection). The most direct application would be (as Lucas suggested) that Camillo, having riches in the beauty of his wife, is thereby worse off than having no wife at all. Monticelso, however, gives (l. 329) another interpretation, more in keeping with the emblem as a whole; this may be paraphrased as 'being plentifully a cuckold (an allusion to the cuckold's horn), Camillo has no sexual satisfaction' (for the double sense of *horns*, cf. Partridge, *Shakespeare's Bawdy* (1947), p. 129), or, possibly, 'the plentiful sexual satisfaction others have received has meant that he has received none at all'.

333. *keep . . . doors*] Camillo puns weakly on two senses of 'given out' (ll. 330–1): (1) 'to publish, report', and (2) 'to send forth'.

334. *You . . . happier*] reversing the common proverb that 'barnes are blessings' (cf. Tilley C331 and C338).

By his excessive heat; 'twas lamentable.
They came to Jupiter all in a sweat   345
And do forbid the bans; a great fat cook
Was made their speaker, who entreats of Jove
That Phoebus might be gelded, for if now
When there was but one sun, so many men
Were like to perish by his violent heat,   350
What should they do if he were married
And should beget more, and those children
Make fireworks like their father ?—so say I,
Only I will apply it to your wife,—
Her issue (should not providence prevent it)   355
Would make both nature, time, and man repent it.

Mont. Look you cousin,
Go change the air for shame, see if your absence
Will blast your cornucopia,—Marcello
Is chosen with you joint commissioner   360
For the relieving our Italian coast
From pirates.

Mar.   I am much honour'd in't.

Cam.   But sir
Ere I return the stag's horns may be sprouted,
Greater than these are shed.

Mont.   Do not fear it,
I'll be your ranger.

Cam.   You must watch i'th'nights,   365
Then's the most danger.

Fran.   Farewell good Marcello.
All the best fortunes of a soldier's wish
Bring you a'ship-board.

---

364. these] *Q;* those *Q2.*

---

353. *fireworks*] alluding both to the 'fire' of Phoebus and the 'fire' of
sexual ardour.
358. *Go . . . air*] i.e., leave this place.
359. *cornucopia*] The association with a cuckold's horn was common;
cf. l. 329 above.
365. *ranger*] (1) 'game-keeper', and (2) 'rake, libertine' (cf. *O.E.D.*, s.v., 1).

Cam. Were I not best now I am turn'd soldier,
    Ere that I leave my wife, sell all she hath,   370
    And then take leave of her ?
Mont.   I expect good from you,
    Your parting is so merry.
Cam. Merry my lord, a'th'captain's humour right—
    I am resolved to be drunk this night.

                           Exit [CAMILLO *with* MARCELLO].
Fran. So,—'twas well fitted, now shall we discern   375
    How his wish'd absence will give violent way
    To Duke Bracciano's lust,—
Mont.   Why that was it;
    To what scorn'd purpose else should we make choice
    Of him for a sea-captain ? and besides,
    Count Lodowick which was rumour'd for a pirate,   380
    Is now in Padua.
Fran.   Is't true ?
Mont.   Most certain.
    I have letters from him, which are suppliant
    To work his quick repeal from banishment,—
    He means to address himself for pension
    Unto our sister duchess.
Fran.   O 'twas well.   385
    We shall not want his absence past six days,—
    I fain would have the Duke Bracciano run
    Into notorious scandal, for there's nought
    In such curst dotage, to repair his name,
    Only the deep sense of some deathless shame.   390
Mont. It may be objected I am dishonourable,

369. turn'd] *Q;* turned *conj. Samp, Thorn.*   373. lord,] *Q;* Lord ? *Q2;*
Lord! *Dod i.*   374.1.] *Dyce i subs.; Exit Q.*

---

385. *sister*] Greg (*M.L.Q.*, i (1900), 123) thought that Webster had confused Monticelso with Cardinal de Medici, Isabella's brother; but, as
Lucas pointed out, *sister* can be a mere courtesy title.
388–90. *there's . . . shame*] i.e., Bracciano can only recover his good name
by becoming aware of some exceptional and public shame. *deathless* is not
recorded in this usage (= 'everlasting') in *O.E.D.* until 1646.

> To play thus with my kinsman, but I answer,
> For my revenge I'd stake a brother's life,
> That being wrong'd durst not avenge himself.

Fran. Come to observe this strumpet.

Mont.   Curse of greatness,—   395
> Sure he'll not leave her.

Fran.   There's small pity in't—
> Like mistletoe on sere elms spent by weather,
> Let him cleave to her and both rot together.   *Exeunt.*

[II. ii]

Enter BRACCIANO *with one in the habit of a Conjurer.*

Brac. Now sir I claim your promise,—'tis dead midnight,
> The time prefix'd to show me by your art
> How the intended murder of Camillo,
> And our loathed duchess grow to action.

Con. You have won me by your bounty to a deed   5
> I do not often practise,—some there are,
> Which by sophistic tricks, aspire that name
> Which I would gladly lose, of nigromancer;
> As some that use to juggle upon cards,
> Seeming to conjure, when indeed they cheat: 10

396. her.] *Q;* her ? *Dod ii.*

II. ii] *Samp; not in Q;* Actus Tertius. Scena Prima. *Q4;* Scene iii. *Sym.*
3. murder] *Q;* murders *Luc.*   8. lose] *Q4;* loose *Q.*   nigromancer] *Q;*
necromancer *Dod i.*

---

395. *of*] possibly = 'on' (cf. *All's W.*, IV. iii. 332: 'a plague of all drums').
396. *pity*] cause for pity.

II. ii.] located in Vittoria's house (cf. ll. 50–1).
3. *murder*] Compositor A often omitted a final letter (cf. II. i. 305 n.) but
the text is not necessarily corrupt; *murder* can be taken as referring to the
slaying of both victims.
8. *nigromancer*] Q's spelling (which was common at the time) may indicate an association with L. *niger* and 'black art'; cf. IV. i. 33 n.
9. *juggle*] practise the art of magic.
10. *conjure*] Cf. J. Mason, *Anatomy of Sorcery* (1612), G1–1ᵛ: 'these men

Others that raise up their confederate spirits
'Bout windmills, and endanger their own necks,
For making of a squib, and some there are
Will keep a curtal to show juggling tricks
And give out 'tis a spirit: besides these   15
Such a whole ream of almanac-makers, figure-flingers,—
Fellows indeed that only live by stealth,
Since they do merely lie about stol'n goods,—
They'd make men think the devil were fast and loose,
With speaking fustian Latin: pray sit down,   20
Put on this night-cap sir, 'tis charm'd,—and now

16. ream] reame *Q;* realm *Dyce ii.*

---

were nothing but meere wicked magitians, and namely, of that sort which
we cal coniurers . . . these . . . will make as though they commaunded the
diuell, howbeit they profit nothing thereby, sauing that they serue his
turne herein, and sometime their own: . . .'

12. *windmills*] fanciful schemes or projects (so *O.E.D.*, s.v., 4, for which
this passage is the first quotation).

14–15. *keep . . . spirit*] an allusion to a 'Mr Banks', a travelling showman,
who, from 1591 onwards, exhibited a performing horse, first a white horse,
and then, by 1595, a docked bay gelding (*curtal* = 'docked horse'), called
Morocco. Eye-witness reports say that Morocco could 'do many rare and
uncouth tricks', as to dance, feign death, count money, and beck at the
name of Queen Elizabeth and bite and strike at that of the King of Spain.
Report went round that Morocco was a familiar spirit; some said that, in
the end, he devoured his master, others that both horse and master were
burned at Rome for witchcraft (so Jonson, *Epigrams* (1640), no. 133). In
fact, Mr Banks retired from show-business to be a vintner in Cheapside,
London. (See S. H. Atkins, *N. & Q.*, clxvii (1934), 39–44.)

16. *ream*] This spelling used to denote both mod. 'ream' (i.e., of paper,
sometimes, imprecisely, a 'large quantity') or 'realm'; both words may be
appropriate here, the first with reference to the voluminous writings of
these tricksters.

figure-flingers] casters of horoscopes (contemptuous).

17–18. *only . . . goods*] i.e., only live by secret cunning and by taking what
is not theirs, that is by lying about spirits and powers which are not theirs
by right.

19. *fast and loose*] shifty, inconstant (originally the name of a cheating
game involving a knotted string which, to the person gulled, seemed to be
'fast' tied, but was, in fact, 'loose'). Cf. Florio, III, viii (p. 473a), of pedantic
wrangling: '[it] may fitly be compared unto juglers play of fast and loose'.

20. *fustian*] inflated, bombastic (especially used of cant jargon); for its
primary sense, see III. ii. 46 n.

I'll show you by my strong-commanding art
The circumstance that breaks your duchess' heart.

A dumb show.

Enter suspiciously, JULIO *and another, they draw a curtain where*
BRACCIANO'*s picture is, they put on spectacles of glass, which cover
their eyes and noses, and then burn perfumes afore the picture, and wash
the lips of the picture, that done, quenching the fire, and putting off
their spectacles they depart laughing.*

Enter ISABELLA *in her nightgown as to bed-ward, with lights after her,
Count* LODOVICO, GIOVANNI, *and others waiting on her, she kneels
down as to prayers, then draws the curtain of the picture, does three
reverences to it, and kisses it thrice, she faints and will not suffer them
to come near it, dies; sorrow express'd in* GIOVANNI *and in Count*
LODOVICO; *she's convey'd out solemnly.*

Brac. Excellent, then she's dead,—
Con.   She's poisoned,
    By the fum'd picture,—'twas her custom nightly,   25
    Before she went to bed, to go and visit

22. strong-commanding] *hyphened Q.*   23.2 *another*] *This ed.; Christophero Q.*   23.3. *Bracciano*'s] *Brachian's Q.*   23.3–4. *spectacles . . .
noses,] Q*b *(. . . glasse,* | *which couer . . .); spectacles, which couers* | *their eyes
and noses, of glasse, Q*a.   23.7. *with lights] Q*b; *lighs Q*a.   23.8. *and*] *This
ed.; Guid-antonio and Q; Gasparo, Antonelli, and Samp.*   23.11. *express'd] Q*b *(exprest); expresse Q*a.

23.1. dumb show] This device was originally an allegorical or simplified
presentation of events which were to follow·in fully dramatized action (cf.
Gorboduc and 'The Mouse-Trap' in *Hamlet*), but it came to be used as a
means of compressing the action of a drama (cf. Heywood, *Brazen Age*
(pf. *c.* 1609–13), I3ᵛ: 'Our last Act comes, which lest it tedious grow, |
What is too long in word, accept in show').

Webster's Conjurer recalls Greene's *Friar Bacon* (pf. *c.* 1589), II. iii, and
IV. iii. Webster probably used the device for compression and variety, and,
possibly, to illustrate Bracciano's impatience, by showing his eagerness to
know the outcome of his plots.

23.2. another] Q's '*Christophero*' and '*Guid-antonio*' (of l. 23.8, below)
are 'ghost' characters (cf. II. i. 0.3 n.).

23.2 curtain] Pictures were often protected by curtains; cf. *Tw.N.*, I. iii.
134 and I. v. 251.

Your picture, and to feed her eyes and lips
On the dead shadow,—Doctor Julio
Observing this, infects it with an oil
And other poison'd stuff, which presently   30
Did suffocate her spirits.

Brac.   Methought I saw
Count Lodowick there.

Con.   He was, and by my art
I find he did most passionately dote
Upon your duchess,—now turn another way,
And view Camillo's far more politic fate,—   35
Strike louder music from this charmed ground,
To yield, as fits the act, a tragic sound.

The second dumb show.

Enter FLAMINEO, MARCELLO, CAMILLO, *with four more as Captains, they drink healths and dance; a vaulting-horse is brought into
the room;* MARCELLO *and two more whisper'd out of the room while*
FLAMINEO *and* CAMILLO *strip themselves into their shirts, as to vault;
compliment who shall begin; as* CAMILLO *is about to vault,* FLAMINEO
*pitcheth him upon his neck, and with the help of the rest, writhes his
neck about, seems to see if it be broke, and lays him folded double as
'twere under the horse, makes shows to call for help;* MARCELLO *comes
in, laments, sends for the Cardinal* [MONTICELSO] *and Duke*

35. fate] *Q4;* face *Q.*   37.6. compliment] *Q;* they complement *Q2.*   37.9.
shows] *Q* (shewes); *shew Dod i.*

---

30. *presently*] immediately.
37.3 vaulting-horse] In fact, Vittoria's husband was shot.
G. Baldini (*John Webster* (Rome, 1953), pp. 291–2) suggested that Webster misunderstood the story he had heard or read, and that 'Montecavallo',
the place of Peretti's assassination, has thus been transfigured into a
vaulting-horse. But Webster may have altered his source wittingly. In
a dumb show an audience must be intrigued in order to follow the action;
they must want to find out what is going to happen. A curious and cumber-
some means of murder was just what Webster required (cf. 1st Dumb
Show).
37.9. shows] Compositor A's tendency to add extra letters at the ends of
words (cf. I. ii. 282 n.) makes Dodsley's emendation attractive; yet the
plural may imply repeated and vigorous action.

[FRANCISCO], *who comes forth with armed men; wonder at the act;*
[FRANCISCO] *commands the body to be carried home, apprehends*
FLAMINEO, MARCELLO, *and the rest, and* [all] *go as 'twere to*
apprehend VITTORIA.

Brac. 'Twas quaintly done, but yet each circumstance
    I taste not fully.
Con.   O 'twas most apparent,
    You saw them enter charged with their deep healths   40
    To their boon voyage, and to second that,
    Flamineo calls to have a vaulting-horse
    Maintain their sport. The virtuous Marcello
    Is innocently plotted forth the room,
    Whilst your eye saw the rest, and can inform you   45
    The engine of all.
Brac. It seems Marcello, and Flamineo
    Are both committed.
Con.   Yes, you saw them guarded,
    And now they are come with purpose to apprehend
    Your mistress, fair Vittoria; we are now   50
    Beneath her roof: 'twere fit we instantly
    Make out by some back postern:—
Brac.   Noble friend,
    You bind me ever to you,—this shall stand

37.11. *comes*] *Q, Q3; come Q4.*   *wonder*] *Q, Q4; wonders Q2.*   37.11-
12. *act; Francisco*] *This ed.; act, Q.*   37.12. *commands*] *Q, Q2; command*
Q4.   *apprehends*] *Q, Q2; apprehend Q4.*   37.13. *all*] *This ed.; not in Q.*
go] *Q, Q4; goes Q2.*   45. *eye*] *Q; eyes Par.*   47. *Brac.*] *Q4; Mar. Q.*

37.11. *wonder . . .*] Compositor A did confuse singular and plural verbs
elsewhere, yet the change from the plural '*wonder*' to the singular '*com-*
mands' and '*apprehends*' and the reversion to the plural '*go*' for an '*exeunt*'
(cf. '*they*' of l. 49) all seem appropriate; instead of emending the verbs it is
probably better to clarify the terse style by adding subjects (cf. the
omission of subjects for other verbs in the directions of these two dumb
shows).
37.12. *apprehends*] seizes, arrests.
38. *quaintly*] skilfully.
41. *boon*] prosperous.
46. *engine*] means, contrivance.
53. *this*] i.e., this service you have done, or the memory of it; or, pos-

As the firm seal annexed to my hand.
It shall enforce a payment.

Con.   Sir I thank you. *Exit* BRACCIANO.
Both flowers and weeds spring when the sun is warm,   56
And great men do great good, or else great harm.

Exit Conjurer

[III. i]

Enter FRANCISCO, *and* MONTICELSO, *their Chancellor and Register.*

Fran. You have dealt discreetly to obtain the presence
Of all the grave lieger ambassadors
To hear Vittoria's trial.

Mont.   'Twas not ill,
For sir you know we have nought but circumstances
To charge her with, about her husband's death,—   5
Their approbation therefore to the proofs
Of her black lust, shall make her infamous
To all our neighbouring kingdoms,—I wonder
If Bracciano will be here.

Fran.   O fie,
'Twere impudence too palpable.   [*Exeunt.*] 10

---

55. S.D.] *so Q4; at end of l. 54 Q; after* payment *Dod* i.

III. i] *Samp; not in Q;* Act. 3. Scen. 2. *Q4;* [II.] Scene iv. *Sym.*   9–10. If
. . . palpable] *so Dyce* i; *one line Q; . . .* here ? / *Fran. . . . Scott.*   10. S.D.]
Dod ii; *not in Q.*

---

sibly, in view of 'bind', this hand-shake (with a quibble on 'hand' of l. 54;
see note).

54. *annexed . . . hand*] i.e., affixed to my signature.

55. S.D.] a clear example of Compositor A's misplacing of a direction
for lack of room in the text-space of the printed page.

56–7.] From W. Alexander (cf. App. IV), *J.C.*, v. i. 2643–50: 'As in fine
fruits, or weeds, fat earth abounds, / Even as the Labourers spend, or spare
their paine, / The greatest sprits (disdaining vulgar bounds) / Of what they
seek the highest height must gaine; / . . . Great sprits must do great good, or
then great ill'.

III. i.] This appears to be located in some ante-chamber adjoining the
papal consistory, or court-room.

2. *lieger*] resident.

Enter FLAMINEO *and* MARCELLO *guarded, and*
a Lawyer.

Law. What are you in by the week? so—I will try now
whether thy wit be close prisoner,—methinks none should
sit upon thy sister but old whore-masters,—

Flam. Or cuckolds, for your cuckold is your most terrible
tickler of lechery: whore-masters would serve, for none   15
are judges at tilting, but those that have been old tilters.

Law. My lord duke and she have been very private.

Flam. You are a dull ass, 'tis threat'ned they have been very
public.

Law. If it can be proved they have but kiss'd one another.   20

Flam. What then?

Law. My lord cardinal will ferret them,—

Flam. A cardinal I hope will not catch conies.

Law. For to sow kisses (mark what I say) to sow kisses, is to

---

20. another.] *Q;* another—*Dyce i.*

10.2. Lawyer] This lawyer is so different from the one in III. ii that they
may be two distinct characters. This one knows so little of law and affects to
know so much about the court that the stage-direction may be an error from
the copy (as elsewhere; cf. Intro., p. lxvii) and should read *'Courtier'*
(the speech-prefixes might have been altered to agree with the erroneous
direction).

11. *in . . . week*] i.e., ensnared (a common phrase; cf. *O.E.D., week*, 6).

15. *tickler*] possibly a quibble: (1) 'chastiser' (cf. *Tw.N.*, v. i. 198), and
(2) 'exciter, provoker'.

16. *tilting*] Cf. *W.Ho*, I. i. 3–6: *'Mistress Birdlime.* Shee that must
weare this gowne . . . is Maister *Justinianos* wife . . . my good old Lord and
Maister, that hath beene a Tylter this twenty yeere, hath sent it'.

17. *private*] secret, intimate.

19. *public*] (1) 'unconcealed, manifest', and (2) 'licentious' (a 'public
woman' was a prostitute; and cf. *Oth.*, IV. ii. 73).

22. *ferret*] search after, question searchingly; or, possibly, simply 'go for'
(cf. *N.Ho*, v. i. 26: 'weele ferrit them and firk them in-faith').

23. *catch conies*] a common cant phrase meaning 'to cozen dupes', here
used because (1) 'ferret' of the previous line was an associated cant term
(ferrets being used to catch conies, or rabbits), and (2) 'cony' was used for
'woman', either in endearment or indecently (cf. S.S., *Honest Lawyer* (pf.
before 1615), C3: 'Now am I in quest of some vaulting house. I would
faine spend these crownes, as I got them, in cony-catching').

reap lechery, and I am sure a woman that will endure 25
kissing is half won.

Flam. True, her upper part by that rule,—if you will win her
nether part too, you know what follows.

Law. Hark the ambassadors are lighted,—

Flam. [*aside*] I do put on this feigned garb of mirth 30
To gull suspicion.

Mar. O my unfortunate sister!
I would my dagger's point had cleft her heart
When she first saw Bracciano: you 'tis said,
Were made his engine, and his stalking horse 35
To undo my sister.

Flam.　　　　　　I made a kind of path
To her and mine own preferment.

Mar.　　　　　　　　　　Your ruin.

Flam. Hum! thou art a soldier,
Followest the great duke, feedest his victories,
As witches do their serviceable spirits, 40
Even with thy prodigal blood,—what hast got?
But like the wealth of captains, a poor handful,
Which in thy palm thou bear'st, as men hold water—

---

27. part] *Q;* part; *Dod i.*　　30. *aside*] *Dyce ii; not in Q; at end of line Q4.*
36. made] *Q;* am *Q2.*　　39. feedest] *Q;* feed'st *Q4.*　　41. got?] *Q;* got,
Dyce ii.　　43. water] *Q;* water? *Dyce ii.*

25-6. *woman . . . won*] Sampson quoted Sharpham, *Cupid's Whirligig*
(1607), ed. 1926, p. 13: 'The French prouerbe saies, *Fame baissee est
demie ioyee*, a woman kis'd is halfe injoyed'.

31. *gull*] deceive.

35. *engine*] instrument, tool.

39-41. *feedest . . . blood*] Cf. G. Giffard, *Witches and Witchcrafts* (1593),
B4ᵛ: 'witches haue their spirits, . . . whome they nourish . . . by letting them
sucke now and then a drop of blood'.

42. *wealth of captains*] Sampson quoted *N.Ho*, v. i: 'whose reward is not
the rate of a Captaine newly come out of the Low-Countries, . . . some angel'
(i.e., 8 or 10 shillings).

43. *palm . . . bear'st*] There may be a quibbling allusion to 'bearing the
palm' (i.e., gaining the victory).

43-5. *men . . . fingers*] Cf. Florio, II, xii (p. 309ᵃ): 'as if one should go about
to graspe the water: for, how much the more he shal close and presse that

    Seeking to gripe it fast, the frail reward
    Steals through thy fingers.

Mar.   Sir,—

Flam.   Thou hast scarce maintenance
    To keep thee in fresh chamois.

Mar.   Brother!

Flam.   Hear me,—   46
    And thus when we have even poured ourselves
    Into great fights, for their ambition
    Or idle spleen, how shall we find reward ?
    But as we seldom find the mistletoe   50
    Sacred to physic on the builder oak
    Without a mandrake by it, so in our quest of gain.

51. physic on] *Luc;* physicke: Or *Q.*   52. gain.] *Q;* gain, *Dod iii.*

---

which by its owne nature is ever gliding, so much the more he shall loose what he would hold and fasten'.

    46. *chamois*] i.e. chamois jerkins worn under armour; cf. Florio, I, xliii (p. 134ᵃ): 'How soone doe plaine chamoy-jerkins and greasie canvase doublets creepe into fashion and credit amongst our souldiers if they lie in the field ?'

    50–2. *seldom . . . it*] i.e., there's always a fly in the ointment (so Lucas).

    Q's 'Or' can hardly be correct, for there is little sense in saying that *most* oak trees have mandrakes by them (so Lucas, who quoted Chéruel, *Dictionnaire* (1899), II, 726, for an 18th-century story connecting mandrakes with mistletoe-bearing oaks). Presumably Compositor A misread his copy ('r' and 'n' are easily confused in Elizabethan secretary hands), and added the heavy punctuation in an effort to make sense.

    For the medicinal properties of *mistletoe*, Lucas quoted Pliny, tr. Holland, XVI, xliv: 'They call it in their language All-Heale, (for they have an opinion of it, that it cureth all maladies whatsoever).'

    builder = 'used for building' (*O.E.D.*, s.v., quotes Spenser, *F.Q.* (1596): 'The builder oake, sole king of forrests all', and Collier noted the epithet in Chaucer, *Parl. of Foules*, l. 176).

    mandrake (i.e., mandragora) is a poisonous plant but formerly was used medicinally for its narcotic and emetic properties. When forked its root offers some resemblance to the human form, and it was thought to utter a shriek when pulled from the ground. It was thought to promote fruitfulness in women. Gerarde's *Herbal* (1597), S4ᵛ–5, recounts several 'ridiculous tales' concerning it, as that 'it is neuer or verie seldome to be founde growing naturally but vnder a gallows, where the matter that hath fallen from the dead bodie, hath giuen it the shape of a man: and the matter of a woman, the substaunce of a female plant;...' Webster, it may be noticed, fastens on the plant's mysterious qualities, not its medicinal; he mentions its shriek

Alas the poorest of their forc'd dislikes
At a limb proffers, but at heart it strikes:
This is lamented doctrine.

Mar.   Come, come.   55

Flam. When age shall turn thee
White as a blooming hawthorn,—

Mar.   I'll interrupt you.

For love of virtue bear an honest heart,
And stride over every politic respect,
Which where they most advance they most infect.   60
Were I your father, as I am your brother,
I should not be ambitious to leave you
A better patrimony.

Enter Savoy [Ambassador].

Flam.   I'll think on't,—
The lord ambassadors.

*Here there is a passage of the lieger Ambassadors over
the stage severally.
Enter French Ambassador.*

Law. O my sprightly Frenchman, do you know him? he's an   65
admirable tilter.

59. over] *Q;* o'er *Dod i.*   63–4. A . . . ambassadors] *so Dod i subs.;*
. . . on't, The . . . (*one line*) *Q.*   63.1.] *This ed.; Enter Sauoy (at end of
l. 62) Q,* (*at end of l. 63*) *Dod i.*   64.3. *Ambassador*] *Q4; Embassadours
Q.*

(v. vi. 67), its feeding on blood (III. iii. 114–15), its power to madden (*D.M.*,
II. v. 1–2). He calls it 'mandragora' when he alludes to its use as a narcotic
(cf. *D.M.*, IV. ii. 242).

53–4.] i.e., when great men take offence at the most trivial action, they
appear to give light punishment to the offender, but in fact the loss of their
favour destroys all his hopes of future success.

63.1.] Compositor A probably misplaced this direction for lack of room
in the text-space in Q.

64.1–2. passage . . . severally] i.e., as if on their way to Vittoria's arraignment.

66. *tilter*] Flamineo seems to take this as a *double entendre,* as at ll. 15–16
above.

Flam. I saw him at last tilting, he showed like a pewter candle-
stick fashioned like a man in armour, holding a tilting-
staff in his hand, little bigger than a candle of twelve i'th'
pound.   70

Law. O but he's an excellent horseman.

Flam. A lame one in his lofty tricks,—he sleeps a'horseback
like a poulter,—

Enter English and Spanish [Ambassadors.]

Law. Lo you my Spaniard.

Flam. He carries his face in's ruff, as I have seen a serving-   75
man carry glasses in a cypress hat-band, monstrous steady
for fear of breaking,—he looks like the claw of a blackbird,
first salted and then broiled in a candle.   *Exeunt.*

78. candle] *Q;* caudle *conj. Thorn.*

67–70. *pewter . . . pound*] Sykes compared *H5*, IV. ii. 45–6: 'The horse-
men sit like fixed candlesticks, / With torch-staves in their hand'.

71. *horseman*] taken as a *double entendre* by Flamineo; cf. the sequence of
similar allusions in *H5*, III. vii. 46–69.

72. *lofty tricks*] used literally of acrobatics or tumbling; for the figurative
usage, cf. Chapman, *May-Day* (1611), V. i. 92: 'there was a reveller, I shall
never see man do his lofty tricks like him. . .'

72–3. *sleeps . . . poulter*] Steevens noted that he had seen 'several country
poulterers [*poulter* = poulterer] asleep over the baskets which they carried
on horseback before them, a position sufficiently commodious to solicit
repose, and safe enough to allow of it'. Allowing for the run of *doubles
entendres*, there might be a pun on 'palterer' (cf. v. iii. 56–7 n.).

75. *carries . . . ruff*] Spanish pomposity and predilection for wide ruffs
were often alluded to; Lucas quoted Jonson, *Alchemist* (pf. 1610), IV. iii. 244
(of Surly dressed as a Spaniard): 'He lookes in that deepe ruffe, like a head
in a platter'.

76. *cypress*] cobweb lawn or crêpe (often worn as a hatband in sign of
mourning).

78. *broiled . . . candle*] Lucas quoted a stage-direction from Fletcher's
Women Pleased (I. ii), which requires a miser to be shown roasting an
egg 'by a Candle'.

[III. ii]

THE ARRAIGNMENT OF VITTORIA.

Enter FRANCISCO, MONTICELSO, *the six lieger Ambassadors,*
BRACCIANO, VITTORIA, [ZANCHE, FLAMINEO, MARCELLO],
Lawyer, and a guard.

Mont. Forbear my lord, here is no place assign'd you,
This business by his holiness is left
To our examination.

Brac.   May it thrive with you.
                                        Lays a rich gown under him.

Fran. A chair there for his lordship.

Brac. Forbear your kindness, an unbidden guest   5
Should travail as Dutch women go to church:
Bear their stools with them.

Mont.   At your pleasure sir.
Stand to the table gentlewoman: now signior
Fall to your plea.

Law. *Domine judex converte oculos in hanc pestem mulierum*   10
corruptissimam.

Vit. What's he?

Fran.   A lawyer, that pleads against you.

Vit. Pray my lord, let him speak his usual tongue—
I'll make no answer else.

III. ii] *Samp; not in Q; Act III. Dod ii; Act the Third. Scene i. Sym.*
0.2. Monticelso] *Montcelso Q.*   six] *Q; four Dod ii.*   0.3. *Zanche . . .*
Marcello] *Luc; Isabella Q; not in Q 4; Flamineo, Marcello Dyce i.*   3.1.] *so*
Q 4; to right of ll. 3–4 Q.   6.] travail *Q;* travel *Q 3.*   8. gentlewoman]
Q 4; gentlewomen *Q.*   10. *Law.] Q 2; not in Q.*

III. ii.] Located in a consistory, or ecclesiastical court-room, in Rome.
0.3. Zanche] Cf. Intro., p. lxvii, n. 5; Zanche's presence seems to be
required by ll. 264–5 below.
8. *gentlewoman*] Q might just possibly be right; but the case proceeds
only against Vittoria.
10–11.] i.e., 'My lord, turn your eyes upon this plague, the most corrupted of women'.
13.] Shakespeare's Katharine (*H8*, III. i. 42–50) also insists on English
for proceedings with her judges.

Fran.   Why you understand Latin.

Vit. I do sir, but amongst this auditory   15
　　　Which come to hear my cause, the half or more
　　　May be ignorant in't.

Mont.   Go on sir:—

Vit.   By your favour,
　　　I will not have my accusation clouded
　　　In a strange tongue: all this assembly
　　　Shall hear what you can charge me with.

Fran.   Signior,   20
　　　You need not stand on't much; pray change your language.

Mont. O for God sake: gentlewoman, your credit
　　　Shall be more famous by it.

Law.   Well then have at you.

Vit. I am at the mark sir, I'll give aim to you,
　　　And tell you how near you shoot.   25

Law. Most literated judges, please your lordships,
　　　So to connive your judgements to the view
　　　Of this debauch'd and diversivolent woman
　　　Who such a black concatenation
　　　Of mischief hath effected, that to extirp   30
　　　The memory of't, must be the consummation
　　　Of her and her projections—

Vit.   What's all this—

22. God] *Q;* God's *Q4.*

---

21. *stand on't*] i.e., insist on speaking Latin.

22. *God*] In view of Compositor A's certain omissions of final letters elsewhere (e.g., l. 100 below), Q4 may be right; but Q's form occurs commonly,
and seems appropriately abrupt.

　　credit] reputation.

24. *give aim*] act as a marker at the butts.

26. *literated*] learned (*O.E.D.*, s.v., first quotes Florio, *New World of
Words* (1611), '*Alletterato*').

27.] The lawyer is trying to be more pompous than he is able to be; no
satisfactory sense can be made of this, for *connive* (L. *conivere*) means 'to
overlook', 'pass over' (a fault, etc.) and so what little sense the line yields
seems to be the opposite of what the lawyer would wish to convey.

28. *diversivolent*] desiring strife (a nonce-word according to *O.E.D.*).

32. *projections*] projects.

Law. Hold your peace.
    Exorbitant sins must have exulceration.
Vit. Surely my lords this lawyer here hath swallowed   35
    Some pothecary's bills, or proclamations.
    And now the hard and undigestible words
    Come up like stones we use give hawks for physic.
    Why this is Welsh to Latin.
Law.   My lords, the woman
    Knows not her tropes nor figures, nor is perfect   40
    In the academic derivation
    Of grammatical elocution.
Fran.   Sir your pains
    Shall be well spared, and your deep eloquence
    Be worthily applauded amongst those
    Which understand you.
Law.   My good lord!
Fran.   Sir,   45
    Put up your papers in your fustian bag,—   FRANCISCO *speaks*
    Cry mercy sir, 'tis buckram,—and accept   *this as in scorn.*
    My notion of your learn'd verbosity.
Law. I most graduatically thank your lordship.
    I shall have use for them elsewhere.   [*Exit.*] 50
Mont. I shall be plainer with you, and paint out
    Your follies in more natural red and white
    Than that upon your cheek.

---

47. buckram] *Q4* (Buck'ram); buckeram *Q*.   50. S.D.] *Thorn; not in Q.*

34. *exulceration*] ulceration (literally), exasperation; Leech suggests that the lawyer means, vaguely, 'extirpation' (cf. l. 30).

38.] Cf. Markham, *Husbandry* (1614), S3, where the dose is seven to fifteen fine white pebbles from a river (quoted Sampson).

39. *to*] compared with.

42. *elocution*] expression.

46. *fustian*] a quibble: (1) 'coarse cloth', and (2) 'inflated, bombastic' (cf. II. ii. 20). Francisco purposely mistakes the stuff in order to introduce the quibble; the bags were traditionally of buckram (cf. *D.L.C.*, IV. ii. 38).

49. *graduatically*] in the manner of a graduate (a nonce-word, according to *O.E.D.*).

51–3. *plainer . . . cheek*] i.e., eschew the 'colours' of rhetoric (because the mere names of her *follies* will be appalling enough). *paint out* = 'depict'.

Vit.   O you mistake.
   You raise a blood as noble in this cheek
   As ever was your mother's.   55
Mont. I must spare you till proof cry whore to that;
   Observe this creature here my honoured lords,
   A woman of a most prodigious spirit
   In her effected.
Vit.   Honourable my lord,
   It doth not suit a reverend cardinal   60
   To play the lawyer thus.
Mont. O your trade instructs your language!
   You see my lords what goodly fruit she seems,
   Yet like those apples travellers report
   To grow where Sodom and Gomorrah stood,   65
   I will but touch her and you straight shall see
   She'll fall to soot and ashes.
Vit.   Your envenom'd
   Pothecary should do't.
Mont.   I am resolved
   Were there a second paradise to lose
   This devil would betray it.
Vit.   O poor charity!   70

59. In her effected.] *Q; not in Q3;* In her affections. *conj. Luc;* In her
infected. *conj. Luc;* In her offences. *conj. Luc;* In her affected. *conj. this
ed.;* In her effected . . . *conj. this ed.*   67–8. Your . . . do't] *so Dyce i;*
one line Q.   68. do't.] doo't *Q.*   resolved] resolued. *Q.*   69. lose]
Q4; loose *Q.*

---

   59. *effected*] possibly, 'put into effect', or 'fulfilled', but the usage is
clumsily abrupt and not paralleled in *O.E.D.*
   Of the possible emendations, 'affected' offers the simplest palaeogra-
phical explanation of Q's error and renders good sense in its common 16th-
and 17th-century meanings of 'desired', or 'cherished, beloved' (cf.
O.E.D., s.v., I, 1608: 'It is at once had and affected'); it is, indeed, possible
that Webster confused 'effect' with 'affect', for there is evidence that the
verbs were not always kept distinct (cf. *O.E.D.*, *effect*, vb., 4, and *effected*).
   64–7. *apples . . . ashes*] The legend has been traced to Deuteronomy,
xxxii. 32. Mandeville (xxx) was among the many who repeated and
developed it (so Reed).
   68. *resolved*] satisfied, convinced.

Thou art seldom found in scarlet.

Mont. Who knows not how, when several night by night
Her gates were chok'd with coaches, and her rooms
Outbrav'd the stars with several kind of lights,
When she did counterfeit a prince's court   75
In music, banquets and most riotous surfeits ?
This whore, forsooth, was holy.

Vit.   Ha ? whore—what's that ?

Mont. Shall I expound whore to you ? sure I shall;
I'll give their perfect character. They are first,
Sweet-meats which rot the eater: in man's nostril   80
Poison'd perfumes. They are coz'ning alchemy,
Shipwrecks in calmest weather. What are whores ?
Cold Russian winters, that appear so barren,
As if that nature had forgot the spring.
They are the true material fire of hell,   85
Worse than those tributes i'th'Low Countries paid,
Exactions upon meat, drink, garments, sleep;
Ay even on man's perdition, his sin.
They are those brittle evidences of law

74. kind] *Q;* kinds *Dod i.*   75. court] *Dod i, Dyce ii, Wheel;* Court. *Q;*
Court, *Q4;* court ? *Samp.*   76. surfeits ?] *Dyce ii;* surfets *Q;* surfets:
Q2, Q4; surfeits, *Samp, Wheel.*   77. holy.] *Q, Q2, Q4, Dyce ii, Samp;*
holy ? *Wheel.*   80. nostril] *Q;* nostrils *Q2.*

---

71. *scarlet*] the colour of the legal faculty as well as that of a cardinal's
vestments.

79. *character*] i.e., a formal delineation like those in *New Characters*
(1615) to which Webster almost certainly contributed.

80. *Sweet-meats . . . eater*] Dyce compared Dekker, *Whore of Babylon*
(1607), v. i. 80–1: 'Good words / (Sweet meates that rotte the eater)'.

86.] Cf. Moryson, *Itinerary* (1617), iv, 61: 'By reason of the huge im-
positions (especially upon wines,) the passengers expence [in the Low
Countries] is much increased, for the exactions often equall or passe the
value of the things for which they are paid'.

88. *perdition*] i.e., prostitution.

89–91. *brittle . . . syllable*] D. P. V. Akrigg (*N. & Q.*, cxciii (1948), 427–8)
suggested that this is an allusion to Sir Walter Raleigh, who lost his estate
of Sherborne because a clerk had omitted ten words from an early transfer
to his wife; this would have been apt at several stages in the proceedings,
which began in 1608.

But the idea was common enough not to need a special occasion; cf.

Which forfeit all a wretched man's estate   90
For leaving out one syllable. What are whores?
They are those flattering bells have all one tune,
At weddings, and at funerals: your rich whores
Are only treasuries by extortion fill'd,
And empty'd by curs'd riot. They are worse,   95
Worse than dead bodies, which are begg'd at gallows
And wrought upon by surgeons, to teach man
Wherein he is imperfect. What's a whore?
She's like the guilty counterfeited coin
Which whosoe'er first stamps it brings in trouble   100
All that receive it.

Vit.   This character scapes me.

Mont. You gentlewoman?
    Take from all beasts, and from all minerals
    Their deadly poison—

Vit.   Well what then?

Mont.   I'll tell thee—
    I'll find in thee a pothecary's shop   105
    To sample them all.

Fr. Amb.   She hath lived ill.

Eng. Amb. True, but the cardinal's too bitter.

Mont. You know what whore is—next the devil, Adult'ry,
    Enters the devil, Murder.

Fran.   Your unhappy
    Husband is dead.

92. flattering] *Q; flatt'ring Q4.*   99. guilty] *Q; gilt Q2.*   100. brings]
Q2; bring Q.   104. poison] poison. *Q.*   108. devil, Adult'ry,] *Samp;*
deuell; Adultry. *Q; Divel adultery, Q3; Devil: Adultery Q4.*   109.
Enters ..., Murder] *Samp; ... deuell, murder Q, Q3 subs.;* Enters, the
Devil and Murder *Q4.*   109–10. Your ... dead] *so Dyce i; ...* husband /
Is ... *Q.*

Atheist's Tragedy (pf. 1607–11), IV. ii: 'a superfluous Letter in the Law, /
Endangers our assurance', or Florio, II, xii (p. 268ª): 'How many weighty
strifes and important quarels hath the doubt of this one sillable, *hoc,*
brought forth'.

   99. *guilty*] with, possibly, a quibble on 'gilt'.

   108–9. *next ... Murder*] Lucas compared *Oth.,* II. iii. 297–8: 'It hath
pleased the devil drunkenness to give place to the devil wrath'.

Vit.   O he's a happy husband   110
    Now he owes nature nothing.
Fran. And by a vaulting engine.
Mont.   An active plot—
    He jump'd into his grave.
Fran.   What a prodigy was't,
    That from some two yards' height a slender man
    Should break his neck?
Mont.   I' th' rushes.
Fran.   And what's more,   115
    Upon the instant lose all use of speech,
    All vital motion, like a man had lain
    Wound up three days. Now mark each circumstance.
Mont. And look upon this creature was his wife.
    She comes not like a widow: she comes arm'd   120
    With scorn and impudence: is this a mourning habit?
Vit. Had I foreknown his death as you suggest,
    I would have bespoke my mourning.
Mont. O you are cunning.
Vit. You shame your wit and judgement   125
    To call it so; what, is my just defence
    By him that is my judge call'd impudence?
    Let me appeal then from this Christian court
    To the uncivil Tartar.

---

110. husband] *Q;* Husband; *Q4.*   112–13. An . . . grave] *so Q; one line*
Dyce i.   116. lose] *Q4;* loose *Q.*   126. what,] What *Q.*

110–11. *happy . . . nothing*] Cf. *Honour's Academy* (cf. App. IV), Nn3^v:
'That debtor, that is still vexed, haunted, and abused by his Creditor, because hee should pay what he oweth, is he not happie, when he hath made
euen with all men, that he may (after) liue in quiet? If so, why (then) farre
more blessed are they, who pay their due vnto Nature, vnto whom they are
indebted . . .'

115. *rushes*] Floors were customarily strewn with rushes instead of
carpets.

118. *Wound up*] i.e., in his winding-sheet.

128. *Christian*] a quibble: (1) ecclesiastical, and (2) civilized. Reed suggested a direct allusion to the 'Courts Christian', the English Ecclesiastical
Courts which dealt with adultery.

129. *uncivil*] barbarous.   *Tartar*] Cf. *Mer.V.*, IV. i. 32–3.

Mont.   See my lords,
    She scandals our proceedings.
Vit.   Humbly thus,   130
    Thus low, to the most worthy and respected
    Lieger ambassadors, my modesty
    And womanhood I tender; but withal
    So entangled in a cursed accusation
    That my defence of force like Perseus,   135
    Must personate masculine virtue—to the point!
    Find me but guilty, sever head from body:
    We'll part good friends: I scorn to hold my life
    At yours or any man's entreaty, sir.
Eng. Amb. She hath a brave spirit.   140
Mont. Well, well, such counterfeit jewels
    Make true ones oft suspected.
Vit.   You are deceived;
    For know that all your strict-combined heads,
    Which strike against this mine of diamonds,
    Shall prove but glassen hammers, they shall break,— 145

135. Perseus] *Q;* Portia's *conj. Mitford (ap. Dyce i), Haz;* Perseus' *Sp.*
136. virtue] *Q;* virtue. *Dod i.*   140. spirit.] spirit *Q.*   143. strict-
combined] *hyphened Dyce i;* strickt combined *Q.*

---

130. *scandals*] abuses, disgraces.
135. *of force*] i.e., perforce.
Perseus] P. Simpson (*M.L.R.*, ii (1907), 162–3) pointed out that Jonson's
Masque of Queens (1609) presented Perseus 'expressing heroique and
masculine Vertue'; a marginal note in the printed text of the masque links
Perseus with Hercules and Bellerophon as types of 'brave and masculine
Vertue'.
    Crawford pointed out that Webster was probably indebted to the dedi-
cation of this masque in *Monumental Column* (1613), ll. 23–30.
136. *virtue*—] Webster's use of the phrase 'to the point' elsewhere
(*D.L.C.*, IV. ii. 126, 163, and 370, and *A.V.*, IV. i. 213) suggests that a break
in the sense is intended (so Lucas). However, 'to the point' can mean 'in
every detail', so Q's punctuation *could* stand.
138–9. *scorn . . . entreaty*] Sykes (quoted by Lucas) compared Florio,
III, x: 'How many gallant men have rather made choice to lose their life
than to be indebted for the same'.
143. *strict-combined*] i.e., closely (possibly, secretly) allied. The word-
play is double: (1) military ('heads' = military forces), and (2) mechanical
('heads' = hammer-heads).

These are but feigned shadows of my evils.
Terrify babes, my lord, with painted devils,
I am past such needless palsy,—for your names
Of whore and murd'ress they proceed from you,
As if a man should spit against the wind,　　　　　150
The filth returns in's face.
Mont.　Pray you mistress satisfy me one question:
　Who lodg'd beneath your roof that fatal night
　Your husband brake his neck?
Brac.　　　　　　　　　That question
　Enforceth me break silence,—I was there.　　　　155
Mont.　Your business?
Brac.　　　　　　　Why I came to comfort her,
　And take some course for settling her estate,
　Because I heard her husband was in debt
　To you my lord.
Mont.　　　　　He was.
Brac.　　　　　　　　　And 'twas strangely fear'd
　That you would cozen her.
Mont.　　　　　　　　Who made you overseer?　　160
Brac.　Why my charity, my charity, which should flow
　From every generous and noble spirit,
　To orphans and to widows.
Mont.　　　　　　　Your lust.
Brac.　Cowardly dogs bark loudest. Sirrah priest,
　I'll talk with you hereafter,—Do you hear?　　　165
　The sword you frame of such an excellent temper,

165. hereafter,—Do] *Q.*

---

146. *shadows*] often used of portraits as contrasted with their originals; cf. II. ii. 28.
147.] Cf. *Mac.*, II. ii. 54–5.
150–1.] Lucas compared Heywood, *Challenge for Beauty* (1636), G3ᵛ: 'all my attempts / Like curses shall against the winde flie back / In mine owne face and soile it'.
161. *charity*] Webster may have echoed this at v. iii. 172–3.
164. *Cowardly . . . loudest*] a common proverb; cf. Tilley D528.
166. *sword*] commonly used meaning 'instrument of justice' (cf. *Meas.*, III. ii. 275 and *Oth.*, v. ii. 17).

I'll sheathe in your own bowels:
There are a number of thy coat resemble
Your common post-boys.

Mont.   Ha?

Brac.   Your mercenary post-boys,—
Your letters carry truth, but 'tis your guise   170
To fill your mouths with gross and impudent lies.

Serv. My lord your gown.

Brac.   Thou liest—'twas my stool.
Bestow't upon thy master that will challenge
The rest a'th'household stuff—for Bracciano
Was ne'er so beggarly, to take a stool   175
Out of another's lodging: let him make
Valance for his bed on't, or a demi-foot-cloth
For his most reverend moil,—Monticelso,
Nemo me impune lacessit.   *Exit* BRACCIANO.

168–71.] Dent quoted from Foxe, *Acts and Monuments* (1563), ed. Pratt, vi, 92–3, of Stephen Gardiner, Bishop of Winchester: 'I mislike that preachers which preach by the king's licence . . . talk against the Mass, . . . I may liken them unto posts; for the proverb says, that posts "do bear truth in their letters, and lies in their mouths" . . .'

Lucas noted the change to the scornful second person singular in *thy* (l. 168). *guise* = custom, practice.

172.] G. A. Parry noted (*N. & Q.*, xi ser., vii (1913), 326) a similar incident in the *Percy Anecdotes*, Chandos Reprint, p. 179: Robert, Duke of Normandy, was invited to a feast by the Emperor at Constantinople; he and his followers were not provided with seats, so they sat on their cloaks, and left them behind at the end of the meal; when the Emperor sent the cloaks after them, the Duke returned answer 'Go and tell your master it is not the custom of the Normans to carry about with them the seats which they use at an entertainment'.

Lucas noted a similar episode in Lope de Vega's *El honrado hermano* (published 1623, but perhaps written before 1604).

173. *challenge*] lay claim to.

177. *Valance*] bed-curtain, drapery around the canopy.

demi-foot-cloth] half-length covering for a horse (cf. I. ii. 51 n.).

178. *moil*] a common 17th-century form of 'mule', which may be retained here for its association with the idea of drudgery (cf. vb. 'to moil').

Mules were the traditional mounts for cardinals, and jests were often made at these humble beasts in the rich equipages of some cardinals; cf. Tofte's Ariosto (cf. I. ii. 78–92 n.), D4 (of a great cardinal): 'if his moiles doe not most ready stand, / . . . He rages straight, his honor is disgrac't'.

179.] i.e., 'No one injures me with impunity'; Lucas noted that this

Mont. Your champion's gone.

Vit.   The wolf may prey the better.   180

Fran. My lord there's great suspicion of the murder,
         But no sound proof who did it: for my part
         I do not think she hath a soul so black
         To act a deed so bloody,—if she have,
         As in cold countries husbandmen plant vines,   185
         And with warm blood manure them, even so
         One summer she will bear unsavoury fruit,
         And ere next spring wither both branch and root.
         The act of blood let pass, only descend
         To matter of incontinence.

Vit.   I discern poison,   190
         Under your gilded pills.

Mont. Now the duke's gone, I will produce a letter,
         Wherein 'twas plotted he and you should meet,
         At an apothecary's summer-house,
         Down by the river Tiber:—view't my lords:—   195
         Where after wanton bathing and the heat
         Of a lascivious banquet... I pray read it,
         I shame to speak the rest.

Vit.   Grant I was tempted,
         Temptation to lust proves not the act,
         Casta est quam nemo rogavit,—   200
         You read his hot love to me, but you want
         My frosty answer.

193. he] *Q3;* her *Q.*   197. banquet . . .] banquet.— *Q.*

---

motto first appeared on the 'Thistle-mark', a coin issued by James VI of
Scotland in 1578.
    180. *prey*] Lucas suggested a pun on 'pray'.
    185–6. *As . . . them*] Lucas compared Marston, *Sophonisba* (1606), II. iii:
'Through rottenst dung best plants both sprout & live / By blood vines
grow.'
    190–1. *I . . . pills*] Cf. *D.M.,* IV. i. 23–4: 'why do'st wrap thy poysond
Pilles / In Gold, and Sugar ?'
    194. *summer-house*] arbour, garden-house.
    200.] i.e., 'She is chaste whom no man has solicited' (Ovid, *Amores,*
I, viii, 43).

Mont.   Frost i'th'dog-days! strange!

Vit. Condemn you me for that the duke did love me?
      So may you blame some fair and crystal river
      For that some melancholic distracted man   205
      Hath drown'd himself in't.

Mont.   Truly drown'd indeed.

Vit. Sum up my faults I pray, and you shall find
      That beauty and gay clothes, a merry heart,
      And a good stomach to a feast, are all,
      All the poor crimes that you can charge me with: 210
      In faith my lord you might go pistol flies,
      The sport would be more noble.

Mont.   Very good.

Vit. But take you your course, it seems you have beggar'd me
          first
      And now would fain undo me,—I have houses,
      Jewels, and a poor remnant of crusadoes,   215
      Would those would make you charitable.

Mont.   If the devil
      Did ever take good shape behold his picture.

---

209. to a] *Dod. ii;* to *Q.*   213. you your] *Q;* your *Haz.*   you have] *Q;*
you've *Haz.*

---

202. *dog-days*] days during the heliacal rising of the Dog-star, renowned
as the hottest and most unwholesome time of the year; usually reckoned
as the forty days following 11 Aug. For their incitation to lust, cf. II. i.
161 n.

204–6.] Cf. *Honour's Academy* (cf. App. IV), Ee2: 'O you blinde and
frantike Louers, who alwayes make your Mistresses the motiues of all your
misfortunes. As if a faire Christall Riuer, and such a one, as is profitable
vnto the whole Common-wealth, should be condemned, for drowning such
as cast themselues headlong into the same, and not their owne foolish and
desperate fault'.

209. *to a*] Cf. note on II. i. 108 (also set by Compositor A).

213. *you your*] Hazlitt's emendation is attractive in view of Compositor
A's clearly erroneous 'you, you' of I. i. 19 and *A.V.*, III. ii. 237: 'Nay, take
your course'; but the irregular metre and the sentiment may seem to
require the emphatic, repetitive phrasing.

215. *crusadoes*] Portuguese coins of gold or silver.

216–17. *devil . . . shape*] a direct reference to the play's title; cf. also,
2 Corinthians, xi. 14: 'Satan himself is transformed into an angel of light'.

Vit. You have one virtue left,
　　You will not flatter me.

Fran.　　　　　　　Who brought this letter?

Vit. I am not compell'd to tell you.　　　　　　　220

Mont. My lord duke sent to you a thousand ducats,
　　The twelfth of August.

Vit.　　　　　　　'Twas to keep your cousin
　　From prison, I paid use for't.

Mont.　　　　　　　I rather think
　　'Twas interest for his lust.

Vit. Who says so but yourself? if you be my accuser　　225
　　Pray cease to be my judge, come from the bench,
　　Give in your evidence 'gainst me, and let these
　　Be moderators: my lord cardinal,
　　Were your intelligencing ears as long
　　As to my thoughts, had you an honest tongue　　230
　　I would not care though you proclaim'd them all.

Mont. Go to, go to.
　　After your goodly and vain-glorious banquet,
　　I'll give you a choke-pear.

Vit.　　　　　　　A' your own grafting?

Mont. You were born in Venice, honourably descended　　235

218–19. You . . . me] *so Q; one line Samp.*　　225. Who . . . accuser] *so Q;*
. . . so / But . . . *Dyce i.*　　229–30. as . . . As] *Luc;* as louing / As *Q;* as
loving / And *Deighton.*　　233. vain-glorious] *hyphened Q.*

---

223. *use*] interest, usury.

225–6. *if . . . judge*] Cf. Jonson, *Sejanus*, III. 200–1: 'is he my accuser? /
And must he be my judge?'

229. *intelligencing*] spying, acting as informer.

long] Lucas compared Jonson, *Sejanus* (1605), II. 453–6: 'Yea, had
Sejanus both his eares as long / As to my in-most closet; I would hate / To
whisper any thought, or change an act, / To be made Juno's riuall'. Q's
error is readily understandable, for in normal secretary handwriting, 'u'
and 'n' were often identical.

234. *choke-pear*] rough and unpalatable pear (often used figuratively for
a 'severe rebuke' or 'set-back').

235–6. *born . . . Vitelli*] In fact, Vittoria was born at Gubbio and descended of the Accoramboni (see Intro., p. **xxvi**).

Stoll suggested that Webster was remembering Bianca Capello who was
born at Venice and after her first marriage became the mistress and then the

From the Vitelli; 'twas my cousin's fate,—
Ill may I name the hour—to marry you,
He bought you of your father.

Vit.   Ha?

Mont. He spent there in six months

    Twelve thousand ducats, and to my acquaintance   240
Receiv'd in dowry with you not one julio:
'Twas a hard penny-worth, the ware being so light.
I yet but draw the curtain—now to your picture,—
You came from thence a most notorious strumpet,
And so you have continued.

Vit.   My lord.

Mont.   Nay hear me,   245
You shall have time to prate—my Lord Bracciano, . . .
Alas I make but repetition
Of what is ordinary and Rialto talk,
And ballated, and would be play'd a'th'stage,
But that vice many times finds such loud friends   250
That preachers are charm'd silent.
You gentlemen Flamineo and Marcello,

247. repetition] Q^b; repetion Q^a.

---

second wife of Francesco, Duke of Florence. But Webster may well have wished to associate Vittoria with Venice because that city was famed for its prostitutes; the title-page of the first quarto calls Vittoria 'the famous Venetian Curtizan'.

The Vitelli were a well-known Roman family; they are mentioned in *A Letter* (1585), quoted in App. II, p. 193.

241. *julio*] a coin worth about 6d. (so Moryson, *Itinerary* (1617), ed. 1907, I, xxiv).

242. *light*] a very common quibble (cf. *Mer.V.*, v. i. 130).

243.] Cf. II. ii. 23.2 n.

248. *Rialto talk*] i.e., talk of the town (so Lucas); cf. Coryat, *Crudities* (1611), ed. 1905, I, 312: 'The Rialto, . . . the Exchange of Venice, where the Venetian Gentlemen and the Merchants doe meete twice a day', and *Mer.V.*, I. iii. 39.

249. *ballated*] Ballad writers were the popular journalists of the time; cf. *D.L.C.*, v. iv. 191–4: 'I am sory . . . / That I made not mine owne Ballad: I doe feare / I shall be roguishly abused in Meeter'.

play'd . . . stage] Topical scandals were often so presented; in 1624 Webster himself helped to write such a play (cf. Intro., p. xxv).

The court hath nothing now to charge you with,
Only you must remain upon your sureties
For your appearance.
Fran.   I stand for Marcello.   255
Flam. And my lord duke for me.
Mont. For you Vittoria, your public fault,
Join'd to th'condition of the present time,
Takes from you all the fruits of noble pity.
Such a corrupted trial have you made   260
Both of your life and beauty, and been styl'd
No less in ominous fate than blazing stars
To princes; here's your sentence,—you are confin'd
Unto a house of convertites and your bawd—
Flam. [*aside*] Who I?
Mont.   The Moor.
Flam.   [*aside*] O I am a sound man again.   265
Vit. A house of convertites, what's that?
Mont.   A house
Of penitent whores.
Vit.   Do the noblemen in Rome
Erect it for their wives, that I am sent
To lodge there?
Fran. You must have patience.
Vit.   I must first have vengeance.   270

262. in] *Q;* an *Q2.*   263. princes; here's] *conj. Dyce i* (princes: here's),
Sym; Princes heares; *Q;* Princes, heare *Q2.*   264. Unto] *Q3; Vit.*
Vnto *Q.*   bawd] *Q*ᵃ (baud); baud. *Q*ᵇ.   265. S.D.s] *Dyce ii; not in Q.*
266–7. *Mont.* A . . . whores] *so Dyce i; one line Q.*

257. *public*] Cf. III. i. 19 n.
262–3. *in . . . princes*] Cf. *Cæs.*, II. ii. 30–1.
263. *here's*] Repunctuation of Q is necessary, but this reading involves no
further emendation, for Compositor A used this current spelling, 'heare',
for mod. 'here' at I. ii. 226 and 271. Those editors who have followed
Q2 have *D.L.C.*'s more general 'attend the Sentence of the Court' (v. v. 65;
quoted Lucas) and Compositor A's propensity for adding erroneous final
letters (e.g., l. 276 below) to support them.
270.] Cf. Jonson, *Sejanus* (1605), IV. 1–2: '—You must haue patience,
royall *Agrippina.*—I must haue vengeance, first'.

I fain would know if you have your salvation
By patent, that you proceed thus.

Mont.   Away with her.
Take her hence.

Vit. A rape, a rape.

Mont.   How?

Vit.   Yes you have ravish'd justice,
Forc'd her to do your pleasure.

Mont.   Fie she's mad—   275

Vit. Die with those pills in your most cursed maw,
Should bring you health, or while you sit a'th'bench,
Let your own spittle choke you.

Mont.   She's turn'd Fury.

Vit. That the last day of judgement may so find you,
And leave you the same devil you were before,—   280
Instruct me some good horse-leech to speak treason,
For since you cannot take my life for deeds,
Take it for words,—O woman's poor revenge
Which dwells but in the tongue,—I will not weep,
No I do scorn to call up one poor tear   285
To fawn on your injustice,—bear me hence,
Unto this house of—what's your mitigating title?

Mont. Of convertites.

272-3. Away . . . hence] *so Q; one line Samp.*   276. those] *Q4;* these *Q.*
maw] *Q2;* mawes *Q.*   286. on] *Q2;* one *Q.*

---

272. *patent*] special licence, or title.

274-5. *A rape . . . pleasure*] E. E. Stoll compared *Atheist's Tragedy* (1611),
I. iv: '—A Rape, a rape, a rape!—How now?—What's that?—Why what
is't but a Rape to force a wench to marry?', and R. Brooke compared
Chapman, *Chabot* (pf. *c.* 1613), v. ii. 122: 'a most prodigious and fearful
rape, a rape even upon Justice itself'.

276. *those*] Elizabethan secretary hands often confused 'e' and 'o'; Vittoria, supposing that Monticelso takes pills for his health, wishes they
would kill him and so bring him to judgement (cf. l. 279).

maw] Emendation seems necessary, for Vittoria is addressing Monticelso only; for a similar error by Compositor A, cf. I. ii. 282.

281. *horse-leech*] i.e., blood-sucker; cf. v. vi. 166.

283-4. *O . . . tongue*] Cf. proverb, 'A woman hath no weapon but her
tongue' (Tilley, W675).

Vit. It shall not be a house of convertites—
 My mind shall make it honester to me   290
 Than the Pope's palace, and more peaceable
 Than thy soul, though thou art a cardinal,—
 Know this, and let it somewhat raise your spite,
 Through darkness diamonds spread their richest light.

        Exit VITTORIA [*with* ZANCHE,
             guarded].

     Enter BRACCIANO.

Brac. Now you and I are friends sir, we'll shake hands,   295
 In a friend's grave, together, a fit place,
 Being the emblem of soft peace t'atone our hatred.
Fran. Sir, what's the matter?
Brac. I will not chase more blood from that lov'd cheek,
 You have lost too much already, fare-you-well. [*Exit.*] 300
Fran. How strange these words sound? what's the interpretation?
Flam. [*aside*] Good, this is a preface to the discovery of the
 duchess' death: he carries it well: because now I cannot
 counterfeit a whining passion for the death of my lady, I
 will feign a mad humour for the disgrace of my sister,   305
 and that will keep off idle questions,—treason's tongue
 hath a villainous palsy in't, I will talk to any man, hear
 no man, and for a time appear a politic madman. [*Exit.*]

    Enter GIOVANNI, *Count* LODOVICO.

Fran. How now my noble cousin, what in black?
Giov. Yes uncle, I was taught to imitate you   310

294.1–3.] *so Q4 subs.; one line ('Enter Brachiano' centred, 'Exit Vittoria'*
to right) Q.   294.1–2. *Vittoria . . . guarded*] *This ed.; Vittoria Q; Vittoria.*/
Act. 3. Scen. 3 *Q4; Vittoria Corombona, Lawyer, and Guards Dyce i.*
297. the] *Q;* th' *Dyce i.*   300. fare-you-well] *hyphened Q.*   *Exit*]
Dod ii; not in Q.   302. *aside*] *Q4 (to right of line); not in Q.*   308. *Exit*]
Dod ii; not in Q.

---

 297. *atone*] appease.
 299–300.] It is not clear whether Bracciano speaks of Francisco, or
Isabella, or both.
 307. *palsy*] i.e., uncontrolled nervousness.

In virtue, and you must imitate me
In colours for your garments,—my sweet mother
Is, . . .

Fran. How? Where?

Giov. Is there,—no yonder,—indeed sir I'll not tell you,   315
For I shall make you weep.

Fran. Is dead.

Giov. Do not blame me now,
I did not tell you so.

Lod.   She's dead my lord.

Fran. Dead?   320

Mont. Blessed lady; thou art now above thy woes,—
Will't please your lordships to withdraw a little?

                              [*Exeunt Ambassadors.*]

Giov. What do the dead do, uncle? do they eat,
Hear music, go a-hunting, and be merry,
As we that live?   325

Fran. No coz; they sleep.

Giov.   Lord, Lord, that I were dead,—
I have not slept these six nights. When do they wake?

Fran. When God shall please.

Giov.   Good God let her sleep ever.
For I have known her wake an hundred nights,
When all the pillow, where she laid her head,   330
Was brine-wet with her tears.
I am to complain to you sir.
I'll tell you how they have used her now she's dead:

311. you] *Q; you now Swinburne (ap. Samp), Wheel.*   313. Is, . . .]
Is, *Q.*   315–16. Is . . . weep] *so Q;* . . . sir, / I'll . . . *Wal.*   317. dead.]
Q; dead? *Dod i.*   318–19. Do . . . so] *so Q; one line Wal.*   321. Blessed
. . . woes] *so Dod iii, Samp, Wheel;* . . . Lady; / Thou . . . *Q.*   322. Will't]
Wilt *Q.*   322.1.] *Dyce i; not in Q.*   324–5. Hear . . . live] *so Dod ii;
one line Q.*   328. Giov.] *Q3; not in Q.*   329. For] *Q3;* Gio. For *Q.*
331–2. Was . . . sir] *so this ed.; one line Q.*   333. they have] *Q;* they've
conj. this ed.

322.1.] Cf. the omission of other exits at ll. 300 and 308 above.

They wrapp'd her in a cruel fold of lead,
And would not let me kiss her.

Fran.   Thou didst love her.   335

Giov. I have often heard her say she gave me suck,
And it should seem by that she dearly lov'd me,
Since princes seldom do it.

Fran. O, all of my poor sister that remains!
Take him away for God's sake.   [*Exit* GIOVANNI *attended.*]

Mont.   How now my lord ?   340

Fran. Believe me I am nothing but her grave,
And I shall keep her blessed memory
Longer than thousand epitaphs.   [*Exeunt.*]

---

335. love her.] *Q; love her ? Luc.*   340. S.D.] *Dyce i subs.; not in Q;
Exit Giovanni Dod ii; Exeunt Giovanni, Lodovico, and Marcello Samp.*
343. S.D.] *Luc; not in Q; Exeunt Francisco de Medicis and Monticelso
Dyce i.*

---

334. *fold*] For the sense of 'wrapping', *O.E.D.* (s.v., 3) quotes Ford,
Broken Heart (1633), III. v: '. . . a winding-sheet, a fold of lead, / And some
untrod-on corner in the earth'; but, in view of 'cruel' and 'kiss' (ll. 334–5),
a sense of 'clasp' or 'embrace' might be suggested (cf. *Troil.*, III. iii. 223, and
A. Stafford, *Niobe* (1611), B9ᵛ–10: 'when your delicate, smooth body shall
be enfolded in earths rugged armes').

335. *love her.*] Q's punctuation may stand, for, although Compositor B
did omit question marks elsewhere, in this section (F3–4ᵛ) there is no
certain example.

336–8.] Cf. *W.Ho*, I. ii: 'if a Woman of any markeable face in the Worlde
giue her Childe sucke, looke how many wrinckles be in the Nipple of her
breast, so many will bee in her forheade by that time twelue moneth', and
Pettie, III, 48: 'women at this daye are so curious of their comlinesse, or
rather of their vanitie, that they hadde rather perverte the nature of their
Children, then chaunge the fourme of their fyrme, harde, and rounde
pappes, . . .'

343.] The *Exeunt* is required if the entries following are to be taken as
a separate 'ante-chamber' scene with 'passages over the stage' as in III. i (cf.
ll. 64.1–2); see also l. 322.1 n.

[III. iii]

Enter FLAMINEO *as distracted* [, MARCELLO,
and LODOVICO].

Flam. We endure the strokes like anvils or hard steel,
Till pain itself make us no pain to feel.
Who shall do me right now? Is this the end of service?
I'd rather go weed garlic; travail through France, and be
mine own ostler; wear sheep-skin linings; or shoes that   5
stink of blacking; be ent'red into the list of the forty
thousand pedlars in Poland.

Enter Savoy [*Ambassador*].

Would I had rotted in some surgeon's house at Venice,
built upon the pox as well as on piles, ere I had serv'd
Bracciano.   10
Sav. Amb. You must have comfort.
Flam. Your comfortable words are like honey. They relish
well in your mouth that's whole; but in mine that's
wounded they go down as if the sting of the bee were in
them. O they have wrought their purpose cunningly, as if   15
they would not seem to do it of malice. In this a politician
imitates the devil, as the devil imitates a cannon. Wheresoever he comes to do mischief, he comes with his back-
side towards you.

III. iii] *Samp; not in Q, Sym.*   0.1–2. *Marcello, and Lodovico*] *Luc; not in
Q; after l. 7.1 Samp.*   4. travail] *Q; travel Q3.*   7.1.] *Haz; Enter
Sauoy Q; Enter Ambassadors Dyce i.*

III. iii.] The location is an ante-chamber, as in III. i.

1–2.] G. K. Hunter (*N. & Q.*, n.s., iv (1957), 53) compared *Orlando
Furioso* (tr. 1591), XXX, vii: 'That with his fist he made the herdman reele, /
Till paine it selfe made him no paine to feele'.

6–7. *forty . . . Poland*] Sugden (*Topographical Dict*[y].) suggested that the
poverty of Poles gave point to this gibe; cf. the 'Scotch tailor' in *Fair Maid
of the Inn* (IV. ii. 142) who had 'travail'd far, & was a pedlar in *Poland*'.

9. *piles*] in two senses.

12–15. *Your . . . them*] probably a (second-hand) allusion to Seneca,
Epistles, 109, 7 (so Dent).

17–19. *Wheresoever . . . you*] In token of obedience, witches 'kisse the
diuels bare buttocks' (so R. Scot, *Discovery of Witchcraft* (1584), E6).

Enter the French [Ambassador].

Fr. Amb. The proofs are evident.   20

Flam. Proof! 'twas corruption. O gold, what a god art thou!
   and O man, what a devil art thou to be tempted by that
   cursed mineral! Yon diversivolent lawyer; mark him,
   knaves turn informers, as maggots turn to flies,—you may
   catch gudgeons with either. A cardinal;—I would he   25
   would hear me,—there's nothing so holy but money will
   corrupt and putrify it, like victual under the line.

                                                    vittle

Enter English Ambassador.

   You are happy in England, my lord; here they sell justice
   with those weights they press men to death with. O
   horrible salary!   30

Eng. Amb. Fie, fie, Flamineo.

Flam. Bells ne'er ring well, till they are at their full pitch, and
   I hope yon cardinal shall never have the grace to pray well,
   till he come to the scaffold.   [*Exeunt Ambassadors.*]

19.1.] *Q4; Enter the French Q; not in Dyce i.*   23. Yon] *Haz;* You *Q;*
Your *Q4.*   25. cardinal;] *Q;* Cardinall! *Q2.*   I] *Q; not in Luc.*
27. victual] *Q* (vittell)*; victuals *Q2.*   27–8. line. / You] *so Luc; as con-*
tinuous prose Q.   27. line] *Q2;* liue *Q.*   27.1.] *so Luc; outer margin, to*
left of ll. 26–30 approx. Q; not in Q2.   32. Bells . . . pitch] *so Dod ii;*
as separate line Q.   34. S.D.] *This ed.; not in Q; after l. 31 Dyce i.*
34–5. scaffold. / If] *so Q; as continuous prose Dod ii.*

---

23. *Yon*] It is hazardous to correct a supposedly distracted speech, but
'u' and 'n' are confused elsewhere (e.g., l. 27 below, also set by B) and there
are parallels in the 'yon' of l. 33 below (also spoken as distracted) and in
'Yonder . . .' of v. iii. 97 (which is truly distracted).
   diversivolent] Flamineo echoes the lawyer; cf. III. ii. 28.
   25. *gudgeons*] small fish, easily caught and used as bait; the word was
often used of gullible simpletons.
   27. *under the line*] i.e., at the equator.
   29. *weights . . . with*] the *peine forte et dure* inflicted by English law up to
1772 on those who refused to plead either guilty or not guilty, when they
were charged with felonies other than treason (so Lucas). If the victim
remained obdurate and died under this torture, his goods were not con-
fiscated because he had not been convicted.
   30. *salary*] reward.
   32. *at . . . pitch*] i.e., pulled up, inverted at their full height.
   34.] The break in the consecutive prose of Q suggests that Compositor B

If they were rack'd now to know the confederacy! But 35
your noblemen are privileged from the rack; and well
may. For a little thing would pull some of them a'pieces
ofore they came to their arraignment. Religion; O how it
is commeddled with policy. The first bloodshed in the
world happened about religion. Would I were a Jew. 40

Mar. O, there are too many.

Flam. You are deceiv'd. There are not Jews enough; priests
enough, nor gentlemen enough.

Mar. How?

Flam. I'll prove it. For if there were Jews enough, so many 45
Christians would not turn usurers; if priests enough, one
should not have six benefices; and if gentlemen enough,
so many early mushrooms, whose best growth sprang
from a dunghill, should not aspire to gentility. Farewell.
Let others live by begging. Be thou one of them; practise 50
the art of Wolner in England to swallow all's given thee;

50. them;] *Q;* them *Dyce i.*

intended to place a stage-direction here (he broke prose for directions at
l. 7 above, and at I. ii. 195 and 197, v. iii. 66, and v. iv. 49). The ambassadors
have appeared only for a 'passage over the stage' as in III. i.

35. *know*] make known.

36–7. *well may*] i.e., with good reason.

37. *pull . . . pieces*] Continuing from talk of the 'rack', Flamineo puns on
'to pull a'pieces', meaning 'to destroy by argument' (cf. *O.E.D., pull,* 8b).

39. *commeddled*] mixed together.

39–40. *first . . . religion*] Cf. Genesis, iv. 3–8.

46. *usurers*] 'Jew' had become almost synonymous with 'usurer'.

48. *mushrooms*] upstarts; *O.E.D.* (s.v., 2) quotes Marlowe, *Ed. II* (pf. *c.*
1593), I. iv. 283: 'A night growne mushrump, / Such a one as my Lord of
Cornewall is'. Cf. *D.L.C.,* IV. ii. 129–33: 'he has rankt himselfe / With the
Nobilitie, . . . / . . . and in a kind of sawcy pride, / Which like to Mushromes,
euer grow most ranke, / When they do spring from dung-hills, sought to
oresway . . .' See, also, Tilley, M1319.

50. *them;*] i.e., those who live by begging; Flamineo, in assumed distraction, abruptly changes tack.

51. *Wolner*] a 'singing-man of Windsor', a famous Elizabethan glutton;
he could 'eat iron, glass, oyster-shells, raw fish, raw flesh, raw fruit, and
whatsoever else he would put into his stomach, without offence'; he died
by 'eating a raw eel' (Moffet, *Health's Improvement* (1655); quoted by
Reed).

and yet let one purgation make thee as hungry again as
fellows that work in a saw-pit. I'll go hear the screech-
owl.   *Exit.*

Lod. [*aside*] This was Bracciano's pandar, and 'tis strange   55
          That in such open and apparent guilt
          Of his adulterous sister, he dare utter
          So scandalous a passion. I must wind him.

                    Enter FLAMINEO.

Flam. [*aside*] How dares this banish'd count return to Rome,
          His pardon not yet purchas'd? I have heard   60
          The deceas'd duchess gave him pension,
          And that he came along from Padua
          I'th'train of the young prince. There's somewhat in't.
          Physicians, that cure poisons, still do work
          With counterpoisons.

Mar.   Mark this strange encounter.   65

Flam. The god of melancholy turn thy gall to poison,
          And let the stigmatic wrinkles in thy face,
          Like to the boisterous waves in a rough tide,
          One still overtake another.

Lod.   I do thank thee
          And I do wish ingeniously for thy sake   70
          The dog-days all year long.

Flam.   How croaks the raven?
          Is our good duchess dead?

53. in a] *Q*2; in *Q*.   55, 59. aside] *Dyce ii; not in Q.*   69. overtake] *Q;*
o'ertake *conj. this ed.*

---

    53. *in a*] Compositor B was not prone to omitting single short words (but
cf. IV. ii. 69), but here *in* is at the end of a line of prose, so two pieces of
type (the 'a' and a space) may have dropped out.
    58. *wind*] get wind of, discover the purposes of.
    60. *purchas'd*] obtained (not necessarily by payment).
    67. *stigmatic*] stigmatized, or branded, by nature; deformed.
    70. *ingeniously*] The sense is ambiguous, for the word was often used for
'ingenuously'.
    71. *dog-days*] Cf. III. ii. 202 n.
    croaks . . . raven] proverbially ill-boding; cf. *Mac.*, I. v. 39–40.

Lod.   Dead—

Flam.   O fate!
Misfortune comes like the coroner's business,
Huddle upon huddle.

Lod. Shalt thou and I join housekeeping?

Flam.   Yes, content.   75
Let's be unsociably sociable.

Lod. Sit some three days together, and discourse.

Flam. Only with making faces;
Lie in our clothes.

Lod. With faggots for our pillows.

Flam.   And be lousy.   80

Lod. In taffeta linings; that's gentle melancholy,—
Sleep all day.

Flam.   Yes: and like your melancholic hare
Feed after midnight.

Enter ANTONELLI [*and* GASPARO, *laughing*].

73. coroner's] *Q3;* Crowners *Q.*   78–9. Only . . . clothes] *so Q; as one
line Dyce i.*   81. gentle] gentile *Q;* genteel *Dod i.*   83.1.] *Luc; Enter
Antonelli (to right of l. 96) Q; Enter Antonelli, / and Gasparo (to right of
ll. 96–7) Q4.*

73. *coroner's*] Q's 'Crowners' was a current form; the modern form
(which was also current) probably suits the metre better.

78–9.] Q's lining may stand, for this is a 'strange encounter' (l. 65) and
abrupt, broken and neurotic-seeming dialogue would be appropriate.

Compositor B may have gathered that this dialogue was unusual, for, at
ll. 71–2 and 75–6, above, he twice set Flamineo's speeches correctly as two
short lines, even though there was ample space, in both cases, for running
the two halves together as he usually did.

81. *taffeta*] plain-woven, glossy silk; supposed to be louse-proof (cf. l.80).

gentle] Mod. 'gentile', 'genteel' and *gentle* were not distinguished by
spelling in the early 17th century.

82–3. *melancholic . . . midnight*] Turberville (*Noble Art of Venery* (1611),
K8v) noted that the hare is 'one of the most melancholicke beasts that is' (so
Sykes). Topsell (*History* (1607–8), Aa1v) described how: 'They rest in the
day time, and walk abroad to feed in the night, neuer feeding near home,
either because they are delighted with forren foode, or else because they
woulde exercise their legs in going, or else by secret instinct of nature, to
conceale their forms and lodging places vnknowne, . . .'

83.1.] The break in the verse, together with 'We are observed . . .' of the
next line, suggests an entry here.

We are observed: see how yon couple grieve.

Lod. What a strange creature is a laughing fool,   85

As if man were created to no use

But only to show his teeth.

Flam.   I'll tell thee what,—

It would do well instead of looking-glasses

To set one's face each morning by a saucer

Of a witch's congealed blood.

Lod.   Precious girn, rogue.   90

---

90. Precious girn, rogue] *This ed.;* Pretious grine rouge *Qᵃ;* Pretious gue
Qᵇ, Dyce ii; Pretious Rogue *Q3;* Precious! grin, rogue *Sisson;* Precious
grin, rogue *conj. this ed.*

Q's direction at l. 96 may have originated from the hurried correction
and amplification of the stage-directions before publication (cf. Intro.,
p. lxvii); it occurs just before Antonelli speaks (cf. the incorrect entry for
Monticelso at IV. iii. 83–4) and omits the necessary entrance of Gasparo,
whose presence (without the earlier 'couple' of l. 84) is not shown by the
dialogue until l. 129.

Editors, who have followed Q, have presumed that the ambassadors
remain on stage from the beginning of this scene (but cf. l. 34 n. above)
and that the two laughing people referred to in ll. 84–5 are, for some un-
specified reason, any two of the onlookers; these difficulties are avoided if
Antonelli enters as directed in this edition, for he has cause for laughter in
his news (cf. ll. 98ff.).

84. *grieve*] ironically.

89. *saucer*] The receptacle for blood in blood-letting was so called.

90. *girn*] referring to a face 'set' in a mirror of blood (cf. l. 89) and used
quibblingly: (1) 'snarl, act of showing teeth' (cf. l. 87 above), and (2) 'snare,
trap, wile'. The two senses are found in Marston, *Antonio and Mellida*
(1602), III. ii (in which Balurdo and Rossaline enter with looking-glasses
and 'stand setting faces'): 'hold up the glass higher, that I may see to
sweare in fashion . . . oh that gerne kils, it kils'.

Some editors follow Qᵇ, but 'gue' (glossed by Dyce as 'rogue, sharper',
from Fr. *gueux*) is only known once elsewhere, in 1651 (so *O.E.D.*), and
there it may be a textual error.

Lucas, following Q3, suggested that 'rogue' was misprinted in Qᵃ twice
(first as 'grine' and then as 'rouge'), but, as C. J. Sisson pointed out (*M.L.R.*
xxiv (1929), 343), 'rouge' was a then current form of 'rogue' and it is hard to
see how 'rogue' could possibly be misprinted as 'grine', especially as it was
repeated as 'rouge'.

Sisson suggested 'Precious! Grin, rogue' because he thought the line
referred to 'the laughing Antonelli and Gasparo'; but it is easier to interpret
with reference to the immediate conversation.

Since 'grin' and *girn* were originally two forms of one word, 'grin' (sb.)

We'll never part.

Flam. Never: till the beggary of courtiers,
    The discontent of churchmen, want of soldiers,
    And all the creatures that hang manacled,
    Worse than strappado'd, on the lowest felly   95
    Of Fortune's wheel be taught in our two lives
    To scorn that world which life of means deprives.

Ant. My lord, I bring good news. The Pope on's death-bed,
    At th'earnest suit of the great Duke of Florence,
    Hath sign'd your pardon, and restor'd unto you—   100

Lod. I thank you for your news. Look up again
    Flamineo, see my pardon.

Flam.   Why do you laugh?
    There was no such condition in our covenant.

Lod. Why?

Flam. You shall not seem a happier man than I,—   105
    You know our vow sir, if you will be merry,
    Do it i'th'like posture, as if some great man
    Sate while his enemy were executed:
    Though it be very lechery unto thee,

96. lives] *Q*ª; liues. *Q*ᵇ.   100. you—] *Q*.

---

might be read for *Q*ª's 'grine', but Marston's 'gerne' tells against this and,
moreover, the substantive in the form 'grin' is not found for a facial
expression before 1635–56 (so *O.E.D.*); it is easier to suppose that Compositor B, for once, muddled the order of 'i' and 'r'.

    *Q*ᵇ's 'gue' is probably an ill-executed miscorrection of an obscure pass-
age (i.e., intending to read the commoner spelling 'rogue' and dropping
(either intentionally or by accident) the puzzling 'grine'); there is no other
variant which suggests that the MS. copy was consulted for correcting this
forme.

    95. *strappado'd*] hung up by the hands after they had been tied across the
back.

    felly] felloe, section of the circular rim of a wheel.

    96. *Fortune's wheel*] Fortune was fabled to turn a wheel, an emblem of
mutability; so she raised men from the lowest 'felly' to the highest, and
then down again. Flamineo intensifies the common idea by alluding to the
wheel as an instrument of torture (as in v. vi. 295); this allusion is made
clear by the sequence of 'manacled', 'strappado'd' (ll. 94–5).

    lives] *Q*ᵇ added a full stop to separate the stage-direction from the text;
the direction is placed as close to Antonelli's first speech as the text-space
in Q permits. See collation to l. 83.1.

Do't with a crabbed politician's face.   110

Lod. Your sister is a damnable whore.

Flam.   Ha?

Lod. Look you; I spake that laughing.

Flam. Dost ever think to speak again?

Lod.   Do you hear?

Wilt sell me forty ounces of her blood,

To water a mandrake?

Flam.   Poor lord, you did vow   115

To live a lousy creature.

Lod.   Yes;—

Flam.   Like one

That had for ever forfeited the daylight,

By being in debt,—

Lod.   Ha, ha!

Flam. I do not greatly wonder you do break:

Your lordship learnt long since. But I'll tell you,—   120

Lod. What?

Flam.   And't shall stick by you.

Lod.   I long for it.

Flam. This laughter scurvily becomes your face,—

If you will not be melancholy, be angry.   *Strikes him.*

See, now I laugh too.

Mar. You are to blame, I'll force you hence.

Lod.   Unhand me: 125

Exit MARCELLO *and* FLAMINEO.

---

114. Wilt] Wil't *Q.*   120. learnt] learn't *Q;* learn'd it *Dod i;* learn'd't
Dod iii.   125. to] *Q;* too *Q4.*

---

115. *mandrake*] Cf. III. i. 50–2 n.

117. *for . . . daylight*] i.e., been imprisoned for life.

119. *break*] i.e., break your oath, with a quibble on *break* = 'to go bankrupt' (cf. l. 118, 'debt'). Sykes noted T. May, *The Heir* (1622), C3: 'He will
not break.—He needes not, he is rich enough . . . —Breake promise, . . . I
meane'.

120. *learnt*] Cf. v. i. 44 n.

125. *to blame*] In the 16–17th centuries, *blame* was often taken as an
adjective (='blameworthy') and so Q's *to* may stand for 'too'. Cf. v. iii. 87,
for 'too blame', set by B.

That e'er I should be forc'd to right myself,
Upon a pandar. > Unhand me.

Ant.   My lord.

Lod. H'had been as good met with his fist a thunderbolt.

Gasp. How this shows!

Lod.   Ud's death, how did my sword miss him?
These rogues that are most weary of their lives,   130
Still scape the greatest dangers, . . .
A pox upon him: all his reputation;—
Nay all the goodness of his family;—
Is not worth half this earthquake.
I learnt it of no fencer to shake thus;   135
Come I'll forget him, and go drink some wine.   *Exeunt.*

[IV. i]

Enter FRANCISCO *and* MONTICELSO.

Mont. Come, come my lord, untie your folded thoughts,
And let them dangle loose as a bride's hair.
Your sister's poisoned.

Fran.   Far be it from my thoughts
To seek revenge.

Mont.   What, are you turn'd all marble?

Fran. Shall I defy him, and impose a war   5
Most burdensome on my poor subjects' necks,
Which at my will I have not power to end?
You know: for all the murders, rapes, and thefts,

131. dangers, . . .] dangers, *Q;* dangers. *Q2.*

IV. i] *Samp; not in Q;* Act. 3. Scen. 4. *Q4;* Scene III. *Haz;* [III.] Scene ii.
Sym.

─────────────────────────────

130–1.] Cf. *Honour's Academy* (cf. App. IV), Ff3: '(Often) is it seene,
that such desperate persons as are wearie of their liues, scape the soonest
the greatest dangers, . . .'

IV. i. 2.] In Jacobean times virgin brides wore their hair so: cf. H.
Peacham, *Nuptial Hymns* (1613), H2–2ᵛ, describing Princess Elizabeth at
her marriage with the Palsgrave: 'her haire discheueled, and hanging downe
ouer her shoulders'.

Committed in the horrid lust of war,
He that unjustly caus'd it first proceed,   10
Shall find it in his grave and in his seed.

Mont. That's not the course I'd wish you: pray, observe me,—
We see that undermining more prevails
Than doth the cannon. Bear your wrongs conceal'd,
And, patient as the tortoise, let this camel   15
Stalk o'er your back unbruis'd: sleep with the lion,
And let this brood of secure foolish mice
Play with your nostrils, till the time be ripe
For th'bloody audit, and the fatal gripe:
Aim like a cunning fowler, close one eye,   20
That you the better may your game espy.

Fran. Free me my innocence, from treacherous acts:
I know there's thunder yonder: and I'll stand,
Like a safe valley, which low bends the knee
To some aspiring mountain: since I know   25
Treason, like spiders weaving nets for flies,
By her foul work is found, and in it dies.
To pass away these thoughts, my honour'd lord,
It is reported you possess a book
Wherein you have quoted, by intelligence,   30
The names of all notorious offenders
Lurking about the city,—

Mont.   Sir I do;
And some there are which call it my black book:
Well may the title hold: for though it teach not

20–1.] Dent compared Du Bartas, *Divine Weeks*, tr. Sylvester (ed. 1608),
P1ᵛ: 'Following good Archers guise, who shut one ey, / That they better
may their mark espy.'

33. *black book*] originally used of certain official books bound in black,
among which was one used for recording abuses in monasteries under
Henry VIII: later it was widely used of lists of rogues and villains (so
O.E.D.).

Lucas, noting the quibble on 'black art' (cf. 'conjuring', and 'devils',
ll. 35–6), compared W. Fennor, *Compter's Commonwealth* (1617), B2ᵛ:
'A fellow . . . called mee to a booke (no Bible or Divinity, but rather of
Negromancy, for all the Prisoners called it a *Blacke-booke*)'.

The art of conjuring, yet in it lurk   35
The names of many devils.

Fran.   Pray let's see it.

Mont. I'll fetch it to your lordship.   *Exit* MONTICELSO.

Fran.   Monticelso,
I will not trust thee, but in all my plots
I'll rest as jealous as a town besieg'd.
Thou canst not reach what I intend to act;   40
Your flax soon kindles, soon is out again,
But gold slow heats, and long will hot remain.

> [*Re-*]*enter* MONTICELSO; *presents* FRANCISCO
> *with a book.*

Mont. 'Tis here my lord.

Fran. First your intelligencers—pray let's see.

Mont. Their number rises strangely,   45
And some of them
You'd take for honest men.
Next are panders.

---

37. S.D.] *so* Dod i; *after* Monticelso Q.   38. I will] Q^b; I'le Q^a.   42.1–
2. Re-enter . . . book.] Dod i subs.; Enter Mont. (*to right of l.* 43) Q^a; Enter
Mont. presents | Fran. with a booke (*to right of ll.* 43–4) Q^b.   45–6. Their
. . . them] *so* Q; *one line* Dod iii.   47–8. You'd . . . panders] *so* Q; . . . men.
The next, . . . (*one line*) Q3.

---

37. S.D.] Compositor A probably placed this direction half a line too late
for lack of convenient space at the correct point (cf. II. i. 93.1 n.).

38. *will*] a press-correction in a forme probably corrected by Webster
himself (see Intro., p. lxviii); the metre suggests that the line should be
pronounced with an emphasis on this word.

39. *jealous*] suspicious, watchful.

41–2.] Hunter (cf. ll. 20–1 n. above) compared Du Bartas, *Judith*, tr.
Hudson (1584), IV, 189f.: 'The straw enkendles soone, and slakes againe: /
But yron is slow, and long will hote remaine'.

45–8.] No satisfactory typographical reason suggests itself for Q's line-
arrangement; Compositor A might have been filling out a page after the
excision of some error, but he could have done that more conveniently by
centring the previous stage-direction. Presumably, therefore, it represents
the lining of the MS. It may have been written in short lines, as a kind of
dramatic pointing; Monticelso should, perhaps, pause while silently pointing out details in his book to Francisco. Q's long line (51–2) and a further
short line (57) can bear similar interpretations.

These are your pirates: and these following leaves,
For base rogues that undo young gentlemen　　　　50
By taking up commodities:
For politic bankrupts:
For fellows that are bawds to their own wives,
Only to put off horses and slight jewels,
Clocks, defac'd plate, and such commodities,　　　　55
At birth of their first children.
Fran.　　　　　　　　　　　Are there such?
Mont.　These are for impudent bawds,
That go in men's apparel: for usurers
That share with scriveners for their good reportage:
For lawyers that will antedate their writs:　　　　60
And some divines you-might find folded there,
But that I slip them o'er for conscience' sake.
Here is a general catalogue of knaves.
A man might study all the prisons o'er,
Yet never attain this knowledge.
Fran.　　　　　　　　　　　Murderers.　　　　65
Fold down the leaf I pray,—
Good my lord let me borrow this strange doctrine.

51–2. By . . . bankrupts] so this ed.; one line Q.　　65. Murderers.] Q;
Murderers? Dod i.

---

51. *taking up commodities*] Swindlers lent goods instead of money, placing
an exaggerated value on them, and then required repayment in cash at
their valuation; cf. *Meas.*, IV. iii. 5–8.

52. *politic bankrupts*] Sykes compared Dekker, *Seven Deadly Sins* (1606),
i; by hiding their assets and then absconding, swindlers were 'bankrupt'
many times to their own gain.

54–6. *put . . . children*] i.e., force their wives' lovers to buy 'commodities'
at inflated prices in return for silence and amenability. *put off* is not
recorded in *O.E.D.* in the sense of 'to sell away fraudulently', until 1653.

59. *share . . . reportage*] i.e., give a 'cut' to scriveners for recommending
them to their clients; cf. *Characters* (1615), 'A Divellish Usurer': 'He puts
his money to the unnaturall Act of generation; and his Scrivener is the
supervisor Bawd to't'. *O.E.D.* glosses *reportage* (s.v., 1) as 'repute', but
cites only this occurrence.

60. *antedate . . . writs*] i.e., fake the evidence in order, perhaps, to enforce
a writ of execution more quickly, or to give precedence to a minor or supposed offence (cf. II. i. 293–8 n.; so Lucas).

Mont. Pray use't my lord.

Fran.   I do assure your lordship,
    You are a worthy member of the state,
    And have done infinite good in your discovery   70
    Of these offenders.

Mont.   Somewhat sir.

Fran.   O God!
    Better than tribute of wolves paid in England;
    'Twill hang their skins o'th'hedge.

Mont.   I must make bold
    To leave your lordship.

Fran.   Dearly sir, I thank you,—
    If any ask for me at court, report   75
    You have left me in the company of knaves.

                                    Exit MONTICELSO.

    I gather now by this, some cunning fellow
    That's my lord's officer, one that lately skipp'd
    From a clerk's desk up to a justice' chair,
    Hath made this knavish summons; and intends,   80
    As th'Irish rebels wont were to sell heads,
    So to make prize of these. And thus it happens,
    Your poor rogues pay for't, which have not the means
    To present bribe in fist: the rest o'th'band
    Are raz'd out of the knaves' record; or else   85
    My lord he winks at them with easy will,
    His man grows rich, the knaves are the knaves still.

78. one] *Q*b*; and *Q*a.   81. wont were] *Q*; were wont *Q*2.

72.] King Edgar ordered the Welsh to pay 'Three hundred wolves a year
for tribute' in order to free the land of the ravenous animals (Drayton
Polyolbion (1612), ix; quoted by Reed).

73. *hang . . . hedge*] 'He that hath a dogge that is a sheepe biter, must by
lawe either hang him vp, or else pay for the sheepe . . .' (L. Wright, *Sum-
mons for Sleepers* (1589), D1); possibly wolves were also 'hung up' (cf.
Mer.V., IV. i. 133–5). Cf. Tilley, H362: 'To hang on the hedge'.

78. *one*] See note, l. 38 above.

81.] Lucas quoted Mountjoy to Cecil, 9 April 1600: 'I have heard you
complain that you could not hear of one head brought in for all the Queen's
money; but I assure you now the kennels of the streets are full of them'.

But to the use I'll make of it; it shall serve
To point me out a list of murderers,
Agents for any villainy. Did I want   90
Ten leash of courtezans, it would furnish me;
Nay laundress three armies. That in so little paper
Should lie th'undoing of so many men!
'Tis not so big as twenty declarations.
See the corrupted use some make of books: 95
Divinity, wrested by some factious blood,
Draws swords, swells battles, and o'erthrows all good.
To fashion my revenge more seriously,
Let me remember my dead sister's face:
Call for her picture: no; I'll close mine eyes,   100
And in a melancholic thought I'll frame
Her figure 'fore me.

Enter ISABELLA's *Ghost.*

                Now I ha't – – – how strong
Imagination works! how she can frame

89. list] *Q*ᵇ; life *Q*ᵃ.   92.] *so Q; . . .* armies. / That . . . *conj. this ed.*
in so] *Q₂;* so *Q*ᵃ; so in *Q*ᵇ.   93. lie] *Q*ᵇ (lye); be *Q*ᵃ.   100. Call] *Q*ᵇ;
Looke *Q*ᵃ.   102.1.] *so Ol; after l. 101 Q.*   102. ha't – – –] *Q₃* (hav't—);
– – –d'foot *Q*ᵃ; – – – ha'te *Q*ᵇ.

91. *leash*] set of three (originally a sporting term, as of hounds, hawks,
etc.).

92. *laundress*] furnish with laundresses (a nonce-usage, according to
O.E.D.); laundresses were, proverbially, of easy virtue.

92–100. *so . . . lie . . . Call*] Cf. l. 38 n. above.

94. *declarations*] official proclamations.

101–3. *melancholic . . . works*] In melancholy men, 'Phantasy, or imagination . . . is most powerful and strong, and often hurts, producing many
monstrous and prodigious things, especially if it be stirred up by some
terrible object, presented to it from common sense or memory' (Burton,
Anatomy, ed. Jackson, I, 159).

102. *ha't – – –*] If the press-correction were solely concerned with eliminating profanity (as Lucas suggested), there would be good reason to
retain *Q*ᵃ's '– – –d'foot'; but the change also clarifies the dialogue, ensuring
that the audience, or reader, knows at once that Francisco sees Isabella.
This is the more likely cause for the correction, for in this very forme
Webster let other profanities stand (cf. l. 71 above, and IV. ii. 42 and 75).

The form 'ha'te' is analogous to the form 'Ile hate' in Q2 of *Ham.* (O1).

Things which are not! methinks she stands afore me;
And by the quick idea of my mind,   105
Were my skill pregnant, I could draw her picture.
Thought, as a subtle juggler, makes us deem
Things supernatural, which have cause
Common as sickness. 'Tis my melancholy,—
How cam'st thou by thy death ?—how idle am I   110
To question mine own idleness ? – – – did ever
Man dream awake till now ? – – remove this object—
Out of my brain with't: what have I to do
With tombs, or death-beds, funerals, or tears,
That have to meditate upon revenge ?   [*Exit Ghost.*]   115
So now 'tis ended, like an old wives' story.
Statesmen think often they see stranger sights
Than madmen. Come, to this weighty business.
My tragedy must have some idle mirth in't,
Else it will never pass. I am in love,   120
In love with Corombona; and my suit
Thus halts to her in verse.—   *He writes.*
I have done it rarely: O the fate of princes!
I am so us'd to frequent flattery,
That being alone I now flatter myself;   125
But it will serve, 'tis seal'd;

Enter Servant.

bear this
To th'house of convertites; and watch your leisure
To give it to the hands of Corombona,
Or to the matron, when some followers

108. which] *Q;* which yet *Q3;* all which *conj. Luc.*   cause] *Q;* a cause
conj. Luc.   110. death ?—] *Q.*   115. S.D.] *Dyce i; not in Q.*   122.
verse.—] *Q.*   *He writes.*] *Dyce i; he writes (to right of l. 124) Q.*   126.1.]
so Dyce ii; at end of line Q.

105. *quick*] (1) 'lively, living', and (2) 'rapid'.
idea] mental picture.
107. *juggler*] magician.
111. *idleness*] light-headedness, folly.

Of Bracciano may be by. Away——   *Exit Servant.*   130
He that deals all by strength, his wit is shallow:
When a man's head goes through each limb will follow.
The engine for my business, bold Count Lodowick:——
'Tis gold must such an instrument procure,
With empty fist no man doth falcons lure.   135
Bracciano, I am now fit for thy encounter.
Like the wild Irish I'll ne'er think thee dead,
Till I can play at football with thy head.
Flectere si nequeo superos, Acheronta movebo.   *Exit.*

[IV. ii]

        Enter the Matron, and FLAMINEO.

Mat. Should it be known the duke hath such recourse
        To your imprison'd sister, I were like
        T'incur much damage by it.
Flam.   Not a scruple.
        The Pope lies on his death-bed, and their heads

139. S.D.] *Dyce i; Exit Mon Q; Exit Mon.*/The end of the Third Act *Q3.*

IV. ii] *Samp; not in Q;* Act 4 *Q3;* Actus Quartus. Scena Prima. *Q4, Sym subs.*

132.] a proverb, usually said of a 'fox' (i.e., politician); cf. *Wyatt* (1607), III. i. 120–1: 'The Fox is suttle, and his head once in, / The slender body easily will follow', and Tilley F655.

135.] commonly applied to human behaviour (cf. Tilley H111). Falcons were recalled by use of a lure, a bunch of feathers or other material resembling their prey, which was attached to a long cord or thong; so the vb. *lure* was often used figuratively for 'to entice, tempt' (so *O.E.D.*).

139.] i.e., 'If I cannot prevail upon the gods above, I will move the infernal regions' (*Æneid*, VII, 312). Cf. Intro., p. xxi, n. 2.

Acheron, the name of a river at the entrance to the lower world, came to be used for the lower world itself, or for the Christian hell.

IV. ii.] This scene is located at first at the entrance to the house of convertites in Rome; later, at l. 72, it seems to be located within the house itself (cf. ll. 128.1–2).

3. *scruple*] very small quantity.

4. *Pope . . .-bed*] Gregory XIII died 10 April 1585.

Webster's source for the papal election (cf. App. III, p. 197) stresses the civil disorder which followed such events; see also ll. 209–12 below.

  Are troubled now with other business   5
  Than guarding of a lady.

Enter Servant.

CARLO
?

Serv. [*aside*] Yonder's Flamineo in conference
  With the matrona. [*to the Matron*] Let me speak with you.
  I would entreat you to deliver for me
  This letter to the fair Vittoria.   10
Mat. I shall sir.

Enter BRACCIANO.

Serv.   With all care and secrecy,—
  Hereafter you shall know me, and receive
  Thanks for this courtesy.   [*Exit.*]
Flam.   How now ? what's that ?
Mat. A letter.
Flam.   To my sister: I'll see't delivered. [*Exit Matron.*]
Brac. What's that you read Flamineo ?
Flam.   Look.   15
Brac. Ha ? [*reads*] '*To the most unfortunate his best respected*
  Vittoria'—
  Who was the messenger ?
Flam.   I know not.
Brac. No! Who sent it ?
Flam.   Ud's foot you speak, as if a man
  Should know what fowl is coffin'd in a bak'd meat   20
  Afore you cut it up.

---

7. aside] *Thorn; not in Q.* 8. S.D.] *Luc subs.; not in Q.* 11.1.] *so Q;
not in Q3; after l. 14 Q4.* 13. S.D.] *Dod ii; not in Q.* 14. S.D.] *Wheel;
not in Q.* 16–18. Ha . . . messenger] *so Q* (Ha . . . Vittoria *one line*)*;
Ha! / To . . . respected / Vittoria . . . Samp.* 16. reads] *Dyce ii; not in Q.
To . . . Vittoria*] *roman type, except* '*Vittoria*' *Q.*

 11.1.] The entry is placed in the most convenient position in the text-space of Q, but if the copy had shown the entry immediately before Bracciano speaks, one would have expected it to be placed two lines lower, where space could have been found.

 20–1.] Lucas compared Chapman, *May-Day* (pf. *c.* 1609), v. i. 142: 'she must have better skill in baked meats than I, that can discern a woodcock

Brac. I'll open't, were't her heart. What's here subscribed—
　　'*Florence*' ? This juggling is gross and palpable.
　　I have found out the conveyance; read it, read it.

Flam. [*reads*] '*Your tears I'll turn to triumphs, be but mine.*　　25
　　Your prop is fall'n; I pity that a vine
　　Which princes heretofore have long'd to gather,
　　Wanting supporters, now should fade and wither.'
　　Wine i' faith, my lord, with lees would serve his turn.
　　'*Your sad imprisonment I'll soon uncharm,*　　30
　　And with a princely uncontrolled arm
　　Lead you to Florence, where my love and care
　　Shall hang your wishes in my silver hair.'
　　A halter on his strange equivocation!
　　'*Nor for my years return me the sad willow,—*　　35
　　Who prefer blossoms before fruit that's mellow ?'
　　Rotten on my knowledge with lying too long i'th'bed-straw.
　　'*And all the lines of age this line convinces:*
　　The gods never wax old, no more do princes.'
　　A pox on't—tear it, let's have no more atheists for God's　　40
　　sake.

22–3. I'll ... palpable] *so Dyce i;* ... Florence? / This ... *Q.*　　23. *Flor-ence*] *roman type Q.*　　25. *reads*] *so Dyce ii; Reades the | letter. (outer margin, to right of ll. 25–6) Q.*　　25–8, 30–3, 35–6, and 38–9.] *so italicized Q.*　　40–1. A ... sake] *so Dyce ii; one line Q;* ... Atheists / For ... *Samp.*

---

through the crust'. *coffin'd* is not necessarily a macabre image, for the noun, 'coffin', was a common term in cookery for the crust or paste of a pie; for this use of the verb, the earliest reference in *O.E.D.* (s.v., 3) is dated 1621.

24. *conveyance*] device, contrivance (as often), with a quibble on the sense of 'means of communicating'.

34. *equivocation*] presumably in 'love and care' and 'hang'; Flamineo's 'halter' picks up the equivocation in 'hang'.

35. willow] 'worne of forlorne Paramours' (Spenser, *F.Q.*, I. i. 9).

37. *bed-straw*] Fruit was ripened in straw.

38.] a quibble: this maxim (1) 'confutes all old maxims to the contrary', and (2) 'is of more force than the wrinkles which suggest old age'. For *convince,* cf. *O.E.D.,* s.v., 1 and 6.

40. *atheists*] commonly used, in a general sense, for impious or wicked persons; but Flamineo also means that Francisco has 'misbelieved' in equating princes with gods (cf. II. i. 198–201).

Brac. Ud's death, I'll cut her into atomies
    And let th'irregular north-wind sweep her up
    And blow her int' his nostrils. Where's this whore?
Flam. That – – –? what do you call her?
Brac.   O, I could be mad;   45
    Prevent the curst disease she'll bring me to,
    And tear my hair off. Where's this changeable stuff?
Flam. O'er head and ears in water, I assure you,—
    She is not for your wearing.
Brac.   In you pander!
Flam. What me, my lord, am I your dog?   50
Brac. A blood-hound: do you brave? do you stand me?
Flam. Stand you? let those that have diseases run;
    I need no plasters.
Brac. Would you be kick'd?
Flam.   Would you have your neck broke?
    I tell you duke, I am not in Russia;   55
    My shins must be kept whole.
Brac.   Do you know me?
Flam. O my lord! methodically.
    As in this world there are degrees of evils:

45. That – – – ?] That? *Q*b; What? *Q*a; That *Dod iii.*   49. In] *Q*b; No
*Q*a.   pander!] Pandar? *Q.*

---

43. *irregular*] wild, unconfined.

45. *That*] Qb is to be preferred since Webster was probably responsible for press-corrections in the same forme (cf. Intro., p. lxviii).

46–7. *Prevent ... off*] Cf. I. ii. 29 n.

47. *changeable stuff*] i.e., fickle woman.

48. *O'er ... water*] i.e., in deep water. Flamineo puns (cf. 'wearing', l. 49) on *changeable* = 'shot' as in 'watered or shot silk'; the same quibble is found in *Tw.N.*, II. iv. 76.

49. *In*] Flamineo's 'am I your dog?' (l. 50) shows that Bracciano commands him to go into the house to fetch Vittoria. For Qb's authority, see l. 45 n. above.

51. *stand*] withstand.

52. *run*] a quibble on the 'running' of a sore.

55. *Russia*] Sykes quoted Dekker, *Seven Deadly Sins* (1606), *Wks*, II, 28: 'The *Russians* haue an excellent custome; they beate them on the shinnes, that haue mony, and will not pay their debts'.

57. *methodically*] i.e., all is worked out, I have it taped.

  So in this world there are degrees of devils.

  You're a great duke; I your poor secretary.   60

  I do look now for a Spanish fig, or an Italian sallet daily.

Brac. Pander, ply your convoy, and leave your prating.

Flam. All your kindness to me is like that miserable cour-

  tesy of Polyphemus to Ulysses,—you reserve me to be

  devour'd last,—you would dig turves out of my grave to 65

  feed your larks: that would be music to you. Come, I'll

  lead you to her.

Brac. Do you face me?

Flam. O sir I would not go before a politic enemy with my

  back towards him, though there were behind me a whirl- 70

  pool.

    Enter VITTORIA *to* BRACCIANO *and* FLAMINEO.

Brac. Can you read mistress? look upon that letter;

  There are no characters nor hieroglyphics.

  You need no comment, I am grown your receiver,—

  God's precious, you shall be a brave great lady,   75

  A stately and advanced whore.

Vit.   Say sir?

Brac. Come, come, let's see your cabinet, discover

---

61. I . . . daily] *one line Q; as verse Scott; as prose Samp.* 69. O sir] Q^b;
Sir Q^a. 70–1. whirlpool] *Q;* whirlpool. / Scene II *Haz;* whirlepoole. /
Exeunt. / Scene III *Samp.*

---

61. *look . . . sallet*] i.e., expect to be poisoned; cf. *Noble Soldier* (pf. before
1631), $H2^v$: 'Is [a poison] speeding?—As all our Spanish figs are'. *sallet* =
'salad'.

 62.] i.e., attend to your trade and bring us together.

 64. *Polyphemus*] a Cyclops, one of a race of savage one-eyed giants; cf.
Odyssey, IX, 369–70.

 65–6. *dig . . . larks*] Cf. *D.M.*, IV. ii. 128–31: 'Didst thou ever see a lark
in a cage? such is the soul in the body: this world is like her little turf of
grass, and the heaven o'er our heads, like her looking-glass, . . .'

 73. *characters*] emblematic, or magical, signs or writings (cf. Spenser,
F.Q., III. xii. 31); or, possibly, *character* = 'cipher' (so Lucas who cited
O.E.D., s.v., 7, for which the first certain quotation is 1659–60).

 74. *receiver*] i.e., pimp, receiving love letters for you (so Lucas).

 75. *God's precious*] i.e., God's blood.

 77. *cabinet*] casket.

> Your treasury of love-letters. Death and furies,
> I'll see them all.

Vit.   Sir, upon my soul,
>   I have not any. Whence was this directed?   80

Brac. Confusion on your politic ignorance!   [*Gives her the*
>   You are reclaimed, are you? I'll give you the bells   *letter.*]
>   And let you fly to the devil.

~~*Flam.*   Ware hawk, my lord.~~

Vit. '*Florence*'! This is some treacherous plot, my lord,—
>   To me, he ne'er was lovely I protest,   85
>   So much as in my sleep.

Brac.   Right: they are plots.
>   Your beauty! O, ten thousand curses on't.
>   How long have I beheld the devil in crystal?
>   Thou hast led me, like an heathen sacrifice,
>   With music, and with fatal yokes of flowers   90

81–2. S.D.] *Luc subs.; not in Q.*   84. *Florence*] *roman type Q.*   85.
lovely] Q^b; thought on Q^a.   88. crystal?] *Q;* Christal! *Q3.*

---

82. *reclaimed*] a quibble: the verb was used for (1) 'to bring back from an evil course', and (2) as a technical term in falconry, 'to call back' a hawk which has been let fly, or 'to tame' a hawk.

82–3. *give . . . fly*] continuing the use of falconry terms: bells were tied to a hawk's legs to aid recovery and to frighten prey. The usual form of the phrase was 'take off your bells and let you fly' (cf. Tilley B282) but the same variation is found in Dekker's *Patient Grissill* (1603), A4; possibly this means 'let you go, bells and all'.

83. *hawk*] Flamineo continues the word-play; *hawk*, especially in this phrase, was used for 'sharper, swindler' (cf. Tilley H227).

85–6. *ne'er . . . sleep*] Q^b's correction (probably by Webster; cf. Intro., p. lxviii) changes the sense from 'I never dreamt of marrying him', to 'I never found him attractive, not even in my dreams'.

88. *devil in crystal*] Probably an allusion to the play's title, and also to the belief that devils could be enclosed and revealed in crystals; R. Scot, *Discovery of Witchcraft* (1584) gives several charms for making 'a spirit to appeare in a christall', one of them (xv, 19) for making it appear in the form of 'a white angell, a greene angell, a blacke angell, a man, a woman, . . . a diuell with great hornes', etc.

G. P. V. Akrigg (*N. & Q.*, cxcix (1954), 52) noted that small shrines were made of crystals, with the figure of a saint inside; he suggested that such a shrine might be alluded to (cf. the religious imagery following). But Dent quoted passages showing that 'to behold the devil in crystal' was a set phrase = 'to be deceived'.

To my eternal ruin. Woman to man
Is either a god or a wolf.

Vit.   My lord.

Brac.   Away.

We'll be as differing as two adamants;
The one shall shun the other. What? dost weep?
Procure but ten of thy dissembling trade,   95
Ye'd furnish all the Irish funerals
With howling, past wild Irish.

Flam.   Fie, my lord.

Brac. That hand, that cursed hand, which I have wearied
With doting kisses! O my sweetest duchess
How lovely art thou now! [*to Vittoria*] Thy loose thoughts
Scatter like quicksilver, I was bewitch'd;   101
For all the world speaks ill of thee.

Vit.   No matter.

I'll live so now I'll make that world recant

---

93. We'll] Q^b (Wee'l); Well Q^a.   96. Ye'd] Q^b (Yee'ld); ee'ld Q^a; Wee'l
$Q2$; Wee'ld *Samp.*   100. S.D.] *Luc; not in Q.*   Thy] Q; my $Q4$.

91–2. *Woman . . . wolf*] In its usual form of 'Man unto man . . .', this proverb is found in Florio, III, v (p. 433ᵃ)—it is used there of marriage, and is
within a line or two of a passage Webster used earlier in *W.D.* (I. ii. 43–6).
See, also, Tilley M247.

93. *adamants*] magnets (cf. I. ii. 171 n.).

96–7. *furnish . . . Irish*] Webster may have got this idea from Stanyhurst's
'Description of Ireland' (as he certainly derived I. ii. 30–2; see note); but a
fuller account is found in B. Riche, *A New Description* (1610) and *Procure*
and *furnish* suggest that it is to this that he was indebted. Stanyhurst reads:
'They follow the dead corp[se] to the graue wᵗ howlyng and barbarous out-
cries, . . . whereof grew, as I suppose, the proverbe, to weepe Irish' (D4);
Riche adds: 'in Citties and Townes where any deceaseth that is of worth or
worthinesse, they wil hyre a number of women to bring the corps to the
place of buriall, that, for some small recompence giuen them, will furnish
the cry, with greater shriking & howling, then those that are grieued
indeede, . . .' (p. 13; cf. H. D. Sykes, *N. & Q.*, xi ser., vii (1913), 342–3).

100. *Thy*] There is no need to emend; with the added stage-direction
Q makes good sense; moreover the line was set by B, the more careful of the
two compositors.

102–4. *all . . . speeches*] Cf. Florio, III, v (p. 439ᵃ): 'Some told Plato that
all the world spake ill of him: "Let them say what they list," quoth hee, "I
will so live that Ile make them recant and change their speeches."'

And change her speeches. You did name your duchess.
Brac.   Whose death God pardon.
Vit.   Whose death God revenge   105
On thee most godless duke.
Flam.   Now for two whirlwinds.
Vit. What have I gain'd by thee but infamy?
Thou hast stain'd the spotless honour of my house,
And frighted thence noble society:
Like those, which sick o'th'palsy, and retain   110
Ill-scenting foxes 'bout them, are still shunn'd
By those of choicer nostrils.
What do you call this house?
Is this your palace? did not the judge style it
A house of penitent whores? who sent me to it?   115
Who hath the honour to advance Vittoria
To this incontinent college? is't not you?
Is't not your high preferment? Go, go brag
How many ladies you have undone, like me.
Fare you well sir; let me hear no more of you.   120
I had a limb corrupted to an ulcer,
But I have cut it off: and now I'll go
Weeping to heaven on crutches. For your gifts,
I will return them all; and I do wish

---

106. two] *Dod iii;* ten *Q*ᵃ; tow *Q*ᵇ; the *Q2.*   112-13. By . . . house] *This ed.; one line Q.*

105.] Dyce compared *R3*, I. iii. 135-7.
110. *sick*] are sick; this usage is last quoted in *O.E.D.* (s.v., 1) from *2H4* (pf. *c.* 1597), IV. iv. 128.
111. *foxes*] Lucas quoted Jonson, writing to the Earl of Newcastle: 'I being strucken with the Palsey in the Yeare 1628. had . . . a Foxe sent mee for a present; wᶜʰ Creature, by handling, I endeauored to make tame, aswell for the abateing of my disease, as the delight I tooke in speculation of his Nature' (*Wks*, I, 213), and H. King, *Poems* (ed. 1925), 'Madam Gabrina': 'If a Fox cures the Paralyticall, / Had'st thou ten Palsies, she'd outstink them all'.
116. *advance*] possibly remembering Bracciano's first taunt, l. 76 above.
118-19. *Go . . . me*] Cf. *D.M.*, I. i. 448-9: 'Go, go brag / You have left me heartless . . .'
121-3. *I . . . crutches*] a reminiscence of Mark, ix. 45.

That I could make you full executor   125
To all my sins,—O that I could toss myself
Into a grave as quickly: for all thou art worth
I'll not shed one tear more;—I'll burst first.

*She throws herself upon
a bed.*

Brac. I have drunk Lethe. Vittoria?
My dearest happiness? Vittoria?   130
What do you ail my love? why do you weep?
Vit. Yes, I now weep poniards, do you see?
Brac. Are not those matchless eyes mine?
Vit.   I had rather
They were not matches.
Brac.   Is not this lip mine?
Vit. Yes: thus to bite it off, rather than give it thee.   135
Flam. Turn to my lord, good sister.
Vit.   Hence you pander.
Flam. Pander! Am I the author of your sin?
Vit. Yes: he's a base thief that a thief lets in.
Flam. We're blown up, my lord,—
Brac.   Wilt thou hear me?
Once to be jealous of thee is t'express   140
That I will love thee everlastingly,
And never more be jealous.

128. more;—] *Q.*   128.1–2.] *so Dod i; to right of ll. 128–9 Q.*   129–30.
I . . . Vittoria ?] *so Dyce i; . . .* Lethe. / Vittoria . . . *Q.*   134. matches] *Q;*
matchles *Q2.*

129–30.] Compositor B probably altered the lining from that of his copy
in order to avoid confusing the text with the stage-direction (see also
v. i. 85 and v. iii. 151).

132. *poniards*] Cf. *Ado*, II. i. 255: 'She speaks poniards, and every word
stabs'.

134. *matches*] Cf. *A.V.*, III. ii. 43–4: 'she hath a matchlesse eye sir – –
True, her eyes are not right matches'.

138.] G. K. Hunter compared R. Southwell, 'Mary Magdalen's Blush'
(1595), st. vi (*Works*, ed. A. B. Grosart (1872), p. 60): 'For theefe he is that
theefe admitteth in.'

139. *blown up*] Cf. *D.M.*, III. ii. 155–6: 'I stand / As if a mine, beneath
my feet, were ready / To be blown up'.

Vit.   O thou fool,
    Whose greatness hath by much o'ergrown thy wit!
    What dar'st thou do, that I not dare to suffer,
    Excepting to be still thy whore ? for that,   145
    In the sea's bottom sooner thou shalt make
    A bonfire.
Flam.   O, no oaths for God's sake.
Brac. Will you hear me ?
Vit.   Never.
Flam. What a damn'd imposthume is a woman's will ?
    Can nothing break it ? fie, fie, my lord.   150
    [*aside to Bracciano*] Women are caught as you take tortoises,
    She must be turn'd on her back. [*aloud*] Sister, by this hand
    I am on your side. Come, come, you have wrong'd her.
    What a strange credulous man were you, my lord,
    To think the Duke of Florence would love her ?   155
    [*aside*] Will any mercer take another's ware
    When once 'tis tous'd and sullied ? [*aloud*] And, yet sister,
    How scurvily this frowardness becomes you!
    [*aside*] Young leverets stand not long; and women's
        anger
    Should, like their flight, procure a little sport;   160
    A full cry for a quarter of an hour,
    And then be put to th'dead quat.
Brac.   Shall these eyes,

145. for] *Q*; 'fore *conj. this ed.*   150. it ?] *Q*; it ? *aside Luc.*   151, 156,
157, 159. S.D.s] *This ed.; not in Q.*   152. aloud] *This ed.; not in Q; Aside
Haz; to Vittoria Luc.*   155. would] *Q*b; could *Q*a.

---

149. *imposthume*] abscess, festering swelling.
155. *would*] The suspicious Vittoria might have inferred from Qa's
'could' that Flamineo was saying that she was not attractive enough to
ensnare Francisco; perhaps Webster (cf. Intro., p. lxviii) corrected it to
avoid this impression—though he may only have been correcting a compositor's slip.
159. *leverets*] young hares.
    stand] hold out (hunting term); the usual form is 'stand up' for which
Lucas quoted Turberville, *Book of Hunting* (1611), L3: 'I haue also seene
an Hare run and stand vp two houres before a kennell of hounds'.
162. *quat*] squat (hunting term).

Which have so long time dwelt upon your face,
Be now put out?

Flam. No cruel landlady i'th'world, which lends forth groats   165
to broom-men, and takes use for them, would do't.
[*aside to Bracciano*] Hand her, my lord, and kiss her: be
not like
A ferret to let go your hold with blowing.

Brac. Let us renew right hands.

Vit.   Hence.

Brac. Never shall rage, or the forgetful wine,   170
Make me commit like fault.

Flam. [*aside to Bracciano*] Now you are i'th'way on't, follow't
hard.

Brac. Be thou at peace with me; let all the world
Threaten the cannon.

Flam.   Mark his penitence.
Best natures do commit the grossest faults,   175
When they're giv'n o'er to jealousy; as best wine
Dying makes strongest vinegar. I'll tell you;
The sea's more rough and raging than calm rivers,
But nor so sweet nor wholesome. A quiet woman

165–6. No . . . do't] *This ed.*; . . . world, / Which . . . them. / Would . . .
Q; . . . world, / Which . . . use / For . . . *Dod ii.*   167. S.D.] *Ol subs;*
not in Q.   170–1. Never . . . fault] *so Q;* . . . rage / Or . . . commit / Like
. . . *Wheel.*   172. S.D.] *Ol subs.; not in Q.*   179. nor so] *Q;* not
so *Q2.*

---

166. *use*] interest, usury.

168.] It is a superstition, but not a fact, that if one blows upon a ferret
it will relinquish anything that its teeth are fixed in (so Lucas, who also
reports that, in fact, pinching its tail does the trick).

170. *forgetful wine*] i.e., inducing forgetfulness; the phrase is repeated in
C.C., III. i. 26.

174. *Threaten the cannon*] i.e., threaten us with the use of force.

175–7. *Best . . . vinegar*] Cf. *Honour's Academy,* Ff3ᵛ: 'There is no better
vineger, then that which is made of good wine when it sowreth. Euen so,
the best Natures commit the grossest faults, when they giue themselues
ouer vnto euill'. The idea was proverbial; cf. Tilley W470.

178–9. *sea's . . . wholesome*] Cf. *Honour's Academy,* D1ᵛ: 'Doest thou
make account of Loue, because hee is strong and violent? why so is the
Sea, tempestuous, strong, violent, rough, and of great power: but are his

Is a still water under a great bridge.   180
A man may shoot her safely.

Vit. O ye dissembling men!

Flam.   We suck'd that, sister,
From women's breasts, in our first infancy.

Vit. To add misery to misery.

Brac.   Sweetest.

Vit. Am I not low enough?   185
Ay, ay, your good heart gathers like a snowball
Now your affection's cold.

Flam.   Ud's foot, it shall melt
To a heart again, or all the wine in Rome
Shall run o'th'lees for't.

Vit. Your dog or hawk should be rewarded better   190
Than I have been. I'll speak not one word more.

Flam. Stop her mouth,
With a sweet kiss, my lord.
So now the tide's turned the vessel's come about—
He's a sweet armful. O we curl'd-hair'd men   195
Are still most kind to women. This is well.

Brac. That you should chide thus!

---

180. a great bridge] *Q;* London-Bridge (*italicized*) *Q3.*   182–3. We...
infancy] *so Dod ii; as prose Q; one line Q4.*   184. misery.] *Q;* misery?
Scott.   192–4. Stop... about] *so Q;* ... So, / Now... *Dyce i.*

---

waters, as wholesome, fresh, sweet, and good, as are those of springs and
lesser fountaines [?]'

180–1.] Q3's reading shows how readily this would evoke the picture
of London Bridge, which was difficult or impossible to pass through,
or *shoot,* when tides ran high; Lucas compared the proverb 'London
Bridge was made for wise men to go over and fools to go under' (Tilley
L417).

182–3. *We ... infancy*] All editors agree in this line-arrangement which
is satisfactory metrically; but Q may well be right in view of Flamineo's
frequent use of prose fragments in this scene.

190. *rewarded*] a technical usage in hunting; cf. *D.M.,* I. i. 59–60: 'There
are rewards for hawks, and dogs, when they have done us service'. The
'reward' was part of the prey; Crawford quoted Florio, II, xii (p. 232a):
'We share the fruits of our prey with our dogges and hawkes, as a meed of
their paine and reward of their industry'.

196. *still*] always, continually.

Flam.   O, sir, your little chimneys
        Do ever cast most smoke. I sweat for you.
        Couple together with as deep a silence
        As did the Grecians in their wooden horse.   200
        My lord supply your promises with deeds;
        You know that painted meat no hunger feeds.
Brac. Stay—ingrateful Rome!
Flam. Rome! it deserves to be call'd Barbary, for our villain-
        ous usage.   205
Brac. Soft; the same project which the Duke of Florence,
        (Whether in love or gullery I know not)
        Laid down for her escape, will I pursue.
Flam. And no time fitter than this night, my lord;
        The Pope being dead; and all the cardinals ent'red   210
        The conclave for th'electing a new Pope;
        The city in a great confusion;
        We may attire her in a page's suit,

202.] *italicized Q.*   203. Stay . . . Rome!] . . . Rome. *Q;* Stay, . . . *Q4;*
Stay, ingrateful Rome— *Dyce i;* Stay in ingrateful Rome! *conj. Dyce i,
Sym subs.;* Stay in grateful Rome! *Brereton;* Staying in ingrateful Rome?
conj. Luc.   204–5. Rome! . . . usage] *so Dod i; one line Q;* . . . Barbary, /
For . . . *Dod iii;* . . . deserves / To . . . *Samp.*

201–2.] G. K. Hunter (*N. & Q.,* n.s., iv (1957), 54) compared Sharpham, *Cupid's Whirligig* (1607), ed. 1926, p. 12: 'husbands are but like to
painted fruite, which promise much, but still deceaues vs when wee come
to touch'. He further suggested, privately, that Webster has drawn a
second image from Southwell's presentation of the repentant Magdalen
(cf. l. 138 n., above), and compared 'Magdalen's Complaint', st. iv (*Wks,*
ed. Grosart, pp. 62–3): 'Paynted meate no hunger feedes'.
    203.] This seems the simplest way of punctuating Q and avoiding
emendation; for other abrupt changes of tone and address in Bracciano's
speeches, cf. II. i. 78 n. Lucas compared 'Stay, I doe not well know . . .' in
D.L.C., v. v. 10.
    For *ingrateful Rome,* cf. L. Lloyd, *Linceus Spectacles* (1607), F4ᵛ:
'*Scipio* and others spake of vngratefull Rome: *O ingrata patria, non habebis
ossa mea:* for Rome was neuer gratefull to Romanes, . . .' (for Webster's
knowledge of this book, cf. 'To the Reader', ll. 28–33 n.). Shakespeare
several times associated Rome and ingratitude; cf. *Tit.,* I. i. 447, IV. iii. 33,
and v. i. 12, and *Ant.,* II. vi. 22. And cf. *A.V.,* IV. ii. 143.
    206 *project*] plan, scheme.

Lay her post-horse, take shipping, and amain
For Padua.   215
Brac. I'll instantly steal forth the Prince Giovanni,
And make for Padua. You two with your old mother
And young Marcello that attends on Florence,
If you can work him to it, follow me.
I will advance you all: for you Vittoria,   220
Think of a duchess' title.
Flam.   Lo you sister.
Stay, my lord; I'll tell you a tale. The crocodile, which
lives in the river Nilus, hath a worm breeds i'th'teeth of 't,
which puts it to extreme anguish: a little bird, no bigger
than a wren, is barber-surgeon to this crocodile; flies into   225
the jaws of 't; picks out the worm; and brings present
remedy. The fish, glad of ease but ingrateful to her that
did it, that the bird may not talk largely of her abroad

222. Stay . . .] *indented Q.*

---

214. *Lay*] station (cf. *O.E.D.*, s.v., 20).
amain] at once, with all speed.
222-35. *The crocodile . . .*] This story was frequently told; the closest to
Webster's account that has been noted is in Topsell, *History* (1607-8),
N2-2ᵛ: 'besides themselues they [crocodiles] haue few friends in the world,
except the bird *Trochilus* and Swine, . . . As for the little bird *Trochilus*, it
affecteth and followeth them for the benefit of his owne belly: for while the
Crocodile greedilie eateth, there sticketh fast in his teeth some part of his
prey, which troubleth him very much, & many times ingendereth wormes,
then the beast to helpe himselfe taketh land, and lyeth gaping against the
sunne-beames westward, the b[ir]d perceiuing it, flyeth to the iawes of the
beast, and there first with a kind of tickling-scratching, procureth (as it
were) licence of the Crocodile to pull foorth the wormes, and so eateth them
all out, and clenseth the teeth thoroughly, for which cause the Beast is content to permit the Bird to goe into his mouth. But when all is clensed, the
ingratefull Crocodile endeuoureth suddainely to shut his chappes together
vppon the Bird, and to deuoure his friend, like a cursed wretch which
maketh no reckoning of friendship, but the turne serued, requiteth good
with euill. But Nature hath armed this little bird with sharpe thornes vpon
her head, so that while the Crocodile endeuoureth to shut his chaps
and close his mouth vpon it, those sharpe thornes pricke him into his
palate, so that full sore against his vnkind nature, hee letteth her flye safe
away.'
223. *worm . . . of't*] a current explanation of toothache (so Lucas who
compared *Ado*, III. ii. 26-7).

non-payment, closeth her chaps intending to swallow
her, and so put her to perpetual silence. But nature   230
loathing such ingratitude, hath arm'd this bird with a
quill or prick on the head, top o'th'which wounds the
crocodile i'th'mouth; forceth her open her bloody prison; and away flies the pretty tooth-picker from her
cruel patient.   235

Brac. Your application is, I have not rewarded
    The service you have done me.

Flam.   No, my lord;
    You sister are the crocodile: you are blemish'd in your
    fame, my lord cures it. And though the comparison hold
    not in every particle, yet observe, remember, what good   240
    the bird with the prick i'th'head hath done you; and
    scorn ingratitude.
    [*aside*] It may appear to some ridiculous
    Thus to talk knave and madman; and sometimes
    Come in with a dried sentence, stuff'd with sage.   245
    But this allows my varying of shapes,—
    Knaves do grow great by being great men's apes.   *Exeunt.*

---

243. aside] *Dyce ii (to right of line); not in Q.*   247.] *italicized Q.*

232,241. *prick*] Possibly Flamineo is making a new point by suggesting a
double entendre; cf. N. Breton, *Cornu-copiae* (1612), F4: 'Oh peirce her
(pretie *Cupid*) with thy sting, / That I may pricke her with another thinge',
and Partridge, *Shakespeare's Bawdy* (1947), p. 171.

237–8. *No . . . crocodile*] Flamineo had directed his tale to Bracciano (cf.
l. 222 above) yet, when questioned, he denies its obvious application, suggesting that it is Vittoria who should be grateful to Bracciano for 'curing'
her dishonour by marriage; he may, indeed, have intended both applications.

245. *sentence*] apophthegm, aphorism.
    sage] Cf. I. ii. 136 n.

[IV. iii]

> Enter LODOVICO, GASPARO, *and six Ambassadors.*
> *At another door* [FRANCISCO] *the Duke of*
> *Florence.*

Fran. So, my lord, I commend your diligence—
Guard well the conclave, and, as the order is,
Let none have conference with the cardinals.
Lod. I shall, my lord: room for the ambassadors,—
Gasp. They're wondrous brave today: why do they wear   5
These several habits ?
Lod.   O sir, they're knights
Of several orders.
That lord i'th'black cloak with the silver cross
Is Knight of Rhodes; the next Knight of S. Michael;
That of the Golden Fleece; the Frenchman there   10
Knight of the Holy Ghost; my lord of Savoy

IV. iii] *Haz; not in Q; Act. 4. Scen. 2. Q4, Sym subs.;* [IV.] Scene IV. *Samp.*
0.1. *Enter*] *Luc; Enter Francisco, Q.*   *Gasparo*] *Gasper Q.*   6. they're]
Q (they'r); they are *Dyce ii.*

IV. iii.] located outside the Pope's palace in Rome, near the Sistine chapel.
Webster's source for much of this scene was Hierome Bignon, *Treatise* (tr.
1605); this is reprinted in epitome as Appendix III.

0.2. At another door] From Bignon's *Treatise*, it would appear that
Lodovico, assisted by Gasparo, has been supervising the return of the
ambassadors from the conclave for electing the new Pope. Francisco
appears 'At another door' to show that he has not been within the conclave.
Dramatic time foreshortens events so that one brief scene shows both the
beginning and the end of the conclave.

9. *Rhodes*] The order of the Knights of St John of Jerusalem was founded
during the First Crusade; they moved from Jerusalem to Rhodes, then to
Crete, and finally to Malta, which was granted to them by the Emperor
Charles V in 1530. They continued to fight against the Mohammedan
enemies of Christendom. A black robe with an eight-pointed silver cross
(the Maltese Cross) was their official dress. The 'several institutions' of
this, and the following orders, were described in W. Segar's *Book of
Honour and Arms* (1590) and *Honour, Military and Civil* (1602).

S. Michael] an order founded by Louis XI in 1469.

10. *Golden Fleece*] an order founded by Philip the Good, Duke of Bur-
gundy, on his marriage-day, 10 Jan. 1430.

11. *Holy Ghost*] an order founded by Henri III in 1578, ranking above
that of S. Michael (see l. 9).

Knight of th'Annunciation; the Englishman
Is Knight of th'honoured Garter, dedicated
Unto their saint, S. George. I could describe to you
Their several institutions, with the laws   15
Annexed to their orders; but that time
Permits not such discovery.

Fran.   Where's Count Lodowick?
Lod. Here my lord.
Fran.   'Tis o'th'point of dinner time,
Marshal the cardinals' service,—
Lod.   Sir I shall.

Enter Servants with several dishes covered.

Stand, let me search your dish,—who's this for?   20
Serv. For my Lord Cardinal Monticelso.
Lod. Whose this?
Serv.   For my Lord Cardinal of Bourbon.
French Amb. Why doth he search the dishes?—to observe
What meat is dress'd?
English Amb.   No sir, but to prevent
Lest any letters should be convey'd in   25
To bribe or to solicit the advancement
Of any cardinal,—when first they enter
'Tis lawful for the ambassadors of princes
To enter with them, and to make their suit
For any man their prince affecteth best;   30
But after, till a general election,
No man may speak with them.
Lod. You that attend on the lord cardinals

19.1.] *so Dod i; to right of ll. 19–22 Q.*   22. Whose] *Q; Who's Luc.*

---

12. *Annunciation*] the highest order of knights in Italy, founded by
Amadeus VI of Savoy in 1362; its dress was of white satin with a cloak of
purple velvet.
22. *Whose*] 'Who's' is a possible modernization of Q, but A set 'who's'
and not 'whose' two lines above and 'Whose' is not found for 'Who's' elsewhere in this text.
24. *meat*] food.

Open the window, and receive their viands.

[A Conclavist appears briefly at the window.]

Con. You must return the service; the lord cardinals   35
Are busied 'bout electing of the Pope,—
They have given o'er scrutiny, and are fallen
To admiration.

Lod.   Away, away.

Fran. I'll lay a thousand ducats you hear news
Of a Pope presently,—hark; sure he's elected,—   40

34.1.] *This ed.; not in Q; A cardinal on the terrace Dod iii; at the window (after speech-prefix, l. 35) Dyce ii.*   35. *Con.*] *This ed.; A Car. Q; An officer Ol; Servant Sp.*

---

34. *the window*] Cf. App. III, p. 195. The Red Bull stage had windows and a balcony (cf. 'terrace', l. 40.2 below) overlooking the main stage (cf. Intro., p. xxiii).

34.1. Conclavist] Q's speech-prefix ('A Car.') of the following line has usually been expanded as 'A Cardinal'. But some editors have seen the difficulty of directing a cardinal to do such petty tasks as opening a window and bearing a message—especially when that message says that the 'lord cardinals' are busy elsewhere; these editors have directed the entry of 'An officer' or 'Servant'. But these solutions bring a new difficulty in that it is hard to see how 'An officer' or 'A Servant' in the copy could have been misread by a compositor as 'A Car.'; moreover, when a servant is designated elsewhere in this text, both in this scene and in others, it is as 'Ser.', not as 'A Ser.'

Both the misreading and the strange form of the prefix are explained, however, if Q is emended to 'A Con.' and a Conclavist directed to appear at the window; this word occurs four times in Bignon's *Treatise* as the correct name for those servants who attend the cardinals within the conclave. It may be assumed that Webster, having read and considered the *Treatise,* forgot that others would be unfamiliar with the term, and so wrote it down in his manuscript without explanation; then the compositor, failing to make sense, chose to substitute the more usual personage of 'A Cardinal'. In the present sense, 'Conclavist' is first noted in *O.E.D.* in 1656.

38. *admiration*] The correct technical word was 'adoration'; cf. App. III, p. 195.

The election of Montalto as Sixtus V—the historical event which Webster represents in the election of Monticelso as Paul IV—was effected when two cardinals, as yet one more in a long series of Scrutinies was proposed, precipitated affairs by starting an Adoration (cf. G. Leti, *Life of Sixtus V* (tr. 1754), p. 147); the election of Leo II described by Bignon was effected in much the same way.

[The] Cardinal *[of* ARRAGON *appears] on the*
                    terrace.

Behold! my lord of Arragon appears
  On the church battlements.
Arrag. Denuntio vobis gaudium magnum. Reverendissimus Car-
    dinalis Lorenzo de Monticelso electus est in sedem apostoli-
    cam, et elegit sibi nomen Paulum Quartum.   45
Omnes. Vivat Sanctus Pater Paulus Quartus.

                    [*Enter Servant.*]

Serv. Vittoria my lord—
Fran.   Well: what of her?
Serv. Is fled the city,—
Fran.   Ha?
Serv.   With Duke Bracciano.
Fran. Fled? Where's the prince Giovanni?
Serv.   Gone with his father.
Fran. Let the matrona of the convertites   50
  Be apprehended: fled—O damnable!   [*Exit Servant.*]
  [*aside*] How fortunate are my wishes. Why? 'twas this
  I only laboured. I did send the letter
  T'instruct him what to do. Thy fame, fond duke,
  I first have poison'd; directed thee the way   55

40.1–2. *The . . . terrace.*] *This ed.; A Cardinal on the Tarras (to right of ll. 39–
40) Q, (after l. 38) Dod i; not in Dod iii.*   46.1.] *Q4; not in Q.*   47. lord]
Lord. *Q.*   51. fled] *Q; fled? Q2.*   51. S.D.] *Dyce i; not in Q.*   52.
aside] *Wheel; not in Q.*

40.2. terrace] Cf. l. 34 n. above.

Webster probably designated the balcony because Bignon specifically
says that the announcement is made after 'opening a little windowe, from
whence the people which attend, *may see, and be seene*'.

43–6.] i.e., 'I bring you tidings of great joy. The Most Reverend Cardinal
Lorenzo di Monticelso has been elected to the Apostolic See, and has
chosen the title of Paul IV.—*All.* Long live the Holy Father, Paul IV'.

The phraseology follows Bignon closely; according to him the cardinal
'shewes forth a Crosse' and then pronounces the words 'with a loud voice'
(cf. App. III, p. 196).

51. *apprehended*] arrested.
54. *fond*] infatuated, foolish.

To marry a whore; what can be worse? This follows:
The hand must act to drown the passionate tongue,—
I scorn to wear a sword and prate of wrong.

Enter MONTICELSO *in state.*

Mont. *Concedimus vobis apostolicam benedictionem et remis-*
     sionem peccatorum.   [*Francisco whispers to him.*]   60
     My lord reports Vittoria Corombona
     Is stol'n from forth the house of convertites
     By Bracciano, and they're fled the city.
     Now, though this be the first day of our seat,
     We cannot better please the divine power,   65
     Than to sequester from the holy church
     These cursed persons. Make it therefore known,
     We do denounce excommunication
     Against them both: all that are theirs in Rome
     We likewish banish. Set on.   *Exeunt* [*all except* FRANCISCO
                                  and LODOVICO].

Fran. Come dear Lodovico.   71
     You have ta'en the sacrament to prosecute
     Th'intended murder.

Lod.   With all constancy.
     But, sir, I wonder you'll engage yourself,
     In person, being a great prince.

Fran.   Divert me not.   75

---

58. wrong] *Q; wrong. / Act. 4. Scen. 3 Q4.*   59–60. *Mont. . . . peccatorum*]
*Q*ᵇ (*peccatorem*); *not in Q*ᵃ.   60. S.D.] *conj. Samp, Luc; not in Q.*
61. My] *Q*ᵇ; *Mon.* My *Q*ᵃ.   64. seat] *Q*ᵇ (seate); state *Q*ᵃ.   70.S.D.–
70.1. all . . . Lodovico] *Luc; not in Q; Monticelso, his train, Ambassadors,
&c Dyce i.*   73. murder.] *Q;* murder ? *Luc.*

    58.] Cf. W. Alexander (cf. App. IV), *J.C.*, III. i. 1173–4: 'Let other men
lament, we must revenge, / I scorne to beare a sword, and to complaine'.
    58.1. in state] described in Bignon (App. III, pp. 196–7).
    59–60.] i.e., 'We grant you the Apostolic blessing and remission of sins'.
    64. *seat*] the technical term for the throne or office of a Pope; the com-
positor, apparently, did not recognize it as such, and misread it as 'state'—
an easy misreading in secretary handwriting. Webster would have found
the word in Bignon's *Treatise.*

Most of his court are of my faction,
And some are of my counsel. Noble friend,
Our danger shall be 'like in this design,—
Give leave, part of the glory may be mine.   *Exit* FRANCISCO.

[*Re-*]*enter* MONTICELSO.

Mont. Why did the Duke of Florence with such care   80
    Labour your pardon? say.

Lod. Italian beggars will resolve you that
    Who, begging of an alms, bid those they beg of
    Do good for their own sakes; or't may be
    He spreads his bounty with a sowing hand,   85
    Like kings, who many times give out of measure;
    Not for desert so much as for their pleasure.

Mont. I know you're cunning. Come, what devil was that
    That you were raising?

Lod.   Devil, my lord?

Mont.   I ask you

---

77. counsel] councell *Q*; Council *Q4*.   78. 'like] *Q*; like *Q2*.   79. S.D.–
79.1.] Dod i subs.; *Enter Mon-/ticelso.* (to right of ll. *83–4*) *Q*ᵃ, *Q*ᵇ; *Exit
Fran. Enter / Monticelso.* (to right of ll. *78–9*) *Q*ᵇ; *Exeunt Fran. de Med. and
Gasparo. / Enter . . . Dyce i.*   80. Mont.] *Q*ᵇ; *not in Q*ᵃ.   84. or't] *Q*;
or it *Dyce ii.*   89. Devil . . . you] *so Dod iii;* . . . Lord? / I . . . *Q*.   Mont.
I] *Q3*; I *Q, Dod iii.*   you] you. *Q*.

79.1.] Monticelso's new attitude manifest in his ensuing speeches was
probably suggested by one of Webster's sources; cf. Intro., p. xxx.
  82–4. *Italian . . . sakes*] Cf. Florio, III, vi (p. 455ᵇ): 'I have heard some
beg in Italy: *Fate bene per voi*: "Do some good for your selfe".'
  85–7.] Cf. Webster's *Monumental Column*, ll. 39–40: 'He [Prince Henry]
spread his bounty with a prouident hand; / And not like those that sow th'
ingratefull sand'. See also Florio, III, vi (p. 460ᵃ): 'Not whole sackes, but by
the hand / A man should sow his seed i'the land. / That whosoever will
reape any commodity by it must sow with his hand, and not powre out of
a sacke. . . If the liberality of a prince be without heedy discretion and
measure, I would rather have him covetous and sparing'. Cf. Tilley, H91.
  88. *cunning*] (1) 'crafty, guileful', and (2) 'possessing magical skill' (cf.
v. i. 88 and 90).
  89. *I . . . you*] If these words had continued Lodovico's speech in the
copy, Compositor B's usual practice (since there *was* sufficient space)
would have been to set Lodovico's whole speech in one line; as he did *not*
do this, it may be presumed that they were given to Monticelso in the copy

How doth the duke employ you, that his bonnet   90
Fell with such compliment unto his knee,
When he departed from you?

Lod.   Why, my lord,
He told me of a resty Barbary horse
Which he would fain have brought to the career,
The 'sault, and the ring-galliard. Now, my lord,   95
I have a rare French rider.

Mont.   Take you heed:
Lest the jade break your neck. Do you put me off
With your wild horse-tricks? Sirrah you do lie.
O, thou'rt a foul black cloud, and thou dost threat
A violent storm.

Lod.   Storms are i'th'air, my lord;   100
I am too low to storm.

Mont.   Wretched creature!
I know that thou art fashion'd for all ill,
Like dogs, that once get blood, they'll ever kill.
About some murder? was't not?

Lod.   I'll not tell you;
And yet I care not greatly if I do;   105
Marry with this preparation. Holy father,
I come not to you as an intelligencer,
But as a penitent sinner. What I utter

90. How] *Q3; Mont.* How *Q, Dod iii subs.*

---

and that he has misplaced the speech prefix (as he clearly misplaced one at
III. ii. 329).

Q might be defended on the grounds that Lodovico is parrying a question by returning it to the churchman who should be expert in such matters; but this would be an abrupt way of speaking and thus out of keeping
with the rest of Lodovico's address to the new Pope.

94–5. *career . . . ring-galliard*] exercises in the 'manage' of a horse.

96. *French rider*] Cf. *D.M.,* I. i. 141–2: 'you have excellent riders in
France'.

98. *horse-tricks*] (1) the exercises of the manage, and (2) 'horse-play,
improprieties'.

103.] Cf. W. Alexander, *A.T.,* IV. ii. 2184: 'As dogges that once get
bloud, would always kill'.

107. *intelligencer*] informer, spy.

  Is in confession merely; which you know
  Must never be reveal'd.
Mont.   You have o'erta'en me. 110
Lod. Sir I did love Bracciano's duchess dearly;
  Or rather I pursued her with hot lust,
  Though she ne'er knew on't. She was poison'd;
  Upon my soul she was: for which I have sworn
  T'avenge her murder.
Mont.   To the Duke of Florence? 115
Lod. To him I have.
Mont.   Miserable creature!
  If thou persist in this, 'tis damnable.
  Dost thou imagine thou canst slide on blood
  And not be tainted with a shameful fall?
  Or like the black, and melancholic yew tree, 120
  Dost think to root thyself in dead men's graves,
  And yet to prosper? Instruction to thee
  Comes like sweet showers to over-hard'ned ground:
  They wet, but pierce not deep. And so I leave thee
  With all the Furies hanging 'bout thy neck, 125
  Till by thy penitence thou remove this evil,
  In conjuring from thy breast that cruel devil.
         Exit MONTICELSO.

Lod. I'll give it o'er. He says 'tis damnable:
  Besides I did expect his suffrage,
  By reason of Camillo's death. 130

   Enter Servant and FRANCISCO [*, and stand aside*].

Fran. Do you know that count?
Serv.   Yes, my lord.

123. over-] *Q; o'er- Haz.* 127.1.] *so Q4; to right of l. 128 Q.* 129–30.] *so Q; . . . reason / Of . . . Luc.* 130.1.] *so Q4; to right of ll. 130–1 Q. and . . . aside*] *This ed.; not in Q.*

 110. *o'erta'en*] overreached, got the better of.
 119. *tainted*] (1) 'sullied' or 'injured', and (2) 'attainted, proved guilty'.
 129. *suffrage*] with, perhaps, a quibble: (1) 'support, assistance', and (2) 'prayers, intercessions' (cf. *O.E.D.*, s.v., 1 and 2).

Fran. Bear him these thousand ducats to his lodging;
　　　Tell him the Pope hath sent them. Happily
　　　That will confirm more than all the rest.   [*Exit.*]
Serv. Sir.   135
Lod. To me sir ?
Serv. His Holiness hath sent you a thousand crowns,
　　　And wills you if you travail, to make him
　　　Your patron for intelligence.
Lod.   His creature
　　　Ever to be commanded.   [*Exit Servant.*]   140
　　　Why now 'tis come about. He rail'd upon me;
　　　And yet these crowns were told out and laid ready,
　　　Before he knew my voyage. O the art,
　　　The modest form of greatness! that do sit
　　　Like brides at wedding dinners, with their looks turn'd   145
　　　From the least wanton jests, their puling stomach
　　　Sick of the modesty, when their thoughts are loose,
　　　Even acting of those hot and lustful sports
　　　Are to ensue about midnight: such his cunning!

133. Happily] *Q;* Haply *Q4.*   134. confirm] *Q;* confirm him *Dyce ii.*
S.D.] *so Dod ii; not in Q.*   137–9. His . . . intelligence] *so Q; . . .* you /
A . . . travel, / To . . . *Wheel.*   138. wills] *Q2* (wils); will *Q.*   travail] *Q;*
travel *Q4.*   139–40. His . . . commanded] *so Luc; one line Q.*   140.
S.D.] *Dyce i; not in Q.*   143. art,] Art *Q.*   146. jests] *Q;* iest *Q2.*
stomach] *Q* (stomacke); stomachs *Dod i.*

132. *ducats*] Coryat, who visited Venice in 1608, reported that a *ducat*
was worth 4s. 8d. (*Crudities* (1611), ed. 1905, I, 423).
134. *confirm*] Dyce's emendation is attractive, especially since Compositor A omitted short words on other occasions (e.g., IV. i. 92); but the line
makes good sense without it, and metrical irregularity may be appropriate to Francisco's abrupt exit.
139. *Your . . . intelligence*] At this time statesmen paid travellers or resi-
dents abroad to provide them with foreign news; cf. III. ii. 229.
144. *form*] The word was often used for 'behaviour, manners', but with
Webster it also has the sense of 'merely outward appearance'; cf. *D.M.*,
I. i. 156–7: 'Some such flashes superficially hang on him, for form; but
observe his inward character . . .'
146. *jests*] Q2's 'iest' is attractive in view of 'stomach' in the same line;
but a desire for regularity in such matters is probably an insufficient cause
for emendation. Moreover, Compositor A was capable of both adding *and*
omitting a final letter, and so a reading 'stomachs' has equal claim.

He sounds my depth thus with a golden plummet,—   150
I am doubly arm'd now. Now to th'act of blood;
There's but three Furies found in spacious hell,
But in a great man's breast three thousand dwell.   [*Exit.*]

[v. i]

    A passage over the stage of BRACCIANO, FLAMINEO,
MARCELLO, HORTENSIO, [VITTORIA] COROMBONA,
    CORNELIA, ZANCHE *and others.*
    [FLAMINEO *and* HORTENSIO *remain.*]

Flam. In all the weary minutes of my life,
    Day ne'er broke up till now. This marriage
    Confirms me happy.

151. arm'd . . . Now] *Q;* arm'd. Now *conj. Samp;* arm'd now *Brereton.*
153. S.D.] *Dyce i; not in Q.*

v. i] *Sym; not in Q;* Act. 4. Scen. 4. *Q4, Haz;* Act. V. *Dod i.*   o.4.] *Haz;*
not in Q; exeunt omnes except Flamineo and Hortensio Dyce i; Then re-
enter Flamineo and Hortensio Samp; Flamineo, Marcello and . . . Luc.

150.] G. K. Hunter (*N. & Q.*, n.s., iv (1957), 54) compared Chapman,
Byron's Tragedy (1608), I. iii. 10: '. . . you were our golden plummet / To
sound this gulph of all ingratitude'. The 'golden plummet' that Lodovico
refers to is the thousand ducats sent him by Francisco.
    151. *Now*] There is some support for Sampson's and Brereton's readings
in Compositor A's error at I. i. 19; but this is probably insufficient to displace Q's emphatic line.
    152-3.] Cf. W. Alexander, *A.T.*, v. i. 2625-6: 'Some but three furies
faine in all the hels; / And ther's three thousand in one great mans brest'.

    v. i.] Act V is located in Bracciano's palace in Padua.
    0.3. others] These probably include the ambassadors (cf. ll. 57-61
below). The audience has just seen them attending the papal election and
hearing the new Pope pronounce Bracciano's excommunication, and so
their mere presence on the stage would enforce Webster's often-repeated
comments on the power of great men and the sycophancy of court society.
There would hardly be time for the actors to change their costumes after
their previous appearance only eighty lines earlier, so they would still be
dressed in the 'habits' of their various orders (cf. IV. iii. 5-14), tokens of
holiness, virtue, and honour—an ironical display for the marriage of a proclaimed whore and an excommunicate duke.
    2. *up till*] i.e., until.

Hort.   'Tis a good assurance.
    Saw you not yet the Moor that's come to court?
Flam. Yes, and conferr'd with him i'th'duke's closet,—   5
    I have not seen a goodlier personage,
    Nor ever talk'd with man better experienc'd
    In state affairs or rudiments of war.
    He hath by report, serv'd the Venetian
    In Candy these twice seven years, and been chief   10
    In many a bold design.
Hort.   What are those two
    That bear him company?
Flam. Two noblemen of Hungary, that living in the emperor's
    service as commanders, eight years since, contrary to the
    expectation of all the court ent'red into religion, into the   15
    strict order of Capuchins: but being not well settled in
    their undertaking they left their order and returned to
    court: for which being after troubled in conscience, they
    vowed their service against the enemies of Christ; went to
    Malta; were there knighted; and in their return back, at   20
    this great solemnity, they are resolved for ever to forsake
    the world, and settle themselves here in a house of Capu-
    chins in Padua.
Hort. 'Tis strange.
Flam. One thing makes it so. They have vowed for ever to   25
    wear next their bare bodies those coats of mail they served
    in.
Hort. Hard penance. Is the Moor a Christian?

28. Hard ... Christian] *so Dyce i;* ... pennance. / Is ... *Q.*

---

8. *rudiments*] principles (without the mod. implication of 'rudimentary').
10. *Candy*] Crete.
16. *strict . . . Capuchins*] an austere and poor order which branched off from the Franciscans about 1528; they did not become an independent order until 1619.
20. *knighted*] i.e., in the order of St John of Jerusalem (cf. IV. iii. 9 n.).
25–7.] Florio, I, xl (p. 122ᵇ) tells how 'William our last Duke of Guienne, ... the last ten or twelve yeares of his life, for penance-sake, wore continually a corselet under a religious habit'.
28.] Q's line-arrangement is peculiar. Possibly the following description

Flam. He is.

Hort. Why proffers he his service to our duke?   30

Flam. Because he understands there's like to grow
        Some wars between us and the Duke of Florence,
        In which he hopes employment.
        I never saw one in a stern bold look
        Wear more command, nor in a lofty phrase   35
        Express more knowing, or more deep contempt
        Of our slight airy courtiers. ~~He talks~~
        ~~As if he had travail'd all the princes' courts~~
        ~~Of Christendom; in all things strives t'express~~
        ~~That all that should dispute with him may know~~   40
        ~~Glories, like glow-worms, afar off shine bright~~
        ~~But look'd to near, have neither heat nor light.~~
        The duke!

Enter BRACCIANO, [FRANCISCO *Duke of*] *Florence disguised like*
Mulinassar; LODOVICO, ANTONELLI, [*and*] GASPARO [*disguised,*
and another], *bearing their swords and helmets*[*;* CARLO *and* PEDRO].

33.] *so Q3; Enter Duke Brachiano. (added to right) Q.*   38. travail'd]
Q; travell'd *Q4.*   42. to] *Q;* too *Q3.*   43. duke!] Duke. *Q;* Duke.— /
Act. 4. Scen. 5. *Q4.*   43.1–3.] *This ed.; Enter Brachiano, Florence . . .
Antonelli, Gaspar, Farnese bearing their swordes and helmets Q, (om.
'Farnese') Q3; . . . Mulinassar, Marcello, Lodovico . . . Gasparo, Farnese,
Carlo, and Pedro, bearing . . . helmets Dyce i; . . . Lodovico and Gasparo,
bearing their swords, their helmets down, Antonelli, Farnese Haz; . . .
Lodovico disguised as Carlo, Antonelli, Gasparo disguised as Pedro, Marcello,
bearing . . . helmets Samp.*

---

of Mulinassar, supplementing that of ll. 4–11, was a late addition, and
Hortensio's question was added to his comment on the Hungarians in
order to introduce the new material. If this were so, the redundant entry
for Bracciano at l. 33 might be another relic of the earlier version.

41–2.] Cf. W. Alexander (cf. App. IV), *A.T.,* v. iii. 3428–9: 'Some things
afarre doe like the Glow-worme shine, / Which look't too neere, have of
that light no signe'. The lines in *W.D.* are repeated (with different punctuation but with 'to neere' as before) in *D.M.,* IV. ii. 144–5; and the idea is
varied in *D.L.C.,* IV. ii. 120–1.

'Glow-worm' came to be used contemptuously of persons; *O.E.D.* (s.v.,
b) first quotes Burton, *Anatomy* (1624), II. iii. II. 260: 'an outside, a glo-
worme, a proud foole, an arrant asse'.

43.2. disguised] Probably Lodovico and Gasparo, the two chief con-

Brac. You are nobly welcome. We have heard at full
   Your honourable service 'gainst the Turk.   45
   To you, brave Mulinassar, we assign
   A competent pension: and are inly sorrow
   The vows of these two worthy gentlemen
   Make them incapable of our proffer'd bounty.
   Your wish is you may leave your warlike swords 50
   For monuments in our chapel. I accept it
   As a great honour done me, and must crave
   Your leave to furnish out our duchess' revels.
   Only one thing, as the last vanity
   You e'er shall view, deny me not to stay   55

---

44. You are] *Q2;* You'are *Q;* You're *conj. this ed.* 47. sorrow] *Q;*
sorrie *Q2.* 48. these] *conj. Luc, this ed.;* those *Q.*

---

spirators from Rome, were disguised as the two Hungarians (cf. ll. 11–12
above).

43.3. another] Q's '*Farnese*' is a 'ghost' character (cf. II. i. 0.3 n.).

Carlo and Pedro] These characters are included in the entry direction on
the strength of Q's speech prefixes of ll. 63 and 65 below; Pedro occurs in
full (with 'Car.') at V. ii. 17.1, and both occur in full at V. vi. 167.1–2. They
are some of those in Bracciano's court who are of Francisco's 'faction' and
'counsel' (IV. iii. 76–7); as such, they welcome Francisco and the other
three conspirators from Rome (ll. 63–7 below).

Many editors have assumed that 'Carlo' and 'Pedro' are names taken by
Lodovico and Gasparo when in disguise. But there is no warrant for this in
the text. Moreover this interpretation involves several major difficulties:
(1) at l. 63 below, Lodovico would welcome Francisco to Padua when, in
fact, they have journeyed there together (cf. ll. 11–12 above); (2) at l. 63
below, 'Car.' would stand for Lodovico, but at V. vi. 227 it would have to
stand for Gasparo; (3) more than two conspirators are necessary to kill
Flamineo, Vittoria, and Zanche in the last scene, especially since Flamineo
is armed with two loaded pistols and all three seem to die together with 'a
joint motion' (l. 232); and (4) the 'all' of V. vi. 279 suggests that more than
two conspirators remain alive at the end.

44. *You are*] A formal opening seems preferable (despite metrical irregularity); on several occasions Compositor B added redundant apostrophes.

47. *inly*] to the heart.

sorrow] sorry (cf. *Cym.*, V. v. 298; Folio).

48. *these*] Since Bracciano is about to address the two visitors, Q's 'those'
is unduly distant; cf. confusion (by Compositor A) at III. ii. 276.

51. *monuments*] evidence, tokens (of a fact).

53. *leave*] permission to depart.

To see a barriers prepar'd tonight;
You shall have private standings: it hath pleas'd
The great ambassadors of several princes
In their return from Rome to their own countries
To grace our marriage, and to honour me   60
With such a kind of sport.

Fran.   I shall persuade them
To stay, my lord.

Brac.   Set on there to the presence.

                    Exeunt BRACCIANO, FLAMINEO,
                    and [HORTENSIO].

Car. Noble my lord, most fortunately welcome,   *The conspirators*
You have our vows seal'd with the sacrament   *here embrace*
To second your attempts.

Ped.   And all things ready.   65
He could not have invented his own ruin,
Had he despair'd, with more propriety.

Lod. You would not take my way.

Fran.   'Tis better ordered.

Lod. T'have poison'd his prayer book, or a pair of beads,
The pommel of his saddle, his looking-glass,   70

---

62. To . . . presence] *so Dod iii, Dyce i; . . . Lord. | Set . . . Q.   Brac.*]
Dyce i; not in Q.   62.1–2.] *Haz; . . . Flamineo. | and Marcello (to right
of the two lines of type of l. 62) Q; . . . Flamineo, Marcello, and . . . Dyce i.*
63. *Car.*] *Q; Lod. Q3.*   63–4. S.D.] *so this ed.; outer margin, three
lines of small type, to right of ll. 63–5, approx. Q; after l. 63 Dod i.*   65.
Ped.] *Q; Gas. Q3.*

---

56. *barriers*] Cf. I. ii. 28–9 n.

62. Brac.] For the emendation, see IV. iii. 70 where the new Pope gives a
similar command.

presence] presence-chamber.

62.1–2.] Compositor B misplaced the direction in order to fit it into the
text-space left by the continuous printing of the dialogue; he worked
similarly at ll. 85.1–2 below (dividing a line of verse) and l. 96.1.

69. *pair*] set.

70. *pommel . . . saddle*] Edward Squire was hanged in 1598, convicted of
trying to murder the Queen by putting poison on the pommel of her
saddle; Squire had hoped that by touching the pommel the Queen would
convey the poison to her mouth and nostrils (so Reed, quoting Camden's
Elizabeth (ed. 1629), pp. 226–8). Lucas noted that Squire, like Webster's

Or th'handle of his racket,—O that, that!
That while he had been bandying at tennis,
He might have sworn himself to hell, and struck
His soul into the hazard! O my lord!
I would have our plot be ingenious,   75
And have it hereafter recorded for example
Rather than borrow example.
Fran.   There's no way
More speeding than this thought on.
Lod.   On then.
Fran. And yet methinks that this revenge is poor,
Because it steals upon him like a thief,—   80
To have ta'en him by the casque in a pitch'd field,
Led him to Florence!
Lod.   It had been rare.—And there
Have crown'd him with a wreath of stinking garlic,
T'have shown the sharpness of his government,
And rankness of his lust. Flamineo comes.   85

                    Exeunt [all except FRANCISCO].

Enter FLAMINEO, MARCELLO, *and* ZANCHE.

Mar. Why doth this devil haunt you ? say.

82. rare.—] *Q.*   85. And . . . comes] *so Dyce i;* . . . lust. / Flamineo . . . *Q.*
85.1–2. *Exeunt . . . Zanche] so Ol subs.; Exeunt Lodo-/uico Antonelli. / Enter
. . . Marcello, / and . . . (to right of ll. 84–6) Q.*

---

conspirators, had taken the sacrament to seal his vows to prosecute the
murder.
    74. *soul . . . hazard*] The 'hazards' were openings in the inner wall of the
tennis court, supporting the penthouse; to strike the ball into a *hazard* was
to win a stroke. Here *hazard* is used quibblingly as 'peril, jeopardy'.
    A similar quibble is found in Sharpham, *Cupid's Whirligig* (1607), ed.
1926, p. 13: '—what Tennis-ball ha's fortune taken thee for, to tosse thee
thus into my way ?—I hope yee will not s[t]rike me into any hazard of my
life though'; and in *D.M.*, v. iv. 54: 'We are merely the stars' tennis-
balls . . .'
    Lucas pointed out that murderers of this age often wished to destroy
both soul and body; he compared *Ham.*, III. iii. 88–95 and Nashe, *Unfortunate Traveller* (1594), *Wks*, II, 325–6 (where a victim consigns his soul to
perdition to save his life at his murderer's hands, and is thereupon killed).
    85.] Cf. IV. ii. 129–30 n.

Flam.   I know not.
   For by this light I do not conjure for her.
   'Tis not so great a cunning as men think
   To raise the devil: for here's one up already,—
   The greatest cunning were to lay him down—   90
Mar. She is your shame.
Flam.   I prithee pardon her.
   In faith you see, women are like to burs;
   Where their affection throws them, there they'll stick.
Zan. That is my countryman, a goodly person;
   When he's at leisure I'll discourse with him   95
   In our own language.
Flam.   I beseech you do,—   *Exit* ZANCHE.
   How is't brave soldier ? O that I had seen
   Some of your iron days! I pray relate
   Some of your service to us.
Fran. 'Tis a ridiculous thing for a man to be his own   100
   chronicle,—I did never wash my mouth with mine own
   praise for fear of getting a stinking breath.
Mar. You're too stoical. The duke will expect other dis-
   course from you—
Fran. I shall never flatter him,—I have studied man too   105
   much to do that: what difference is between the duke

96. S.D.] *so Q4; to right of l. 95 Q; after* language *Dod i.*

---

88. *cunning*] occult art, magic.
89–90. *raise . . . down*] Cf. *Rom.*, II. i. 23–9 for the same *double entendre* (so Lucas).
92–3. *burs . . . stick*] proverbial; cf. Tilley B724.
100–1. *'Tis . . . chronicle*] Cf. *D.M.*, III. i. 88–9: 'you / Are your own chronicle too much; and grossly / Flatter yourself'.
101–2. *wash . . . breath*] Cf. Pettie (cf. App. IV), I, 95: 'That hee which washeth his mouth with his owne praise, soyleth himselfe with the suddes that come of it'. See, also, Tilley, M476: 'proper praise stinks'.
106–9. *difference . . . chance*] Cf. Pettie, II, 192: 'they think it no lesse shame to be seene in the company of the baser sort, then to be taken in the common stewes: not knowing that there is no more difference between the gentleman and the yeoman, then there is between two brickes made of self same earth: whereof the one is set in the top of a towre, the other in the bottome of a wel'.

and I ? no more than between two bricks; all made of one
clay. Only't may be one is plac'd on the top of a turret;
the other in the bottom of a well by mere chance; if I
were plac'd as high as the duke, I should stick as fast;   110
make as fair a show; and bear out weather equally.

Flam. If this soldier had a patent to beg in churches, then he
would tell them stories.

Mar. I have been a soldier too.

Fran. How have you thriv'd ?   115

Mar. Faith poorly.

Fran. That's the misery of peace. Only outsides are then
respected: as ships seem very great upon the river,
which show very little upon the seas: so some men i'th'
court seem Colossuses in a chamber, who if they came   120
into the field would appear pitiful pigmies.

Flam. Give me a fair room yet hung with arras, and some
great cardinal to lug me by th'ears as his endeared
minion.

Fran. And thou may'st do the devil knows what villainy.   125

Flam. And safely.

Fran. Right; you shall see in the country in harvest time,

112. *Flam.*] *Q subs.; Flam. (aside) Dyce ii.*   121. pitiful] pittifull. *Q.*
125. do] *Q3;* doe, *Q;* doe— *Luc.*

---

111. *fair*] There may be a quibbling allusion to his disguise as the dark-
skinned Mulinassar.

112. *patent to beg*] Without a proper licence from a J.P., a beggar was
liable to be whipped as a vagabond.

117. *misery of peace*] Those who had served in the wars often complained
against the injustices consequent on peace; such a complaint is B. Riche's
Room for a Gentleman (1609).

118–21. *ships . . . pigmies*] Cf. Pettie, II, 221: 'as some ships seeme great
uppon the ryver, whiche shewe very little uppon the Sea: so some seeme
learned amongst the ignorant, whiche have but a little when they come
amongst the learned'.

122. *arras*] i.e., to hide behind; *arras*, or tapestries, were often hung some
distance from the walls.

125. *do*] Lucas' 'doe—' is probably an unnecessary attempt to rationalize
Q; compare similar oddities in Q at l. 121 above, and I. ii. 95 (both set by B,
as this present passage).

pigeons, though they destroy never so much corn, the
farmer dare not present the fowling-piece to them! why?
because they belong to the lord of the manor; whilst   130
your poor sparrows that belong to the Lord of heaven,
they go to the pot for't.

Flam. I will now give you some politic instruction. The duke
says he will give you pension; that's but bare promise:
get it under his hand. For I have known men that have   135
come from serving against the Turk; for three or four
months they have had pension to buy them new wooden
legs and fresh plasters; but after 'twas not to be had. And
this miserable courtesy shows, as if a tormenter should
give hot cordial drinks to one three-quarters dead o'th'   140
rack, only to fetch the miserable soul again to endure
more dog-days.

Enter HORTENSIO, *a young Lord,* ZANCHE, *and two
more.*

How now, gallants; what are they ready for the barriers?
                                        [*Exit* FRANCISCO.]

Y. Lord. Yes: the lords are putting on their armour.

Hort. What's he?   145

Flam. A new up-start: one that swears like a falc'ner, and
will lie in the duke's ear day by day like a maker of almanacs; and yet I knew him since he came to th'court
smell worse of sweat than an under-tennis-court-
keeper.   150

Hort. Look you, yonder's your sweet mistress.

---

134. you] *Q;* you a *Q2.*   143.1. *Exit Francisco*] *This ed.; not in Q; after
l. 142 Dyce i.*   148. since] *Q;* once ere *conj. Luc.*

---

128. *pigeons*] Lucas quoted Harrison's 'Description of England', in
Holinshed, *Chronicles* (1587), III, ii: 'pigeons [are] now an hurtfull foule by
reason of their multitudes, and number of houses dailie erected for their
increase (which the bowres [i.e., boors] of the countrie call in scorne almes
houses, and dens of theeves, and such like)'.

139. *miserable*] (1) 'compassionate', and (2) 'miserly' (cf. *O.E.D.*, s.v., 7
and 6); the quibble is made three-fold at l. 141.

142. *dog-days*] Cf. III. ii. 202 n.

Flam. Thou art my sworn brother, I'll tell thee,—I do love
that Moor, that witch, very constrainedly: she knows
some of my villainy; I do love her, just as a man holds a
wolf by the ears. But for fear of turning upon me, and 155
pulling out my throat, I would let her go to the devil.

Hort. I hear she claims marriage of thee.

Flam. 'Faith, I made to her some such dark promise, and in
seeking to fly from't I run on, like a frighted dog with a
bottle at's tail, that fain would bite it off and yet dares not 160
look behind him.—Now my precious gipsy!

Zan. Ay, your love to me rather cools than heats.

Flam. Marry, I am the sounder lover,—we have many
wenches about the town heat too fast.

Hort. What do you think of these perfum'd gallants then? 165

Flam. Their satin cannot save them. I am confident
They have a certain spice of the disease,
For they that sleep with dogs, shall rise with fleas.

Zan. Believe it! A little painting and gay clothes make you
loathe me. 170

Flam. How? love a lady for painting or gay apparel? I'll
unkennel one example more for thee. Æsop had a foolish

155. of] *Q; of her Haz.*   165. What ... then] *one line Q; as prose Dod i;
as verse Scott.*   169–70. Believe ... me] *so Dyce i; ... clothes, / Make ...
Q.*   170. loathe] *Q; love Q4.*

154–5. *holds ... ears*] an ancient and common proverb (Tilley W603);
Lucas compared *Arcadia, Wks,* II, 12: 'as the proverbe saith, like them
that hold the wolfe by the eares, bitten while they hold, and slaine if they
loose'.

161. *gipsy*] alluding to her dark skin; see also the quotation in the following note.

162. *your ... heats*] i.e., Flamineo's passion is declining; but Flamineo
takes it to mean that he *cools,* or allays, Zanche's passion (cf. *Ant.,* I. i. 6–10:
'his captain's heart, / ... is become the bellows and the fan / To cool a
gipsy's lust').

166. *satin*] a pun on 'Satan'; cf. Intro., p. xxi, n. 2.

168.] a common proverb (Tilley D537); it is found in Pettie, I, 38.

169–70. *little ... me*] i.e., some one finer than I has taken your love, so
that you now hate me.

172–4. *Æsop ... diners*] i.e., certain physical satisfaction is more important than a desire for finery.

~~dog that let go the flesh to catch the shadow. I would
have courtiers be better diners.~~

Zan. You remember your oaths.   175

Flam. Lovers' oaths are like mariners' prayers, uttered in
extremity; but when the tempest is o'er, and that the
vessel leaves tumbling, they fall from protesting to
drinking. And yet amongst gentlemen protesting and
drinking go together, ~~and agree as well as shoemakers~~   180
~~and Westphalia bacon.~~ They are both drawers on; for
drink draws on protestation; and protestation draws on
more drink. Is not this discourse better now than the
morality of your sunburnt gentleman?

Enter CORNELIA.

Cor. Is this your perch, you haggard? fly to th'stews.   185
                              [*Strikes* ZANCHE.]

Flam. You should be clapp'd by th'heels now: strike i'th'court!
                              [*Exit* CORNELIA.]

---

174. diners] *Samp;* Diuers (*italicized*) Q.   175. oaths.] *Q;* oathes?
Dod i.   184. morality] *Q4;* mortality Q.   your] *Q;* yon *Q4.*   185.1.]
Dyce ii *subs.; not in* Q.   186. court!] Court. *Q;* Court? *Q2.*   186.1.]
Dyce i; *not in* Q.

Cf. Pettie, II, 135 (of one who cares more for words than sense): 'with
Esopes Dogge, letteth fall the fleshe, to catche the shadow'.

176. *Lovers'* . . . *prayers*] Cf. Pettie, I, 95: 'The othes of lovers, carry as
much credite as the vowes of Mariners'.

177. *that*] when.

178. *tumbling*] a *double entendre*; cf. *Ham.,* IV. v. 60–6.

180–1. *agree* . . . *bacon*] i.e., salt bacon draws men on to drink, and shoe-
makers draw shoes on to feet; Sampson quoted *Gammer Gurton* (1575), I. i,
where a 'slyp of bacon' is to be used 'for a shoinghorn to draw on two pots
of ale'.

184. *sunburnt gentleman*] i.e., the dark-skinned Mulinassar (cf. Song of
Solomon, i. 6: 'I am black, because the sun hath looked upon me').

185. *haggard*] wild (female) hawk; often used of a wild, intractable person (cf. *Shr.,* IV. ii. 39), and of a 'wanton' (cf. *Oth.,* III. iii. 260).

186. *clapp'd* . . . *heels*] i.e., put in irons, or in the stocks.

strike i'th'court] an act of contempt; from 1541, malicious striking which
drew blood at the king's court was punishable by life imprisonment, a fine,
and the loss of the striker's right hand (so Stephen, *Commentaries* (ed. 1914),
IV, 156; quoted by Lucas).

Zan. She's good for nothing but to make her maids
    Catch cold a' nights ; they dare not use a bed-staff,
    For fear of her light fingers.
Mar.   You're a strumpet.
    An impudent one.   [*Kicks* ZANCHE.]
Flam.   Why do you kick her ? say,   190
    Do you think that she's like a walnut tree ?
    Must she be cudgell'd ere she bear good fruit ?
Mar. She brags that you shall marry her.
Flam.   What then ?
Mar. I had rather she were pitch'd upon a stake
    In some new-seeded garden, to affright   195
    Her fellow crows thence.
Flam.   You're a boy, a fool,—
    Be guardian to your hound, I am of age.
Mar. If I take her near you I'll cut her throat.
Flam. With a fan of feathers ?
Mar.   And for you ;—I'll whip
    This folly from you.
Flam.   Are you choleric ?   200

190. S.D.] *Dyce ii subs.; not in Q.*   190. her ? say,] *Q;* her, say ? *Dod i.*
195. new-seeded] *hyphened Q.*   196. You're] *Q2* (You'r); Your *Q.*

188. *bed-staff*] either one of the slats which supported the bedding, or a
staff used for beating up the bed in making it ; here it is quibblingly used for
(1) the man who should 'warm' the maids in bed (cf. 'Catch cold a'nights'),
and (2) a stick with which Cornelia could beat them.

191–2.] Cf. Pettie, III, 39: 'A woman, an asse, and a walnut tree, / Bring
the more fruit, the more beaten they bee': a common proverb (cf. Tilley,
W644).

199. *fan of feathers*] i.e., the instrument of a courtier, not of a soldier; cf.
M.C., ll. 93–5.

200. *choleric*] Cf. P. Charron, *Of Wisdom,* tr. S. Lennard (1608), G4:
'Choler is a foolish passion which putteth vs wholly out of ourselues, and
. . . maketh the blood to boile in our hearts, and stirreth vp furious vapors in
our spirits, which blinde vs and cast vs headlong to whatsoeuer may satisfie
the desire which we haue of reuenge. . . A man deceiueth himselfe to thinke
that there is courage where there is violence: violent motions are like the
endeuours of children and olde men . . . a great imbecillitie is it in a man to
be cholericke'.

Flamineo enrages Marcello by treating his moral indignation as a
physical ailment ; cf. next note.

I'll purge't with rhubarb.

Hort.   O your brother!

Flam.   Hang him.

He wrongs me most that ought t'offend me least,—
I do suspect my mother play'd foul play
When she conceiv'd thee.

Mar.   Now by all my hopes,
Like the two slaught'red sons of Œdipus,   205
The very flames of our affection
Shall turn two ways. Those words I'll make thee answer
With thy heart blood.

Flam.   Do—~~like the geese in the progress,~~
You know where you shall find me,—   [*Exit.*]

Mar.   Very good,—
And thou beest a noble friend, bear him my sword,   210

---

207. two] *Q*b; to *Q*a.   208. heart] *Q;* heart's *Dod i.*   Do] *Q; Doe, Q2.*
geese] *Q* (geesse); gesse *Q2;* gestes *Steevens* (*ap. Luc*); Guise *conj. Luc.*
progress,] *Q;* progress; *Dod ii.*   209. S.D.] *so Samp; not in Q; at end of
line Q4.*   210. beest] *Q;* be'st *Q3.*

---

201. *rhubarb*] a common prescription; cf. *D.M.*, II. v. 12–13: 'Rhubarb,
O, for rhubarb / To purge this choler'.

205–7. *two ... ways*] These two died in single combat for their father's
throne (cf. Statius, *Thebais*, XII). Their story is referred to in Pettie (cf.
App. IV), III, 84: 'it is sayde, that the enmity between Eteocles and
Polinices was so great, that their bodyes being burnt together, the flames
were seene most miraculously to part one from another: shewing plainly,
that death was not able to take up their controversies, or set an end to their
cancred hatred'.

208–9. *Do ... me*] *geese* was often used for 'prostitutes' (cf., for example,
LLL., III. i. 100, and Arden ed. (1951), note). Royal progresses were reputed to be occasions for licentiousness (cf. I. ii. 174–5) and so prostitutes were
readily found in the course of one; cf. L. Barrey, *Ram Alley* (1611), B2ᵛ:
'a ritch well-practis'd baud, / May pursse more fees in a summers pro-
gresse, / Then a well traded lawyer in a whole terme, ...'

Spencer interpreted the line as 'Do as the geese do in a procession—
follow me, you goose, you', and compared Hamlet's exit (IV. ii. 33) with
'Hide fox, and all after'; but this scarcely makes sense of 'You know ... find
me', nor does it allow for the fact that Flamineo speaks to Marcello, not to
a whole pack of people.

Lucas suggested reading 'gestes' or 'gesses', a technical term for the
stopping-places on a progress.

210. *And*] if.

And bid him fit the length on't.
Y. Lord.   Sir I shall.

[*Exeunt all but* ZANCHE.]

Enter FRANCISCO *the Duke of Florence* [*disguised*
as Mulinassar].

Zan. [*aside*] He comes. Hence petty thought of my disgrace,—
[*to him*] I ne'er lov'd my complexion till now,
Cause I may boldly say without a blush,
I love you.
Fran.   Your love is untimely sown,—   215
There's a spring at Michaelmas, but 'tis but a faint one,
—I am sunk in years, and I have vowed never to marry.
Zan. Alas! poor maids get more lovers than husbands,—yet
you mistake my wealth. For, as when ambassadors are
sent to congratulate princes, there's commonly sent   220
along with them a rich present; so that though the prince
like not the ambassador's person nor words, yet he likes
well of the presentment: so I may come to you in the
same manner, and be better loved for my dowry than my
virtue.   225

211.1.] *Haz; not in Q; to right of l. 214 Q3.*   211.2. *Enter . . . Florence*]
so this ed.; to right of ll. 213–14 Q; to right of l. 213 Q3 subs.   211.2–3.
disguised as Mulinassar] *This ed.; not in Q.*   212. *aside*] *Luc; not in
Q.*   213. *to him*] *This ed.; not in Q.*   215, 226, *and* 231. *Fran.*] *Q3*
(Fra.); Fla. Q.   215. *Your . . . sown*] *so Q; as prose Dyce i.*   216–17.
There's . . . marry] *so Dyce i; . . . sunck / In . . . Q; . . . one: / I am . . .*
Dod ii.   218. *Alas . . . husbands*] *so Dod iii; as verse Q.*

211.2–3.] Compositor A misplaced this direction for lack of room in the
text-space (cf. IV. i. 37 S.D. n.).
215, etc. Fran.] Q's '*Fla.*' is probably a misprint, or misreading, of
'*Flo[rence]*.'
216. *spring . . . one*] Michaelmas is 29 Sept. For Francisco's usage, cf.
O.E.D., s.v., b, 1669: 'God promised him a Michaelmas Spring (I may say
so) a son in his old age'.
218. *poor . . . husbands*] Cf. Pettie, III, 6: 'you see how now adayes fayre
women without riches fynde more Lovers then Husbandes, and there are
few that take wives for Gods sake, or as the saying is, For their fayre
lookes: . . .'

Fran. I'll think on the motion.

Zan. Do,—I'll now detain you no longer. At your better
    leisure I'll tell you things shall startle your blood.
    Nor blame me that this passion I reveal;
    Lovers die inward that their flames conceal.   230

Fran. [*aside*] Of all intelligence this may prove the best,—
    Sure I shall draw strange fowl, from this foul nest.   *Exeunt.*

[v. ii]

Enter MARCELLO *and* CORNELIA.

Cor. I hear a whispering all about the court,
    You are to fight,—who is your opposite?
    What is the quarrel?

Mar.   'Tis an idle rumour.

Cor. Will you dissemble? sure you do not well
    To fright me thus,—you never look thus pale   5
    But when you are most angry. I do charge you
    Upon my blessing;—nay I'll call the duke,
    And he shall school you.

Mar.   Publish not a fear
    Which would convert to laughter; 'tis not so,—
    Was not this crucifix my father's?

Cor.   Yes.   10

Mar. I have heard you say, giving my brother suck,
    He took the crucifix between his hands,

227–8. Do . . . blood] *so Q; . . .* now / Detain . . . leisure / I'll . . . *Dod iii.*
230. conceal] *Q;* conceal. *Exit Dyce ii.*   231. aside] *Luc; not in Q,*
Dyce ii.   232. S.D.] *Q; Exit Dyce ii.*

v. ii] *Sym; not in Q;* Act. 4. Scen. 6. *Q4;* [IV.] Scene V. *Haz.*   0.1.
Cornelia] *Q;* Cornelia and Page *conj. Lucas, Sp.*   2. You] *Q2;* Your
Q.

---

226. *motion*] proposal, offer.
230. *flames*] i.e., the passions of love (as often; cf., for example, *Tw.N.,*
I. v. 283).

v. ii. 10. *crucifix*] presumably one hanging round Cornelia's neck.

Enter FLAMINEO.

And broke a limb off.
Cor.   Yes: but 'tis mended.
Flam. I have brought your weapon back.   FLAMINEO *runs*
Cor.   Ha, O my horror!   MARCELLO *through.*
Mar. You have brought it home indeed.
Cor.   Help,—O he's murdered.
Flam. Do you turn your gall up? I'll to sanctuary,   16
And send a surgeon to you.   [*Exit.*]

Enter CARLO, HORTENSIO, PEDRO.

Hort.   How? o'th'ground?
Mar. O mother now remember what I told
    Of breaking off the crucifix:—farewell—
    There are some sins which heaven doth duly punish   20
    In a whole family. This it is to rise
    By all dishonest means. Let all men know
    That tree shall long time keep a steady foot
    Whose branches spread no wider than the root.   [*Dies.*]
Cor. O my perpetual sorrow!
Hort.   Virtuous Marcello.   25
    He's dead: pray leave him lady; come, you shall.

12.1.] *so* Q (*Flamineo,*)*; after l. 13 Dyce ii.*   17. *Exit*] *Dod i; not in* Q;
to right of l. 16 Q3.   17.1.] *Dyce i subs.; Enter Car. Hort.* | *Pedro (to right
of ll. 19–20)* Q; *Enter Cor Hort.* | *Pedro (as* Q) Q2; *Enter Hort (to right of
l. 19)* Q3, Q4, (*after you, l. 17*) *Dod ii subs;. Enter Lodovico, Hortensio and
Gasparo Haz.*   19. off] Q; *of* Q2.   24. wider] Q4; wilder Q.   Dies]
Dod ii; not in Q.

12.1.] Q's entry *may* be misplaced, for there was no other place for it in
the text-space near l. 14 (unless another line of type was used); Compositor
A certainly misplaced l. 17.1 for this reason.

16. *turn . . . up*] probably a variant of 'to turn up one's heels' (i.e., to die);
gall was used metaphorically for bitterness of spirit, rancour (cf. *O.E.D.*,
s.v., 3). Or, possibly, the phrase is a literal description of Marcello vomiting
from his wound (so Lucas).

24. *wider*] The emendation is supported by G. K. Hunter's reference to
Chapman, *Byron's Conspiracy* (1608), III. iii. 29–30: 'And being great (like
trees that broadest sproote) / Their owne top-heavy state grubs up their
roote'.

Cor. Alas he is not dead: he's in a trance.
   Why here's nobody shall get any thing by his death. Let
   me call him again for God's sake.

Car. I would you were deceiv'd.   30

Cor. O you abuse me, you abuse me, you abuse me. How
   many have gone away thus for lack of tendance; rear
   up's head, rear up's head; his bleeding inward will kill
   him.

Hort. You see he is departed.   35

Cor. Let me come to him; give me him as he is, if he be turn'd
   to earth; let me but give him one hearty kiss, and you
   shall put us both into one coffin: fetch a looking-glass,
   see if his breath will not stain it; or pull out some feathers
   from my pillow, and lay them to his lips,—will you lose   40
   him for a little pains-taking?

Hort. Your kindest office is to pray for him.

Cor. Alas! I would not pray for him yet. He may live to lay me
   i'th'ground, and pray for me, if you'll let me come to him.

   Enter BRACCIANO *all armed, save the beaver, with*
   FLAMINEO[, FRANCISCO *disguised as Mulinassar, a Page, and*
                LODOVICO *disguised*].

Brac. Was this your handiwork?   45
Flam. It was my misfortune.
Cor. He lies, he lies,—he did not kill him: these have kill'd
   him, that would not let him be better look'd to.
Brac. Have comfort my griev'd mother.
Cor. O you screech-owl!   50
Hort. Forbear, good madam.

27. Alas . . . trance] *so Q; as prose Haz.*   30. *Car.*] *Q; Cor. Q2, Q3; Hor.
Q4; Lod. Haz.*   36. is,] *Q, Q2; is; Dod i.*   37. earth;] *Q; earth, Q2,
Dod i.*   40. lose] *Q4; loose Q.*   44.1-2. *Enter . . . Flamineo] so Q2; to
right of ll. 44–6 Q.*   44.2-3. *Francisco . . . Lodovico disguised] This ed.;
not in Q; and Page Q3; Francisco de Medicis, Lodovico, and Page Dyce i.*
50. you] *Q; yon Q3.*

36–40. *turn'd . . . lips*] Reed compared *Lr.*, v. iii. 261–5.

Cor. Let me go, let me go.   *She runs to* FLAMINEO *with*
                                    her knife drawn and coming
                                    to him lets it fall.

    The God of heaven forgive thee. Dost not wonder
    I pray for thee ? I'll tell thee what's the reason,—
    I have scarce breath to number twenty minutes;   55
    I'd not spend that in cursing. Fare thee well—
    Half of thyself lies there: and may'st thou live
    To fill an hour-glass with his mould'red ashes,
    To tell how thou shouldst spend the time to come
    In blest repentance.

Brac.   Mother, pray tell me   60
    How came he by his death ? what was the quarrel ?

Cor. Indeed my younger boy presum'd too much
    Upon his manhood; gave him bitter words;
    Drew his sword first; and so I know not how,
    For I was out of my wits, he fell with's head   65
    Just in my bosom.

Page. This is not true madam.

Cor.   I pray thee peace.
    One arrow's graz'd already; it were vain
    T'lose this: for that will ne'er be found again.

Brac. Go, bear the body to Cornelia's lodging: 70
    And we command that none acquaint our duchess
    With this sad accident: for you Flamineo,
    Hark you, I will not grant your pardon.

Flam.   No ?

Brac. Only a lease of your life. And that shall last
    But for one day. Thou shalt be forc'd each evening   75

---

52. S.D.–52.2.] *so Dod i; to right of ll. 52–6 Q.*   67. I] *Q; aside* I *Luc.*
68. graz'd] *Q;* grassed *Wheel.*   69. this:] *Q;* this *Dod iii.*

---

    68. *graz'd*] probably a 17th-century form of 'grassed' (i.e., 'lost in the
grass'), a rare verb for which cf. *O.E.D.*, s.v., 1, 1670: 'One Arrow must be
shot after another, though both be grast, and never found again'. Q's form
should be retained since a quibble may be intended on 'to graze' = 'to cut
the surface of' (referring, by litotes, to Marcello's wound).
    For shooting a second arrow to find the first, cf. *Mer.V.*, I. i. 140–4.

To renew it, or be hang'd.

Flam.   At your pleasure.

LODOVICO *sprinkles* BRACCIA-
NO's *beaver with a poison.*

Your will is law now, I'll not meddle with it.

Brac. You once did brave me in your sister's lodging;
I'll now keep you in awe for't. Where's our beaver?

Fran. [*aside*] He calls for his destruction. Noble youth,   80
I pity thy sad fate. Now to the barriers.
This shall his passage to the black lake further,—
The last good deed he did, he pardon'd murther.   *Exeunt.*

[v. iii]

Charges and shouts. They fight at barriers;
first single pairs, then three to three.
Enter BRACCIANO *and* FLAMINEO *with others*[*following,*
including VITTORIA, GIOVANNI, *and* FRANCISCO
disguised as Mulinassar].

Brac. An armourer! Ud's death an armourer!

Flam. Armourer; where's the armourer?

Brac. Tear off my ~~beaver.~~ helmet

Flam.   Are you hurt, my lord?

Brac. O my brain's on fire,

75–6. But . . . hang'd] *so Dod ii; as prose Q;* . . . it, / Or . . . *Dod i.*   76.
pleasure.] *Q;* pleasure. *Enter Lod. and Fra. Q3.*   80. aside] *Dyce ii; not*
in Q.   83.] *indented Q.*   murther] *Q;* murder *Dod i.*

v. iii] *Sym; not in Q;* Act 5. (*after l. o.2*) *Q3.*   0.3–5. Enter . . . *Mulinassar*]
This ed.; Enter . . . others Q; Enter Brachiano, Vittoria Corombona, Gio-
vanni, Francisco de Medicis, Flamineo, with others Dyce i.   4. O . . .
poison'd] *so Wheel;* . . . fire, / The . . . *Q, Samp.*

76.2. *beaver*] lower portion of the face-guard of a helmet. Boklund suggested (p. 29) that Webster derived this method of poisoning from P.
Boaistuau, *Theatrum Mundi* (tr. 1581), p. 168: 'Another Florentine Knight,
after that he had pulled off his helmet for to take aire, . . . an enemie of his
rubbed it with a certayne poyson, which was the occasion that when he put
it on againe, he dyed sodainly'.

78. *You . . . lodging*] Cf. IV. ii. 51.

81. *barriers*] Cf. I. ii. 28–9 n.

Enter Armourer.

the helmet is poison'd.

Arm. My lord upon my soul—

Brac.   Away with him to torture.   5
                                        [*Exit Armourer, guarded.*]

There are some great ones that have hand in this,
And near about me.

Vit.   O my loved lord,—poisoned?

Flam. Remove the bar: here's unfortunate revels,—
Call the physicians;

Enter two Physicians.

                        a plague upon you;
We have too much of your cunning here already.   10
I fear the ambassadors are likewise poison'd.

Brac. O I am gone already: the infection
Flies to the brain and heart. O thou strong heart!
There's such a covenant 'tween the world and it,
They're loth to break.

Giov.   O my most loved father!   15

Brac. Remove the boy away,—
Where's this good woman? had I infinite worlds
They were too little for thee. Must I leave thee?
What say yon screech-owls, is the venom mortal?

5.1.] *Sp; not in* Q.   7. poisoned?] Q; poison'd? *Enter Vittoria.* Q4.
8. revels] Q2; reuls Q.   9.1.] *so Dod i; at end of line* Q.   14. covenant]
Q; cov'nant Q4.   15. father!] Q; Father! *Enter Giovan.* Q4.   19. yon]
Q; you Q2.   owls] Q; owl Q3.

    4.] Compositor A probably set this line as two in order to make space
for the stage-direction (as at l. 266 below); there would have been room
in the text-space two or three lines earlier.
    8. *bar*] i.e., the barriers (so Sampson), or some fastening of Bracciano's
helmet (so Lucas).
    17–18. *had . . . thee*] Lucas compared *Arcadia*, iii (*Wks*, I, 427): 'I sweare,
that Death bringes nothing with it to grieve me, but that I must leave thee,
and cannot remaine to answere part of thy infinit deserts'; but this is probably insufficient to establish Webster's knowledge of the *Arcadia* before
writing *D.M.*
    19. *owls*] The owl foretold death; cf. *R3*, IV. iv. 509, etc.

Phys. Most deadly.

Brac.   Most corrupted politic hangman!   20
    You kill without book; but your art to save
    Fails you as oft as great men's needy friends.
    I that have given life to offending slaves
    And wretched murderers, have I not power
    To lengthen mine own a twelve-month?   25
    [to Vittoria] Do not kiss me, for I shall poison thee.
    This unction is sent from the great Duke of Florence.

Fran. Sir be of comfort.

Brac. O thou soft natural death, that art joint-twin
    To sweetest slumber: no rough-bearded comet   30
    Stares on thy mild departure: the dull owl
    Beats not against thy casement: the hoarse wolf
    Scents not thy carrion. Pity winds thy corse,
    Whilst horror waits on princes.

Vit. I am lost for ever.   35

Brac. How miserable a thing it is to die
    'Mongst women howling!

        [Enter LODOVICO and GASPARO, in the habit of
            Capuchins.]

                What are those?

Flam.   Franciscans.

26. S.D.] *Q4* (*at end of line*); *not in Q.*   27. unction is] *Q;* unction's
Dyce ii.   29. joint-twin] *hyphened Q.*   30. rough-bearded] *hyphened Q.*
34. waits] *Q2* (waites); waights *Q.*   princes] *Q;* princes' *Haz.*   37.1–
2.] *Dyce i; not in Q.*

    21–2. *You . . . you*] i.e., 'You are never at a loss how to kill, but your art
deserts you when you have to save life'; *without book* = 'from memory, by
rote' (cf. *Tw.N.*, I. iii. 28).

    29–30. *death . . . slumber*] a rephrasing of the proverb 'Sleep is the
brother of death' (Tilley S526).

    31–2. *dull . . . casement*] Lucas compared the omens of Edward II's death
in Drayton's *Barons' Wars* (1619), v, xlii: 'Under his Eave, the buzzing
Screech-Owle sings, / Beating the Windowes with her fatall Wings'.

    35.] Cf. *D.L.C.*, II. iii. 102: 'O, I am lost for euer', and *C.C.*, IV. ii. 130:
'I am every way lost', and III. iii. 12: 'And I am lost, lost in't for euer'; each
is a cry from a woman at the loss of her lover.

    37. *Franciscans*] Capuchins were a dependent order of the Franciscans

They have brought the extreme unction.

Brac. On pain of death, let no man name death to me,
It is a word infinitely terrible,—   40
Withdraw into our cabinet.   *Exeunt but* FRANCISCO
                                               and FLAMINEO.

Flam. To see what solitariness is about dying princes. As
heretofore they have unpeopled towns; divorc'd friends,
and made great houses unhospitable: so now, O justice!
where are their flatterers now? Flatterers are but the   45
shadows of princes' bodies—the least thick cloud makes
them invisible.

Fran. There's great moan made for him.

Flam. 'Faith, for some few hours salt water will run most
plentifully in every office o'th'court. But believe it: most   50
of them do but weep over their stepmothers' graves.

Fran. How mean you?

Flam. Why? They dissemble, ~~as some men do that live within~~
~~compass o'th'verge.~~

Fran. Come you have thriv'd well under him.   55

Flam. 'Faith, like a wolf in a woman's breast; ~~I have been fed~~
~~with poultry;~~ but for money, understand me, I had as

42–7. To ... invisible] *so Q;* To see / What ... princes. / As ... townes; /
Divorc'd ... unhospitable: / So ... now? / Flatterers ... bodies / The ...
conj. Samp.   53–4. Why ... verge] *so Q;* ... liue / Within ... *Q2.*
53. Why?] *Q;* Why *Dod i.*

(cf. v. i. 16 n.); the use of this name here is dramatically ironical, for the
supposed friars are indeed the servants of Francisco (who is standing
silently by).

51–3. *weep ... dissemble*] Cf. Pettie (cf. App. IV), II, 137: 'Hee which in
wordes and outward shew pretendeth us great good will, and in his heart
wisheth and worketh us yll, may bee signified, and set foorth by us with this
onely worde (Dissembler) yet you shall heare some fine head (refusing to
use that common worde, whiche very infants understande) which ... will
say, hee maketh shewe of the cuppe, but giveth blowes of the cudgell: or,
that he weepeth over his Stepmothers grave'.

53. *some men*] an ironical understatement (so Lucas).

54. *verge*] area within twelve miles of the king's court and so under the
jurisdiction of the Lord High Steward (from A.F. *la verge* = 'the Steward's
rod of office'; cf. *O.E.D.*, s.v., 10).

56–7. *wolf ... poultry*] Cf. *D.M.*, II. i. 52–4: 'diseases / Which have their

good a will to cozen him, as e'er an officer of them all. But
I had not cunning enough to do it.

Fran. What did'st thou think of him ? 'faith speak freely.   60

Flam. He was a kind of statesman, that would sooner have
reckon'd how many cannon-bullets he had discharged
against a town, to count his expense that way, than how
many of his valiant and deserving subjects he lost before it.

Fran. O, speak well of the duke.   65

Flam. I have done. Wilt hear some of my court wisdom ?

Enter LODOVICO [*disguised as before*].

To reprehend princes is dangerous: and to over-
commend some of them is palpable lying.

Fran. How is it with the duke ?

Lod.   Most deadly ill.

He's fall'n into a strange distraction.   70
He talks of battles and monopolies,
Levying of taxes, and from that descends
To the most brain-sick language. His mind fastens

66–8. I . . . lying] *so Thorn; . . .* done. / Will't . . . wisedome ? / To . . . (*the
rest as prose*) Q; . . . done. / Wilt . . . (*the rest as prose*) *Dyce i; as continuous
prose Dyce ii.*   66. Wilt] *Dod i;* Will't *Q.*   66.1. *Enter Lodovico*] *so Q;
after* done (*l. 66*) *Dyce i; after l. 68 Dyce ii.*   disguised as before] *This ed.;
not in Q.*

---

true names only ta'en from beasts, / As the most ulcerous wolf, . . .' and
Topsell, *History* (1607), Xxxi^v: 'There is a disease called a wolfe, because
it consumeth and eateth vp the flesh in the bodie next the sore, and must
euery day be fed with fresh meat, as Lambes, Pigeons, and such other
things wherein is bloode, or else it consumeth al the flesh of the body,
leauing not so much as the skin to couer the bones'.

The ulcer in the thigh of the real-life Bracciano (cf. Intro., p. xxvii) was
treated with raw meat.

Lucas suggested that *fed with poultry* was used quibblingly for 'fed on
the fat of the land' (he compared 'Chapman', *Revenge for Honour* (*c.* 1640),
I. i. 20–1: '. . . i'th'camp / You do not feed on pleasant poults'). On the
other hand, there might be a 'bad' pun on 'paltry', *sb.* = 'rubbish, trash' (cf.
O.E.D., s.v.).

67–8.] Cf. Pettie, II, 198–9: 'me thinkes you have regarde to that which
is sayde by one, That to reprehend princes it is dangerous, and to commend them, plaine lying'.

On twenty several objects, which confound
Deep sense with folly. Such a fearful end   75
May teach some men that bear too lofty crest,
Though they live happiest, yet they die not best.
He hath conferr'd the whole state of the dukedom
Upon your sister, till the prince arrive
At mature age.

Flam.   There's some good luck in that yet.   80
Fran. See here he comes.

Enter BRACCIANO, *presented in a bed,* VITTORIA *and others*[, *including* GASPARO, *disguised as before*].

There's death in's face already.
Vit. O my good lord!
Brac.   Away, you have abus'd me.

> *These speeches are several*
> *kinds of distractions and in*
> *the action should appear so.*

You have convey'd coin forth our territories;
Bought and sold offices; oppress'd the poor,
And I ne'er dreamt on't. Make up your accounts;   85
I'll now be mine own steward.

Flam.   Sir, have patience.
Brac. Indeed I am too blame.
For did you ever hear the dusky raven

---

81. See . . . already] *so Dyce ii; . . . comes. / There's . . . Q.*   81.1–2.] *so this ed.; Enter . . . others (to right of the two lines of type of l. 81) Q, (after comes, l. 81) Dod i; The traverse is drawn. / Enter . . . others Samp.*   82.1–3.] *so Dyce i; outer margin, to left of ll. 83–90 approx. Q.*   82.3. *appear so*] Q^b; *appeare* Q^a.   87. *too*] *Q; to Q3.*

---

78. *state*] This can mean both 'riches, possessions, property', and 'dignity, power'.

83.] a serious offence; Lucas quoted statutes forbidding it from Henry VI's time to Henry VIII's.

87. *too blame*] Cf. III. iii. 125 n.

88–9. *raven . . . blackness*] Cf. *Troil.*, II. iii. 218–21: '*Ajax.* A paltry, insolent fellow! / *Nestor.* How he describes himself! / *Ajax.* Can he not be sociable ? / *Ulysses.* The raven chides blackness.'

Chide blackness ? or was't ever known the devil
Rail'd against cloven creatures ?

Vit.   O my lord!   90
Brac. Let me have some quails to supper.
Flam.   Sir, you shall.
Brac. No: some fried dog-fish. Your quails feed on poison,—
That old dog-fox, that politician Florence,—
I'll forswear hunting and turn dog-killer;
Rare! I'll be friends with him: for mark you, sir, one dog   95
Still sets another a-barking: peace, peace,
Yonder's a fine slave come in now.
Flam.   Where ?
Brac.   Why there.

In a blue bonnet, and a pair of breeches
With a great codpiece. Ha, ha, ha,
Look you his codpiece is stuck full of pins   100
With pearls o'th'head of them. Do not you know him ?
Flam. No, my lord.
Brac.   Why 'tis the devil.

I know him by a great rose he wears on's shoe

91–2.] *quails* were a great delicacy; cf. Sharpham, *Cupid's Whirligig* (1607), ed. 1926, p. 25: 'O thou pampred Iade! . . . what wouldst thou feede on Quailes ? art thou not Fat ? . . .' In contrast *dog-fish* was one of the cheapest foods.

Lucas suggested a quibble on *quails* = 'loose women'; he quoted *Troil.*, v. i. 56–8: 'Agamemnon . . . that loves quails'. For their feeding *on poison*, cf. Bartholomaeus, *De Proprietatibus Rerum* (tr. 1582), XII, vii: 'His best meate is venemous seede and graines, and for that cause in olde time men forbad eating of them'.

93. *dog-fox*] Cf. *Troil.*, v. iv. 12–13: 'that same dog-fox, Ulysses'.

94. *dog-killer*] Men were hired to kill stray or mad dogs in towns.

95–6. *one . . . a-barking*] Cf. *H8*, II. iv. 158–60: 'you have many enemies . . . / . . . like to village-curs, / Bark when their fellows do'; these are the two earliest citations for the proverb in Tilley (D539). *Still* = 'continually, always'.

100.] This fashion is alluded to in *Gent.*, II. vii. 53–6.

102–4. *devil . . . foot*] A *rose* was a rosette, or knot, of ribbons on a shoe; Lucas compared Jonson, *Devil is an Ass* (1616), I. iii. 7–9: 'my heart was at my mouth, / Till I had view'd his shooes well: for, those roses / Were bigge inough to hide a clouen foote'.

To hide his cloven foot. I'll dispute with him.
He's a rare linguist.

Vit.   My lord here's nothing.   105

Brac. Nothing ? rare ! nothing ! when I want money,
Our treasury is empty; there is nothing,—
I'll not be us'd thus.

Vit.   O ! lie still, my lord—

Brac. See, see, Flamineo that kill'd his brother
Is dancing on the ropes there: and he carries   110
A money-bag in each hand, to keep him even,
For fear of breaking's neck. And there's a lawyer
In a gown whipt with velvet, stares and gapes
When the money will fall. How the rogue cuts capers !
It should have been in a halter.   115
'Tis there; what's she ?

Flam.   Vittoria, my lord.

Brac. Ha, ha, ha. Her hair is sprinkled with arras powder,

114.] *so Q; . . .* fall. / How *. . . conj. this ed.*   115–16. It *. . .* she] *so Q;* one
line *Dyce i.*   117–19. Ha *. . .* he] *so Q; . . .* powder, / That *. . .* pastry. /
What's *. . . Dod iii.*

---

105. *linguist*] Cf. Marston, *Malcontent* (1604), I. iii: '— . . . what doost
thinke to be the best linguist of our age ?—Phew, the Divell, . . . heele teach
thee to speake all languages, most readily and strangely, and great reason
mary, hees traveld greatly ithe worlde: . . .' *linguist* could, however, mean
simply 'good, or free, talker' (cf. *O.E.D.*, s.v., 4).

110. *ropes*] tight-ropes (this is the earliest citation in *O.E.D.*, s.v.,
2b).

113. *whipt*] trimmed, ornamented (of needlework, etc.).

115.] quibbling on 'dancing on the ropes' (l. 110 above); cf. S.S., *Honest
Lawyer* (pf. before 1615), K1ᵛ: 'I shall not dance alone vpon the rope'
(= 'I alone shall not be hanged'). Thus the 'rogue' (l. 114) is Flamineo, not
the lawyer.

117. *hair . . . powder*] Powdered orris, or iris, root was used for whitening
and perfuming hair; cf. *D.M.*, III. ii. 67–8: 'When I waxe gray, I shall haue
all the Court / Powder their haire, with Arras, to be like me'.

Orris and *arras* (a rich tapestry fabric) were not always distinguished in
form in the 17th century; the rich associations of *arras* and its occurrence
again in *D.M.* (surviving both the scribe's and the compositor's changes)
argue for its retention in the present modernized text.

G. Baldini (*John Webster* (Rome, 1953), p. 99) pointed out that this
apparition of an aged, defeated Vittoria exists only in Bracciano's mind, as

that makes her look as if she had sinn'd in the pastry.
What's he?

Flam. A divine my lord.   120

Brac. He will be drunk: avoid him: th'argument is fearful
when churchmen stagger in't.
Look you; six gray rats that have lost their tails,
Crawl up the pillow,—send for a rat-catcher.
I'll do a miracle: I'll free the court   125
From all foul vermin. Where's Flamineo?

Flam. I do not like that he names me so often,
Especially on's death-bed: 'tis a sign
I shall not live long: see he's near his end.

> BRACCIANO *seems here near his end.*
> LODOVICO *and* GASPARO *in the*
> *habit of Capuchins present*
> *him in his bed with a*
> *crucifix and hallowed candle.*

Lod. Pray give us leave: *Attende Domine Bracciane,*—   130
Flam. See, see, how firmly he doth fix his eye
Upon the crucifix.

Vit.   O hold it constant.

121–2. He . . . in't] *so Q; . . . argument / Is . . . Q4.   123–4. Look . . .
-catcher] so Q4; as prose Q.*   128. sign] *Q; sign (Aside. Dyce ii.   129.1–
5.] so this ed.; outer margin, to right of ll. 120–32 approx. Q; after l. 120
Dod i.*   129.2. Gasparo] *Q*b; *Gasparoe Q*a.

_____

the other apparitions. But (as Dent argued) Vittoria's hair would have been
powdered as a bride (cf. Jonson, *Hymenaei*, ll. 57, 184) earlier in the
day.

118. *pastry*] place where pastry is made (cf. *O.E.D.*, s.v., 2).

121. *drunk*] Webster makes the mad priest in *D.M.*, IV. ii, cry: 'He that
drinks but to satisfy nature is damned' (ll. 96–7).

123. *six . . . tails*] Lucas suggested an allusion to the nursery rhyme,
'Three blind mice . . .' But here the *rats* may be witches; witches were said
to be able to turn themselves into any animal they pleased, but the tail
would always be missing (cf. *Mac.*, I. iii. 8–9).

124–6. *send . . . vermin*] possibly an allusion to the Pied Piper of Hamelin.

129.1–5.] Q's direction clearly refers to this moment; l. 132 is the foot of
a page in Q, so the compositor has placed the direction as close as possible
to this line.

130. Attende . . . Bracciane] i.e., 'Listen, Lord Bracciano'.

It settles his wild spirits; and so his eyes
Melt into tears.

Lod. (*by the crucifix*) *Domine Bracciane, solebas in bello tutus*   135
esse tuo clypeo, nùnc hunc clypeum hosti tuo opponas
infernali.

Gasp. (*by the hallowed taper*) *Olim hastâ valuisti in bello; nùnc*
hanc sacram hastam vibrabis contra hostem animarum.

Lod. *Attende Domine Bracciane si nunc quòque probas ea quæ*   140
acta sunt inter nos, flecte caput in dextrum.

Gasp. *Esto securus Domine Bracciane: cogita quantum habeas*
meritorum—denique memineris meam animam pro tua
oppignoratam si quid esset periculi.

Lod. *Si nùnc quoque probas ea quæ acta sunt inter nos, flecte*   145
caput in lævum.

135. *by the crucifix*] *so Wal; outer margin, to left of ll. 135–7 approx.* Q.
138. *by . . . taper*] *so Wal; outer margin, to left of ll. 138–40 approx.* Q.

135–46. Domine . . . lævum] i.e., 'Lord Bracciano, you were accustomed
to be guarded in battle by your shield; now this shield you shall oppose
against your infernal enemy.—Once with your spear you prevailed in
battle; now this holy spear you shall wield against the enemy of souls.—
Listen, Lord Bracciano, if you now also approve what has been done between us, turn your head to the right.—Rest assured Lord Bracciano:
think how many good deeds you have done—lastly remember that my soul
is pledged for yours if there should be any peril.—If you now also approve
what has been done between us, turn your head to the left.'
   A. W. Reed (*T.L.S.*, 14 June 1947) showed that the whole passage was
based on Erasmus' Colloquy, *Funus*, a comparison between the death of the
good Cornelius Montius and that of Georgius Balearicus who 'trusting to
his wealth, sought by purchase to retain his standing beyond the grave'.
The passage concerning the death of Balearicus is: '*Marcolphus:* Obsecro,
quid tum postea ?—*Phaedrus:* Porrecta est ægroto crucis imago & candela
cerea. Ad crucem porrectam dixit ægrotus, soleo in bellis tutus esse meo
clypeo, nunc hunc clypeum opponam hosti meo; & exosculatus admovit
humero lævo. Ad ceream vero sacram, Olim, inquit, hastâ valui in bellis,
nunc hanc hastam vibrabo adversus hostem animarum.—*Ma.:* Satis
militariter.—*Ph.:* Has postremas voces edidit. Nam mox linguam mors
occupavit, simulque cœpit animam agere. Bernardinus [a Franciscan] à
dextris imminebat morienti, Vincentius [a Dominican] à sinistris, uterque
pulchre vocalis . . .—*Ma.:* Quid occlamabant ?—*Ph.:* Hujusmodi ferme
Bernardinus, Georgi Balearice, si nunc quoque probas ea quæ sunt acta
inter nos, flecte caput in dextrum: Flexit. Vincentius contra, . . . Esto
securus. Cogita quantum habeas meritorum, quod diploma, denique

He is departing: pray stand all apart,
And let us only whisper in his ears
Some private meditations, which our order
Permits you not to hear.

> *Here the rest being departed*
> LODOVICO *and* GASPARO *discover*
> *themselves.*

Gasp.   Bracciano.   150
Lod. Devil Bracciano. Thou art damn'd.
Gasp.   Perpetually.
Lod. A slave condemn'd, and given up to the gallows
Is thy great lord and master.
Gasp.   True: for thou
Art given up to the devil.
Lod.   O you slave!
You that were held the famous politician;   155
Whose art was poison.
Gasp.   And whose conscience murder.
Lod. That would have broke your wife's neck down the stairs
Ere she was poison'd.

150.1–3.] *so Dod i; to right of ll. 149–51 Q.*   150.2. *Gasparo*] *Q*ᵇ*; Gasparao*
*or Q*ᵃ*.*   151. Devil . . . damn'd] *so Dyce i; . . . Brachiano. / Thou . . . Q.*
157–8. That . . . poison'd] *so Dod ii; as prose Q.*

---

memineris meam animam pro tua oppignoratam, si quid esset periculi:
hæc si sentis & probas, flecte caput in lævum. Flexit.'
    When the dying were speechless, it was customary for priests to ask for
signs of their faith.
    151.] For Q's line arrangement, cf. IV. ii. 129–30 n.
    156. *conscience*] inmost thought (cf. *H5*, IV. i. 124).
    157–8. *broke . . . poison'd*] Baker (quoted by Lucas) suggested that this
alludes to reports that the Earl of Leicester tried to poison his wife, Amy
Robsart, and then killed her by having her thrown down the stairs at
Cumnor Place (at the foot of which she was found dead on 8 Sept. 1560).
Leicester's Commonwealth (a pamphlet of 1584) names an Italian, 'Doctor
Julio', as one of Leicester's poisoners, and says that he employed two
'atheists' for 'figuring and conjuring'.
    The parallels between Leicester and Bracciano do not imply any sus-
tained 'personal allegory' in the play; they are incidental only, like the
reference to Elizabeth and Essex made *en passant* in *D.L.C.*, III. iii. 303–8.
    For the modern reader or audience, the parallels are important as a

Gasp.   That had your villainous sallets—
Lod. And fine embroidered bottles, and perfumes
        Equally mortal with a winter plague—   160
Gasp. Now there's mercury—
Lod.   And copperas—
Gasp.   And quicksilver—
Lod. With other devilish pothecary stuff
        A-melting in your politic brains: dost hear?
Gasp. This is Count Lodovico.
Lod.   This Gasparo.
        And thou shalt die like a poor rogue.
Gasp.   And stink   165
        Like a dead fly-blown dog.
Lod.   And be forgotten
        Before thy funeral sermon.
Brac.   Vittoria?
        Vittoria!
Lod.   O the cursed devil,
        Come to himself again! We are undone.

159. And . . . perfumes] *so Q2;* . . . bottles, / And . . . *Q.*   161. mercury]
Mercarie. *Q.*   166–7. And . . . sermon] *so Dyce i; one line Q, Samp.*
167–8. Vittoria? / Vittoria] *so Dyce i; one line Q, Samp.*   167. Vittoria?]
Q; Vittoria! Q2.   168. cursed *Q*ᵃ*; cursed, Q*ᵇ*?.*   169. Come] *Q;*
Comes *Q2.*   undone] *Q;* undone. / Act. 5. Scen. 2 *Q4.*

---

reminder that the events of Webster's plays are not out of all relation to life
in England in his day.
   158. *sallets*] Cf. IV. ii. 61 and note.
   159.] Compositor B may have split this line in order to avoid confusion
with the run-over of the previous line.
   160. *winter plague*] 'Almost all the English plagues were virulent in the
summer and declined at the approach of cold weather'; one which 'flourish-
ed in the winter was thought to be most pernicious' (F. P. Wilson, *The
Plague in Shakespeare's London* (1927), p. 7, n. 2).
   161. *mercury*] In view of 'quicksilver' in the same line, Lucas suggested
that *mercury* = 'mercuric chloride', but *O.E.D.* first quotes this usage in
1789 (s.v., 7b). Possibly, the poisonous plant, *Mercurialis perennis*, or 'wild
mercury', is meant; or, more likely, Gasparo repeats himself in trying to
terrify Bracciano with words. ('Copperas' (sulphate of copper, iron, or zinc),
it may be noted, is mortally poisonous only when taken in considerable
quantity.)

Enter VITTORIA *and the Attendants.*

Gasp. [*aside*] Strangle him in private.   170
    [*aloud*] What ? will you call him again
    To live in treble torments ? for charity,
    For Christian charity, avoid the chamber.

                                [*Exeunt* VITTORIA *etc.*]
Lod. You would prate, sir. This is a true-love knot
    Sent from the Duke of Florence.   BRACCIANO *is strangled.*
Gasp.   What—is it done ?   175
Lod. The snuff is out. No woman-keeper i'th'world,
    Though she had practis'd seven year at the pest-house,
    Could have done't quaintlier. My lords he's dead.

        [*Re-enter* VITTORIA, FRANCISCO, *and* FLAMINEO,
                with Attendants.]

Omnes. Rest to his soul.
Vit.   O me! this place is hell.

                    Exit VITTORIA[, *followed
                    by all except* LODOVICO,
                FRANCISCO, *and* FLAMINEO].

169.1.] *so Q; after l. 170 Dyce i.*   Vittoria] *Q; Vittoria, Francisco Q3;
Vittoria, Francisco, Flamineo Dyce i subs.*   Attendants] *Q4; attend Q.*
170. aside] *This ed.; not in Q, Dyce i.*   170–1. Strange . . . again] *so
Dyce i; one line Q.*   171. aloud] *This ed.; not in Q.*   173.1.] *Dyce i subs.;
not in Q; Exeunt Q3.*   174. true-love knot] *Q; true loue-knot Q2.*
176–8. The . . . dead] *so Q; as prose conj. this ed.*   178.1–2. Re-enter . . .
Attendants] *Dyce i subs.; not in Q; They return (to right of ll. 177–8) Q3.*
179. soul] *Q; soule! The traverse is closed Samp.*   179.1–3. Exit . . .
Flamineo] *This ed.; Exit Vittoria Q.*

---

176. *snuff*] Cf. Tilley (C49) who quoted T. More, *Wks* (1557): 'I cannot
licken my life more metely now than to the snuffe of a candle that burneth
within the candlestickes nose.'
    woman-keeper] female nurse; nurses were often suspected of killing off
their patients: Lucas quoted Jonson, *Volpone* (1607), I. v. 68–9: 'Faith, I
could stifle him, rarely, with a pillow, / As well, as any woman, that should
keepe him'.
    177. *the pest-house*] In 1594, the City of London had erected a pest-
house, or hospital, for the confinement of those sick of the plague.
    178. *quaintlier*] more skilfully.

Fran. How heavily she takes it.

Flam.   O yes, yes;   180
    Had women navigable rivers in their eyes
    They would dispend them all; surely I wonder
    Why we should wish more rivers to the city,
    When they sell water so good cheap. I'll tell thee,
    These are but moonish shades of griefs or fears,   185
    There's nothing sooner dry than women's tears.
    Why here's an end of all my harvest, he has given me
       nothing—
    Court promises! Let wise men count them curst
    For while you live he that scores best pays worst.

Fran. Sure, this was Florence' doing.

Flam.   Very likely.   190
    Those are found weighty strokes which come from th'hand,
    But those are killing strokes which come from th'head.
    O the rare tricks of a Machivillian!
    He doth not come like a gross plodding slave
    And buffet you to death: no, my quaint knave,   195
    He tickles you to death; makes you die laughing;

180, 190, 200, and 207. *Fran.*] *Q3 subs.; Flo. Q.*   187.] *so Q (one line); as prose conj. this ed.*   he has] *Qb;* he as *Qa;* h'as *conj. this ed.*   193. Machivillian] *Q;* Machiavelian *Dod i.*

183.] an allusion to Sir Hugh Middleton's 'New River', which ran about thirty-nine miles from Ware to Islington (so Sampson). Work started early in 1609 and the river was finished at Michaelmas 1613.

184. *so . . . cheap*] at such a bargain price, so cheaply.

185. *moonish*] changeable, fickle.

187. *he has*] Press-corrections have no special authority in this forme, so 'h'as' might be the correct reading; cf. 'h'as' at v. iv. 88 (also set by B).

188–9.] Cf. *Honour's Academy* (cf. App. IV), Ee6ᵛ: 'they will not sticke for golden promises. But the old saying is, that he that scoreth best, paieth euer worst'. *score* = 'to run up a score or debt, to obtain on credit'.

193. *Machivillian*] It is desirable to keep Q's spelling for the sake of the metre and a possible quibble on 'villain'.

195–6.] Crawford compared Florio, I, xl (p. 117): 'How many popular persons are seene brought unto death . . . uttering words of jesting and laughter . . . [One] wished the hang-man not to touch his throat, lest hee should make him swowne with laughing, because hee was so ticklish'. *quaint* = 'skilled, ingenious'.

As if you had swallow'd down a pound of saffron—
~~You see the feat,—'tis practis'd in a trice~~
~~To teach court-honesty it jumps on ice.~~

Fran. Now have the people liberty to talk   200
       And descant on his vices.

Flam.   Misery of princes,
       That must of force be censur'd by their slaves!
       Not only blam'd for doing things are ill,
       But for not doing all that all men will.
       One were better be a thresher.   205
       Ud's death, I would fain speak with this duke yet.

Fran. Now he's dead?

Flam. I cannot conjure; but if prayers or oaths
       Will get to th'speech of him, though forty devils
       Wait on him in his livery of flames,   210
       I'll speak to him, and shake him by the hand,
       Though I be blasted.   *Exit* FLAMINEO.

---

198. feat] *Q?*, *Q2;* seat *Q?*   trice] *Q;* trice: *Q2;* trice— *Luc.*   199.
court-honesty] *hyphened Q.*   -honesty] *Luc;* -honestie, *Q.*   205–6.
One . . . yet] *so Q;* . . . I / Would . . . *Samp;* . . . death, / I . . . *Wheel.*
212. S.D.] *so Dod iii; to right of l. 213 Q.*

---

197. *saffron*] Lucas compared Gerarde, *Herbal* (1597), H6ᵛ: 'the moder-
ate vse of it is good for the head, and maketh the sences more quicke and
liuely, . . . and maketh a man merrie'. Sampson quoted Rabelais, *Gargantua,*
I, x: 'saffron . . . doth so rejoice the heart, that if you take of it excessively,
it will by a superfluous resolution and dilation, deprive it altogether of life'.
198–9.] i.e., 'You see the trick of a Machiavellian'—it is carried out in a
moment and so teaches that honesty at court is always in peril'. *court-
honesty* is probably intended ironically; i.e. = 'honesty as the court knows
it, deceitfulness' and hence 'court intriguers'.
        For *jumps on ice* cf. *D.M.,* v. ii. 332–4: 'I must look to my footing: / In
such slippery ice-pavements, men . . . / . . . may break their necks . . .'
        201. *descant*] comment, enlarge.
        201–4. *Misery . . . will*] Cf. W. Alexander (cf. App. IV), *A.T.,* v. i. 2723–
6: '. . . (A prince) for every action that is his / The censure of a thousand
tongues must have, / Not onely damn'd for doing things amisse, / But for
not doing all that all men crave'.
        205.] In *W.Ho,* II. iii. 95–6, a number of 'rustical' disguises are consider-
ed: 'some filthy shape like a Thrasher, or a Thatcher, or a Sowgelder'.
        208–12. *I . . . blasted*] Lucas compared *Tw.N.,* III. iv. 94–6.
        212. S.D.] Misplaced in Q for lack of space at the correct point.

Fran.   Excellent Lodovico!
    What ? did you terrify him at the last gasp ?
Lod. Yes; and so idly, that the duke had like   214
    T'have terrified us.
Fran.   How ?

        Enter [ZANCHE] *the Moor.*

Lod.   You shall hear that hereafter,—
    [*aside*] See! yon's the infernal, that would make up sport.
    Now to the revelation of that secret
    She promis'd when she fell in love with you.
Fran. You're passionately met in this sad world.
Zan. I would have you look up, sir; these court tears   220
    Claim not your tribute to them. Let those weep
    That guiltily partake in the sad cause.
    I knew last night by a sad dream I had
    Some mischief would ensue; yet to say truth
    My dream most concern'd you.
Lod.   Shall's fall a-dreaming ? 225
Fran. Yes, and for fashion sake I'll dream with her.
Zan. Methought sir, you came stealing to my bed.
Fran. Wilt thou believe me sweeting ? by this light
    I was a-dreamt on thee too: for methought
    I saw thee naked.
Zan.   Fie sir! as I told you,   230
    Methought you lay down by me.
Fran.   So dreamt I;
    And lest thou shouldst take cold, I cover'd thee
    With this Irish mantle.

---

216. *aside*] *Ol subs.; not in Q.*   up] *Q; us Q4.*   220, et seq. *Zan.*] *Q3;*
Moo. or *Moore. Q.*

---

    216. *make up*] make good, make complete.
    226. *fashion*] form's; cf. Marston, *Malcontent* (1604), IV. v: 'baudes go to
Church, for fashion sake'.
    233. *Irish mantle*] 'a kind of blanket or plaid worn until 17th. c. by
the rustic Irish, often as their only covering' (*O.E.D., mantle,* 1b); the point
here is that the body was naked under it.

Zan.   Verily, I did dream
    You were somewhat bold with me; but to come to't.
Lod. How? how? I hope you will not go to't here.   235
Fran. Nay: you must hear my dream out.
Zan.   Well, sir, forth.
Fran. When I threw the mantle o'er thee, thou didst laugh
    Exceedingly methought.
Zan.   Laugh?
Fran.   And cried'st out,
    The hair did tickle thee.
Zan.   There was a dream indeed.
Lod. Mark her I prithee,—she simpers like the suds   240
    A collier hath been wash'd in.
Zan. Come, sir; good fortune tends you; I did tell you
    I would reveal a secret,—Isabella
    The Duke of Florence' sister was empoison'd,
    By a 'fum'd picture: and Camillo's neck   245
    Was broke by damn'd Flamineo; the mischance
    Laid on a vaulting-horse.
Fran.   Most strange!
Zan.   Most true.
Lod. The bed of snakes is broke.
Zan. I sadly do confess I had a hand
    In the black deed.
Fran.   Thou kept'st their counsel,—
Zan.   Right,—
    For which, urg'd with contrition, I intend   251
    This night to rob Vittoria.

---

235. to't here] *Q*b (to₁t); to it here *Q*a; to there *Q*2; to't there *Q*3.   240–
1. Mark . . . in] *so Q; as aside Wheel*.   250. kept'st] *Q*2 (keps't); kepts *Q*.
counsel,] *Q; counsel? Dyce ii*.

---

235. *to't*] *Q*b should be preferred since another press-correction (l. 82.3
above) suggests that copy may have been consulted for this forme.
    245. *'fum'd*] perfumed.
    248. *bed*] nest, tangled knot. Sykes quoted Davenport, *City Night-Cap*
(licensed 1624), Hazlitt's Dodsley, XIII, 148: '. . . your eyes are open, lords; /
The bed of snakes is broke, the trick's come out'.

Lod.   Excellent penitence!
Usurers dream on't while they sleep out sermons.
Zan. To further our escape, I have entreated
        Leave to retire me, till the funeral,   255
        Unto a friend i'th'country. That excuse
        Will further our escape. In coin and jewels
        I shall, at least, make good unto your use
        An hundred thousand crowns.
Fran.   O noble wench!
Lod. Those crowns we'll share.
Zan.   It is a dowry,   260
        Methinks, should make that sunburnt proverb false,
        And wash the Ethiop white.
Fran.   It shall, —away!
Zan. Be ready for our flight.
Fran.   An hour 'fore day.

                                    Exit [ZANCHE] *the Moor.*
        O strange discovery! why till now we knew not
        The circumstance of either of their deaths.   265

                [*Re-*]*enter* [ZANCHE *the*] *Moor.*

Zan. You'll wait about midnight in the chapel.
Fran.   There. [*Exit* ZANCHE.]
Lod. Why now our action's justified,—
Fran.   Tush for justice.
        What harms it justice? we now, like the partridge

262. And . . . white] *italicized Q.*   263.1.] *so Q4 subs.; to right of l.* 264 *Q*
(*Exit the Moore*); *not in Dod i.*   265.1.] *Q* (*Enter Moore*); *not in Dod i.*
266. You'll . . . chapel] *so Dyce i;* . . . midnight / In . . . *Q.*   chapel.] *Q;*
chapel ? *Dyce i.*   266. S.D.] *Dyce i; not in Q; after* chapel *Dod i.*

_____

256. *Unto . . . country*] a casual excuse; cf. Heywood, *Wise Woman* (pf.
1604), Mermaid ed., p. 280, of women who, growing near their time, 'get
leave to see their friends in the country, for a week or so'.
    261. *sunburnt*] Cf. v. i. 184 n.
    262. *wash . . . white*] Cf. Jeremiah, xiii. 23 : 'Can the Ethiopian change his
skin, or the leopard his spots ?'
    263.1.] Misplaced in Q for lack of space at the correct point.
    266.] For Q's line arrangement, cf. l. 4 n. above.
    268–70. *like . . . shame*] i.e., 'let the honour of the end justify the injustice

Purge the disease with laurel: for the fame
Shall crown the enterprize and quit the shame. *Exeunt.*   270

[v. iv]

> *Enter* FLAMINEO *and* GASPARO *at one door, another
> way* GIOVANNI *attended.*

Gasp. The young duke: did you e'er see a sweeter prince?
Flam. I have known a poor woman's bastard better favour'd
—this is behind him: now, to his face all comparisons
were hateful: wise was the courtly peacock, that being a
great minion, and being compar'd for beauty, by some   5
dottrels that stood by, to the kingly eagle, said the eagle
was a far fairer bird than herself, not in respect of her
feathers, but in respect of her long tallants. His will grow
out in time,—
My gracious lord.   10
Giov. I pray leave me sir.
Flam. Your grace must be merry: 'tis I have cause to mourn,
for wot you what said the little boy that rode behind his
father on horseback?

v. iv] *Sym; not in Q; Act.* 5. *Scen.* 3. *Q4.*   3. face] *Q;* face— *Luc.*
8. tallants] *Q;* Talons *Q2.*   10. My . . . lord] *so Q; as continuous prose*
Dyce i.

---

of the means'. There is a quibble on *laurel* as a symbol of 'fame', and as a
medicine; Pliny (VIII, xxvii) said that doves, daws, and partridges purged
themselves with laurel.
   quit = 'clear, pay off'.

   v. iv. 4–9. *wise . . . time*] Cf. Pettie (cf. App. IV), II, 203: 'perchaunce he
liked better to yeelde with his tongue, then with his heart, by the example
of the Peacocke, who saide the Eagle was a fayrer byrde then hee, not in
respect of his feathers, but of his beake and talents, which caused that no
other birde durst stand in contention with him.'
   dottrels were a species of plover; the word was often used for 'simpletons,
dotards' (the bird was supposed to imitate the fowler, and so be easy game;
cf. *O.E.D.*, s.v., 1, 1526 and 1659).
   tallants is a 16th–17th-century form of both 'talons' and 'talents'; 'talons'
is obviously the primary sense here, but since, as Lucas suggested, there
may be a pun on 'talents', the equivocal form should stand. Cf. *LLL.*, IV. ii.
64–6.
   13–17. *little . . . saddle*] Cf. Pettie, III, 43: 'the world is now come to this

Giov. Why, what said he ?   15
Flam. 'When you are dead father' (said he) 'I hope then I
        shall ride in the saddle',—O 'tis a brave thing for a man to
        sit by himself: he may stretch himself in the stirrups, look
        about, and see the whole compass of the hemisphere,—
        you're now, my lord, i'th'saddle.   20
Giov. Study your prayers, sir, and be penitent,—
        'Twere fit you'd think on what hath former bin,—
        I have heard grief nam'd the eldest child of sin.

                                          Exit GIOVANNI [*and all
                                          except* FLAMINEO].

Flam. Study my prayers ? he threatens me divinely,—
        I am falling to pieces already,—I care not, though, like   25
        Anacharsis, I were pounded to death in a mortar. And
        yet that death were fitter for usurers' gold and them-
        selves to be beaten together, to make a most cordial cullis
        for the devil.
        He hath his uncle's villainous look already,   30

23.1–2. *and . . . Flamineo*] *This ed.; not in Q.*   26. Anacharsis] *Q;*
Anaxarchus *Sykes, Luc.*   27. usurers'] Vsurers *Q;* usurers, *Dod i;*
usurers,— *Samp.*

---

passe, that the child is no sooner come to any understanding, but that he
beginneth to cast in his head of his fathers death: as a little childe riding
behind his father, sayde simply unto him, Father, when you are dead, I shal
ride in the Saddle'.
    21.] Cf. *2H4,* v. v. 51.
    22–3.] Cf. the Cardinal in *D.M.,* v. v. 54–5: 'I suffer now, for what hath
former been: / *Sorrow is held the eldest child of sin*'.
    26. *Anacharsis*] Sykes (*N. & Q.,* xii ser., iii (1917), 441–2) pointed out
that it was, in fact, Anaxarchus who was 'pounded to death in a mortar' by
order of Nicocreon of whom he had spoken despitefully in front of Alexander. But Webster had read otherwise in *Honour's Academy* (cf. App. IV),
F3ᵛ–4: 'For what trouble can there arise vnto a vertuous man ? . . . *Ana-
charsis*, being pounded to death in a morter, iested at death'. The only
course is, therefore, to read as Q.
    Anacharsis was a Thracian prince of the 6th century B.C., who was
noted for his wisdom.
    27–9. *gold . . . devil*] Cf. *Characters* (1615), 'A Drunken Dutch-Man': 'He
whoords up fayre gold, and pretends 'tis to seethe in his Wives broth for a
Consumption'. Bartholomaeus, *De Proprietatibus Rerum* (tr. 1582), Xx2,
discusses medicinal uses for gold. *cullis* = 'broth'.

Enter Courtier.

In *decimo-sexto*. Now sir, what are you?

Cour. It is the pleasure sir, of the young duke
    That you forbear the presence, and all rooms
    That owe him reverence.

Flam. So, the wolf and the raven   35
    Are very pretty fools when they are young.
    Is it your office, sir, to keep me out?

Cour. So the duke wills.

Flam. Verily, master courtier, extremity is not to be used in
    all offices: say that a gentlewoman were taken out of her   40
    bed about midnight, and committed to Castle Angelo, to
    the tower yonder, with nothing about her, but her smock:
    would it not show a cruel part in the gentleman porter to
    lay claim to her upper garment, pull it o'er her head and
    ears; and put her in nak'd?   45

Cour. Very good: you are merry.   [*Exit.*]

Flam. Doth he make a court ejectment of me? A flaming fire-
    brand casts more smoke without a chimney, than within't.
    I'll smoor some of them.

Enter [FRANCISCO *Duke of*] *Florence*[*, disguised as Mulinassar*].

How now? Thou art sad.   50

30.1.] *so Q; after 'sexto' (l. 31) Dyce ii.*   31. In . . . -sexto] *italicized Q.*
32–4. It . . . reverence] *so Q; as prose Thorn.*   35–7. So . . . out] *so Dyce i;*
as prose Q, Thorn.   41–2. to the] *Q; or to the Sym.*   46. S.D.] *Q4; not*
in Q.   49.1. Enter . . . Mulinassar] *This ed.; Enter Florence Q.*   50. art]
Q2; hart Q.

31. decimo-sexto] technical term for the size of a small book, of which
each leaf is one-sixteenth of a full sheet of paper; for its figurative use,
O.E.D. (s.v.) quotes Jonson, *Cynthia's Revels* (1601), I. i. 51: 'How now!
my dancing braggart in *decimo sexto*!'

33. *presence*] presence-chamber.

41. *Castle Angelo*] i.e., Castle St Angelo at Rome; the real-life Vittoria
was imprisoned for a time in this castle (cf. Boklund, p. 16, etc.).

42. *tower yonder*] Lucas suggested that Webster's audience would have
equated Castle Angelo with the Tower of London (cf. v. vi. 266).

47–8. *flaming firebrand*] Lucas suggested that Flamineo plays on his own
name.

49. *smoor*] suffocate.

Fran. I met even now with the most piteous sight.

Flam. Thou met'st another here—a pitiful
    Degraded courtier.

Fran.   Your reverend mother
    Is grown a very old woman in two hours.
    I found them winding of Marcello's corse;   55
    And there is such a solemn melody
    'Tween doleful songs, tears, and sad elegies:—
    Such, as old grandames, watching by the dead,
    Were wont t'outwear the nights with;—that believe me
    I had no eyes to guide me forth the room,   60
    They were so o'ercharg'd with water.

Flam.   I will see them.

Fran. 'Twere much uncharity in you: for your sight
    Will add unto their tears.

Flam.   I will see them.
    They are behind the traverse. I'll discover
    Their superstitious howling.   *[Draws the traverse curtain.]*

    CORNELIA, [ZANCHE] *the Moor and three other Ladies*
        discovered, winding MARCELLO'*s corse.*
            A song.

Cor. This rosemary is wither'd, pray get fresh;   66
    I would have these herbs grow up in his grave
    When I am dead and rotten. Reach the bays,

52. met'st] *Q* (metst)*; meet'st Q4.*   58. grandames] *Q; Grandams Q4.*
65. howling] *Q; howling. / Act. 5. Scen. 4 Q4.   Draws . . . curtain*]
Dyce ii subs.; not in Q.

---

    52. *met'st*] Emendation is unnecessary; the past tense is appropriate to
Francisco's 'even now' of the preceding line. Moreover, to follow Q4 (as
recent editors have done) involves adding to B's few errors one of a kind
to which his work in the rest of the text does not appear to afford parallels.
    65. S.D.] This is implied by 'discover' of ll. 64 and 65.2 (a verb often
used in 17th-century stage-directions for indicating the opening of some
curtained acting area). 'traverse' (l. 64) was used of curtains or screens
across a room, hall, or stage.
    66ff.] an imitation of Shakespeare's Ophelia (*Ham.*, IV. v.)
    66. *rosemary*] an ever-green herb, an emblem of immortality and used as
a token of remembrance at weddings and funerals (cf. *Rom.*, IV. v. 79–80).

I'll tie a garland here about his head:
'Twill keep my boy from lightning. This sheet   70
I have kept this twenty year, and every day
Hallow'd it with my prayers,—I did not think
He should have wore it.

Zan.   Look you; who are yonder?

Cor. O reach me the flowers.

Zan. Her ladyship's foolish.

Lady.   Alas! her grief   75
Hath turn'd her child again.

Cor.   You're very welcome.
There's rosemary for you, and rue for you,   *To* FLAMINEO.
Heart's-ease for you. I pray make much of it.
I have left more for myself.

Fran.   Lady, who's this?

Cor. You are, I take it, the grave-maker.

Flam.   So.   80

Zan. 'Tis Flamineo.

Cor. Will you make me such a fool? here's a white hand:

> CORNELIA *doth this in*
> *several forms of distrac-*
> *tion.*

73, 75, and 81. *Zan.*] *Dod iii subs.; Moo. Q.*   75. *Lady.*] *Dyce ii; Wom. Q.*
82.1–3.] *so this ed.; to right of ll. 96–8 Q; after l. 94 Dod i.*

68–70. *bays . . . lightning*] A *garland*, or wreath, of bays was given to a conqueror or poet in token of success; but it was also thought to give protection from lightning (so Pliny, II, lv).

70. *sheet*] i.e., winding-sheet.

77. *rue*] This shrub with bitter leaves was often mentioned with a punning allusion to *rue* = 'sorrow, regret' (*O.E.D.*, s.v., *sb²*, 1b quotes J. Davies, *Wks*, ed. Grosart, II, 8: 'So shalt thou / But beare thine own Hartsease, and never Rue').

To Flamineo] It is not clear whether Cornelia gives any one, or all of her gifts to Flamineo; the ambiguous position of this direction in Q is therefore retained.

78. *Heart's-ease*] i.e., pansies; cf. *Ham.*, IV. v. 176–7.

make . . . it] i.e., because you will need it (so Lucas).

82–3. *white . . . out*] Cf. *Mac.*, II. ii. 60–5 and v. i. 30–68; the idea was proverbial (cf. Tilley W85).

82.1–3.] There is little authority for the position of this direction in Q,

Can blood so soon be wash'd out ? Let me see,—
When screech-owls croak upon the chimney-tops,
And the strange cricket i'th'oven sings and hops,   85
When yellow spots do on your hands appear,
Be certain then you of a corse shall hear.
Out upon't, how 'tis speckled! h'as handled a toad sure.
Cowslip-water is good for the memory: pray buy me
three ounces of't.   90

Flam. I would I were from hence.

Cor.   Do you hear, sir ?
I'll give you a saying which my grandmother
Was wont, when she heard the bell toll, to sing o'er
Unto her lute.

---

84. -owls] *Q2;* -howles *Q.*   88. Out . . . sure] *so Q (one line); as prose
Wheel.*   89–90. Cowslip- . . . of't] *so Q, Wheel; as one verse-line Dod i;
. . . memory: / Pray . . . Dod iii.*   91–2. Do . . . grandmother] *so Q; as
prose Wheel.*   93–4. Was . . . lute] *so Dyce i; one line Q; . . . sing / O'er . . .
Dod iii; as prose Wheel.*

---

for l. 96 is the first position in the text-space after l. 73 where there is room
for it. (Space could have been made by opening out the arrangement of the
main text, but both compositors were keen to conserve space; cf. Intro.,
p. lxiv.)

It seems best to place the direction where Cornelia hears Flamineo's
name and begins her long speech (cf. Bracciano's distraction of v. iii).

84–5. *When . . . hops*] Cf. v. iii. 19 n., and *D.M.,* II. ii. 78–9: the 'singing of
a cricket . . . [is] of pow'r / To daunt whole man in us'.

Q's 'howles' was a current spelling and elsewhere might have indicated
a quibble; but 'screech' and 'croak' immediately next to it would seem to
cancel out any such word-play here.

86.] Cf. S.S., *Honest Lawyer* (pf. before 1615), G4: 'Oh the case is
cleare, / A yellow spot doth on your hand appeare'—so proving that
Vaster's wife will hang as a thief.

88. *handled a toad*] Cf. Bartholomaeus, *De Proprietatibus Rerum* (tr.
1582), XVIII, xvii: 'his [the toad's] venime is accounted most cold, and
[a]stonieth, therefore each member that he toucheth, it maketh lesse feeling,
as it were frore [i.e., frozen] . . . and as manye speckes as he hath vnder the
wombe, so many manner wise, his venimme is accompted grieuous'.

89. *Cowslip-water*] Cf. R. Dodoens, *New Herbal* (ed. 1578), L2v: 'Cow-
slips, . . . are now vsed dayly amongst other pot herbes, but in Physicke
there is no great accompt made of them. They are good for the head &
synewes, and haue other good vertues, . . .'

Flam.   Do and you will, do.

Cor.   Call for the robin-red-breast and the wren,   95
    Since o'er shady groves they hover,
    And with leaves and flow'rs do cover
    The friendless bodies of unburied men.
    Call unto his funeral dole
    The ant, the field-mouse, and the mole   100
    To rear him hillocks, that shall keep him warm,
    And (when gay tombs are robb'd) sustain no harm,—
    But keep the wolf far thence, that's foe to men,
    For with his nails he'll dig them up agen.

They would not bury him 'cause he died in a quarrel   105
But I have an answer for them.
    Let holy church receive him duly
    Since he paid the church tithes truly.
His wealth is summ'd, and this is all his store:
This poor men get; and great men get no more.   110
Now the wares are gone, we may shut up shop.

95–104.] *italicized* Q.   95. *robin-red-breast*] *hyphened* Q.   97. *flow'rs*]
Sp; *flowres* Q; *flowers* Q3.   104. *agen*] Q; *again* Dod i.   105–6. They
. . . them] *so* Q; *as prose conj. this ed.*   107–8.] *italicized* Q.

---

95. robin-red-breast . . . wren] Cf. Lupton, *Notable Things* (1595), I,
xxxvii: 'A Robin Redbreast finding the dead body of a man or woman will
cover the face of the same with moss; & as some hold opinion, he will cover
also the whole body'.

The *wren* was believed to be the robin's wife (so Lucas who quoted 'The
robin redbreast and the wren / Are God Almighty's cock and hen').

97. flow'rs] Q's spelling is unique in Compositor B's work in this text and
the metre seems to require elision.

99. dole] rites of funeral (cf. *O.E.D.*, s.v., *sb*², 6).

103–4.] The superstitious believed this was a sign of death by murder;
cf. *D.M.*, IV. ii. 309–11: 'The wolf shall find her grave, and scrape it up: /
Not to devour the corpse, but to discover / The horrid murder'.

109–10.] Cf. W. Alexander (cf. App. IV), *A.T.*, I. i. 75–6: 'For some few
foots of Earth to be a grave, / Which meane men get, and great men get no
more'. *summ'd* = 'reckoned' and, perhaps, 'brought into small compass'
(cf. *O.E.D.*, s.v., 3).

111.] a proverb for which this is the earliest quotation in Tilley (W68).
we . . . shop] Probably the curtains of the stage were closed at this point
(cf. l. 65 S.D. n. above).

Bless you all good people,—   *Exeunt* CORNELIA[, ZANCHE,]
                                  and Ladies.

Flam. I have a strange thing in me, to th'which
     I cannot give a name, without it be
     Compassion,—I pray leave me.   *Exit* FRANCISCO. 115
     This night I'll know the utmost of my fate,
     I'll be resolv'd what my rich sister means
     T'assign me for my service: I have liv'd
     Riotously ill, like some that live in court;
     And sometimes, when my face was full of smiles   120
     Have felt the maze of conscience in my breast.
     Oft gay and honour'd robes those tortures try,—
     We think cag'd birds sing, when indeed they cry.

Enter BRACCIANO's *Ghost, in his leather cassock and breeches,*
     boots, [and] a cowl, [in his hand] a pot of lily-flowers
     with a skull in't.

112. *Cornelia, Zanche,*] *Dyce ii; Cornelia Q.*   113. th'] *Q; the Dod i.*
119. court;] *Court. Q.*   121. maze] *Q2; mase Q.*   123. We] „Wee *Q.*
123.1. *Enter . . . Ghost,*] *Dyce ii; . . . Brachian. Ghost. (to right of l. 124) Q;
after l. 126 Dod i.*   123.1–3. *in . . . in't*] *so Dyce ii; In . . . (outer margin, to
right of ll. 124–31 approx.) Q; after l. 126 Dod i.*   123.2. *in his hand*]
Dyce ii; not in Q.   lily] *Q2 (lilly); Iilly Q; gilly Crow.*

---

112. *Bless . . . people*] Cf. Ophelia's final 'God be wi' ye' (*Ham.*, IV. v. 200)
     116.] Cf. Antonio's 'This night, I meane to venture all my fortune'
(*D.M.*, v. i. 69) and Iago's 'This is the night / That either makes me or for-
does me quite' (*Oth.*, v. i. 128–9).
     117. *resolv'd*] assured, satisfied.
     121. *maze*] 'state of bewilderment' (*O.E.D.*, s.v., 3), or, possibly,
'windings, winding movement' (cf. *O.E.D.*, s.v., 4c).
     122–3.] Cf. W. Alexander, *A.T.*, IV. ii. 2389–90: 'As birds (whose cage of
gold the sight deceives) / Do seeme to sing, whil'st they but waile their
state'. The idea of l. 123 may have been proverbial, for Lucas noted it in
Arcadia (*Wks*, I, 139): 'The house is made a very lothsome cage / Wherein
the birde doth never sing, but cry'.
     Either *robes* = 'great men' (an extremely rare usage; cf. *O.E.D.*, s.v., 5)
and *try* = 'to experience, undergo' (cf. *O.E.D.*, s.v., 14, 1579: 'The quiet
life which I haue tryed being a mayden'), or, more probably, *tortures* is the
subject of the sentence and *try* = 'to test the effect of'.
     123.1. *leather cassock*] customary dress for a ghost; cf. the description of
tragedies in *Warning for Fair Women* (1599), Ind. (A2ᵛ): '. . . a filthie
whining ghost, / Lapt in some fowle sheete, or a leather pelch [i.e., pilch], /

Ha! I can stand thee. Nearer, nearer yet.
What a mockery hath death made of thee?   125
Thou look'st sad.
In what place art thou? in yon starry gallery,
Or in the cursed dungeon? No? not speak?
Pray, sir, resolve me, what religion's best
For a man to die in? or is it in your knowledge   130
To answer me how long I have to live?
That's the most necessary question.
Not answer? Are you still like some great men
That only walk like shadows up and down,
And to no purpose? say:—   *The Ghost throws earth upon*
                               him and shows him the skull.
What's that? O fatal! he throws earth upon me.   136
A dead man's skull beneath the roots of flowers.

125–6. What ... sad] *so this ed.; one line Q.*   130.] *so Q; ... in? / Or ...*
conj. this ed.   135. say:—] *Q.*   135. S.D.–135.1.] *so Dyce i; outer*
margin, to right of ll. 135–9 approx. Q.

Comes skreaming like a pigge halfe stickt'. A 'cassock' was a long coat or
cloak, especially as worn by soldiers; *O.E.D.* first quotes the ecclesiastical
use of this word in 1663.

    123.2. lily-flowers] Normally Q's '*lilly-flowers*' would be modernized as
'Gilly-flowers'. But there are two reasons to suppose that the copy read
'lilly-flowers': (1) the compositor used a capital '*I*' which was so damaged
that every editor has hitherto read it as an '*l*' (the present editor, failed to
read it correctly until Mr John Crow pointed it out to him), and therefore
it may have been sorted into the '*l*' compartment of the lower case and used
as such; and (2) 'gilly-flower' was used of a 'light woman' (so *O.E.D.*) and
the flowers were known as 'nature's bastards' (cf. *Wint.*, IV. iv. 83), but it
would be difficult to wring much significance out of Bracciano's ghost
holding a *pot* of them; *a pot of lily-flowers* was, on the other hand, a common emblem: in G. Wither, *Emblems* (1635), D3ᵛ, Vice is depicted with a
pot of lily flowers and a skull with cross-bones by her side, promising
Youth 'what the wanton *Flesh* desires to have', and in Jonson's *Masque of
Beauty* (pf. 1608), Venus carries lilies which, as the author notes, were
'speciall *Hieroglyphicks* of *louelinesse*'.

    124. stand] withstand; echoing IV. ii. 51–3.

    125. mockery] The primary sense is 'counterfeit, unreal shadow' (cf.
Mac., III. iv. 106–7), but 'sad' (i.e., 'grave, serious') in the next line suggests that Flamineo may, even in such a context as this, quibble on *mockery*
= 'person occasioning ridicule' (cf. *O.E.D.*, s.v., 1b).

    133. still] invariably, always; or 'now as formerly'.

I pray speak sir,—our Italian churchmen
Make us believe dead men hold conference
With their familiars, and many times   140
Will come to bed to them, and eat with them.   *Exit Ghost.*
He's gone; and see, the skull and earth are vanish'd.
This is beyond melancholy.
I do dare my fate
To do its worst. Now to my sister's lodging,   145
And sum up all these horrors; the disgrace
The prince threw on me; next the piteous sight
Of my dead brother; and my mother's dotage;
And last this terrible vision. All these
Shall with Vittoria's bounty turn to good,   150
Or I will drown this weapon in her blood.   *Exit.*

[v. v]

    Enter FRANCISCO, LODOVICO, *and* HORTENSIO
       [*overhearing them*].

Lod. My lord upon my soul you shall no further:
  You have most ridiculously engag'd yourself
  Too far already. For my part, I have paid
  All my debts, so if I should chance to fall
  My creditors fall not with me; and I vow   5
  To quite all in this bold assembly
  To the meanest follower. My lord leave the city,
  Or I'll forswear the murder.
Fran.   Farewell Lodovico.

141. S.D.] *so Q3; outer margin, to right of l. 141 approx. Q.* 143–4. This
. . . fate] *so this ed.; one line Q.*

v. v] *Q4, Sym; not in Q.* 0.2. overhearing them] *Luc; not in Q; apart
Samp.* 8. murder] *Q, Q3; murder. Exit Dod ii.*

---

 143. *beyond melancholy*] i.e., more than a figment of his own imagination;
cf. IV. i. 101–3 n.

 v. v. 6. *quite*] repay, requite.
 7. *To*] i.e., down to, including.

If thou dost perish in this glorious act,
I'll rear unto thy memory that fame   10
Shall in the ashes keep alive thy name.

>   [*Exeunt* FRANCISCO *and*
>   LODOVICO *severally*.]

Hort. There's some black deed on foot. I'll presently
  Down to the citadel, and raise some force.
  These strong court factions that do brook no checks,
  In the career oft break the riders' necks.   [*Exit*.] 15

[v. vi]

> *Enter* VITTORIA *with a book in her hand;* ZANCHE,
>   [*and*] FLAMINEO, *following them.*

Flam. What are you at your prayers ? Give o'er.
Vit.   How ruffin ?
Flam. I come to you 'bout worldly business:
  Sit down, sit down:—nay stay blowze, you may hear it,—

11.1–2.] *Samp; not in Q; Exit Q3, Dod ii.*   15. oft] *Q2;* of't *Q.*   S.D.]
Q3; not in Q.

v. vi] *Sym; not in Q, Q4;* [V.] Scene II. *Haz.*   0.1–2.] *so Dod i; outer
margin, to left of ll. 1–6 approx. Q.*   hand; . . . and] *This ed.; hand.
Zanke, Q.*

10–11.] A relative has been omitted after *fame*; i.e., 'that report which . . .'
keep alive suggests that an underlying meaning of *rear* is 'to foster, bring
up', and that *ashes*, as well as = 'ruin', might also = 'mortal remains' (cf.
O.E.D., s.v., 4).
  12. *presently*] at once, immediately.
  15. *career*] short gallop at full speed.

v. vi. 0.1. book] Flamineo's first remarks show that this is a devotional
book. Such 'business' probably derives from Webster's source (cf. Intro.,
p. **xxix**), but not necessarily so, for, on the stage at this time, the reading of
a book was very commonly used as a sign of melancholy (cf. *Ham.*, III. i.
44–6); in *D.M.*, the Cardinal, troubled in conscience, enters 'with a
book' (v. v. 0.1), and in *D.L.C.*, Jolenta enters 'in mourning', with 'a
Booke' (III. iii. 0.1–2).
  2. *ruffin*] devil (a cant term).
  3. *blowze*] normally a fat, red-faced wench (so Schmidt); here used,
ironically, of the black-faced Zanche (as in *Tit.*, IV. ii. 72 it is used of
Aaron's black-faced child).

The doors are fast enough.

Vit.   Ha, are you drunk?

Flam. Yes, yes, with wormwood water,—you shall taste   5
Some of it presently.

Vit.   What intends the fury?

Flam. You are my lord's executrix, and I claim
Reward, for my long service.

Vit.   For your service?

Flam. Come therefore here is pen and ink, set down
What you will give me.   *She writes.* 10

Vit. There,—

Flam.   Ha! have you done already?—
'Tis a most short conveyance.

Vit.   I will read it.
[*reads*] '*I give that portion to thee, and no other,*
Which Cain groan'd under having slain his brother.'

Flam. A most courtly patent to beg by.   15

Vit. You are a villain.

Flam. Is't come to this? they say affrights cure agues:
Thou hast a devil in thee; I will try
If I can scare him from thee:—nay sit still:
My lord hath left me yet two case of jewels   20
Shall make me scorn your bounty; you shall see them.
                                                    [*Exit.*]

Vit. Sure he's distracted.

Zan.   O he's desperate—
For your own safety give him gentle language.

---

6. the] *Q; thy conj. Luc.*   fury] *Q; Fury Q2.*   8. service?] seruice *Q.*
10. S.D.] *so Ol subs.; outer margin, to left of l. 11 approx. Q.*   13. reads]
Dyce ii (to right of l. 12); not in Q.   13–14. *I . . . brother] italicized Dyce ii;*
roman type (except 'Caine') Q.   17. they] *Q2; the Q.*   21.1.] *Q3; not*
in Q.

---

5. *wormwood*] i.e., *Artemisia Absinthium,* a plant with a bitter taste;
it was an emblem of what is bitter to the soul (cf. *Ham.,* III. ii. 191).
6. *presently*] immediately.
14. Cain] Cf. Genesis, iv. 11–12.
15. *patent*] See v. i. 112 n.
20. *case*] pair.

*[Re-]enter [*FLAMINEO*] with two case of pistols.*

Flam. Look, these are better far at a dead lift
      Than all your jewel house.

Vit.   And yet methinks   25
      These stones have no fair lustre, they are ill set.

Flam. I'll turn the right side towards you: you shall see
      How they will sparkle.

Vit.   Turn this horror from me:
      What do you want? what would you have me do?
      Is not all mine, yours? have I any children?   30

Flam. Pray thee good woman do not trouble me
      With this vain worldly business; say your prayers,—
      I made a vow to my deceased lord,
      Neither yourself, nor I should outlive him
      The numb'ring of four hours.

Vit.   Did he enjoin it?   35

Flam. He did, and 'twas a deadly jealousy,
      Lest any should enjoy thee after him,
      That urg'd him vow me to it:—for my death—
      I did propound it voluntarily, knowing
      If he could not be safe in his own court   40
      Being a great duke, what hope then for us?

Vit. This is your melancholy and despair.

Flam.   Away,—
      Fool thou art to think that politicians
      Do use to kill the effects of injuries
      And let the cause live: shall we groan in irons,   45

23.1. *Re-enter . . . pistols*] Dod *i subs.; He enters with . . . (outer margin, to
right of ll. 22–5 approx.)* Q.   27–8. I'll . . . sparkle] *so* Dod *iii; . . . see /
how . . .* Q; *as prose* Q2; *as one verse-line* Dod *i.*   28. they] Q2; the Q.
32. worldly] Q2; wordly Q.   37. him,] him; Q.   43. Fool] Q2; Foole,
Q; Fool that Wheel.

---

24. *dead lift*] sudden emergency; a proverbial phrase (cf. Tilley L271)
derived from lifting, or pulling, a heavy 'dead' weight. Here there is an
obvious pun on *dead*.

43. *Fool*] Wheeler's emendation is attractive, especially since Compositor
A clearly omitted short words on other occasions (cf., for example, II. i. 27
and note).

> Or be a shameful and a weighty burden
> To a public scaffold ? This is my resolve—
> I would not live at any man's entreaty
> Nor die at any's bidding.

Vit.   Will you hear me ?

Flam. My life hath done service to other men,   50
> My death shall serve mine own turn; make you ready—

Vit. Do you mean to die indeed ?

Flam.   With as much pleasure
> As e'er my father gat me.

Vit. [*aside*] Are the doors lock'd ?

Zan. [*aside*] Yes madam.   55

Vit. Are you grown an atheist ? will you turn your body,
> Which is the goodly palace of the soul
> To the soul's slaughter house ? O the cursed devil
> Which doth present us with all other sins
> Thrice candied o'er; despair with gall and stibium,   60
> Yet we carouse it off;—[*aside to Zanche*] cry out for help,—
> Makes us forsake that which was made for man,
> The world, to sink to that was made for devils,
> Eternal darkness.

Zan.   Help, help!

Flam.   I'll stop your throat
> With winter plums,—

52–3. With . . . me] *so Q; one line Q4.*   54, 55. aside] *Luc; not in Q.*
61. S.D.] *Dod i subs.; not in Q.*

48–9. *I . . . bidding*] echoing III. ii. 138–9.

56–8. *turn . . . house*] inverting the common proverbial saying that the
body is the prison of the soul; cf. Tilley (B497), and *A.V.*, IV. ii. 89–91:
'through a large wide wound, / My mighty soule might rush out of this
prison / To flie more freely to yon christal pallace'.

58–61. *devil . . . off*] i.e., 'The devil makes all sins, except despair, seem
sweet and attractive to the taste, but offers despair mixed with bitterness and poison; nevertheless we accept despair completely, that is we
commit suicide'. Cf. *D.M.*, I. i. 275–7: 'the devil / Candies all sins o'er;
and what heaven terms vile, / That names he complimental.' *candied* =
sugared.

64–5. *stop . . . plums*] i.e., 'know the right time for speaking'. *stop your
throat* = gag you. *winter plums* had to be gathered at just the right time: cf.

Vit.   I prithee yet remember,   65
  Millions are now in graves, which at last day
  Like mandrakes shall rise shrieking.

Flam.   Leave your prating,
  For these are but grammatical laments,
  Feminine arguments, and they move me
  As some in pulpits move their auditory   70
  More with their exclamation than sense
  Of reason, or sound doctrine.

Zan. [*aside*]   Gentle madam
  Seem to consent, only persuade him teach
  The way to death; let him die first.

Vit. [*aside*] 'Tis good, I apprehend it,—   75
  [*aloud*] To kill one's self is meat that we must take
  Like pills, not chew't, but quickly swallow it,—
  The smart a'th'wound, or weakness of the hand
  May else bring treble torments.

Flam.   I have held it
  A wretched and most miserable life,   80
  Which is not able to die.

Vit.   O but frailty!
  Yet I am now resolv'd,—farewell affliction;
  Behold Bracciano, I that while you liv'd

---

72. *aside*] *Dyce ii subs.; not in* Q. 75. *aside*] *Ol subs.; not in* Q. 76.
aloud] *Ol subs.; not in* Q. 77. chew't] Q; chew'd *Haz.*

Raven's Almanac (1609); Dekker, *Wks*, iv, 187: 'know when Winter-
plomes are ripe and ready to be gathered'.
  67. mandrakes] Cf. III. i. 50–2 n.
  68–72. these . . . doctrine] Cf. Florio, III, iv (p. 425[b]): 'When such like
repetitions pinch me, and that I looke more nearely to them, I finde them
but grammaticall laments, the word and the tune wound me. Even as
Preachers exclamations do often move their auditory more then their
reasons: . . .'
  grammatical = 'according to rule, elementary' (often used with reference to the exposition of a text; cf. *O.E.D.*, s.v., 2).
  exclamation = 'formal declamation' (cf. *O.E.D.*, s.v., 3), and also, perhaps, 'vociferation'.
  76–7.] Cf. Florio, II, xiii (p. 312[b]): 'it [the killing of one's self] is a meate
a man must swallow without chewing'.

Did make a flaming altar of my heart
To sacrifice unto you; now am ready   85
To sacrifice heart and all. Farewell Zanche.
Zan. How madam! Do you think that I'll outlive you?
Especially when my best self Flamineo
Goes the same voyage.
Flam.   O most loved Moor!
Zan. Only by all my love let me entreat you;—   90
Since it is most necessary none of us
Do violence on ourselves; —let you or I
Be her sad taster, teach her how to die.
Flam. Thou dost instruct me nobly,—take these pistols:
Because my hand is stain'd with blood already,   95
Two of these you shall level at my breast,
Th'other 'gainst your own, and so we'll die,
Most equally contented: but first swear
Not to outlive me.
Vit. and Zan.   Most religiously.
Flam. Then here's an end of me: farewell daylight   100
And O contemptible physic! that dost take
So long a study, only to preserve
So short a life, I take my leave of thee.
These are two cupping-glasses, that shall draw   *Showing the*
All my infected blood out,—are you ready?   *pistols.* 105

91. none] *Q;* one *Q2.*   97. Th'other] *Q;* The other *Dyce i.*   99. *Zan.*]
Q3; Moo. Q.   104–5. S.D.] *so Q (outer margin); after l. 104 Q4.*   105.
All . . . ready] *so Dyce i;* . . . out, / Are . . . *Q.*

---

91. *none*] Many editors have read 'one' with Q2, but Q makes good sense
if it is interpreted with reference to ll. 76–9 above; i.e., *none* must 'Do
violence' by botching the task ('taster' of the next line also alludes to ll. 76–
9, using and developing its metaphor). Flamineo modifies Zanche's 'instructions' for his own purposes.
96–7. *Two . . . own*] i.e., two pistols should be aimed at him and then the
remaining two (for there were two pairs) aimed by the survivors at each
other.
104. *cupping-glasses*] surgical vessels in which a vacuum is created by the
application of heat, and thus are used to draw off blood.
105. *All . . . blood*] Cf. Florio, III, v (p. 429b): 'cupping-glasses, that
affect and suck none but the worst bloud'.

Vit. and Zan. Ready.

Flam. Whither shall I go now? O Lucian thy ridiculous
    purgatory! to find Alexander the Great cobbling shoes,
    Pompey tagging points, and Julius Caesar making hair
    buttons; Hannibal selling blacking, and Augustus crying   110
    garlic, Charlemagne selling lists by the dozen, and King
    Pippin crying apples in a cart drawn with one horse.
    Whether I resolve to fire, earth, water, air,
    Or all the elements by scruples, I know not
    Nor greatly care,—Shoot, shoot,   115
    Of all deaths the violent death is best,
    For from ourselves it steals ourselves so fast
    The pain once apprehended is quite past.

> *They shoot and run to him*
> *and tread upon him.*

Vit. What—are you dropt?

106. *Vit. and Zan.*] *Dod i; Both.* Q.   107. Lucian] *Q; Lucian to Dod i.*
108. purgatory!] Purgatory *Q*; purgatory? *Dod i.*   112. Pippin] *Q;*
Pepin *Dyce i.*   118.1–2.] *so Dod iii; outer margin, to right of ll. 117–20
approx. Q; to right of ll. 115–16 Q4.*

107–12. *Lucian . . .*] Cf. *Menippos,* tr. Hickes (1634), G4ᵛ–H1: 'I thinke
it would move you to laugh much, if you saw those that were Kings and
Princes amongst us, beg their bread there, sell salt fish, and teach the
A.B.C. for sustenance, and how they are scorned and boxed about the
eares as the basest slaves in the world. It was my fortune to have a sight of
Philip King of Macedon, and I thought I should have burst my heart with
laughing: hee was shewed mee sitting in a little corner, cobling old shoes to
get somewhat towards his living: many other were to be seene there also,
begging by the high waies side, such as *Xerxes, Darius,* and *Polycrates*'
(quoted Sampson).

    109. *tagging points*] tagged laces (*points*) were a common means of
fastening garments.

    110. *crying*] i.e., for sale.

    111. *lists*] bands or strips of cloth (used for garters, ties, etc.).

    112. *Pippin*] the name of a variety of apple, of which 'pepin' was another
spelling; so Webster refers to King Pepin ('The Short') of the Franks, who
died in 768.

    114. *scruples*] small portions.

    116–18.] Cf. W. Alexander (cf. App. IV), *J.C.,* IV. i. 1988–91: 'O! of all
deaths, unlook'd for death is best: / It from our selves doth steale our selves
so fast, / That even the minde no feareful forme can see, / Then is the paine
ere apprehended past'.

Flam. I am mix'd with earth already: as you are noble   120
    Perform your vows, and bravely follow me.

Vit. Whither—to hell?

Zan.   To most assured damnation.

Vit. O thou most cursed devil.

Zan.   Thou art caught—

Vit. In thine own engine,—I tread the fire out
    That would have been my ruin.   125

Flam. Will you be perjur'd? what a religious oath was Styx
    that the gods never durst swear by and violate? O that
    we had such an oath to minister, and to be so well kept
    in our courts of justice.

Vit. Think whither thou art going.

Zan.   And remember   130
    What villanies thou hast acted.

Vit.   This thy death
    Shall make me like a blazing ominous star,—
    Look up and tremble.

Flam.   O I am caught with a springe!

Vit. You see the fox comes many times short home,—
    'Tis here prov'd true.

Flam.   Kill'd with a couple of braches.   135

Vit. No fitter off'ring for the infernal Furies
    Than one in whom they reign'd while he was living.

Flam. O the way's dark and horrid! I cannot see,—

---

132. me] *Q; me, Q4, Dod iii;* men, *conj. Luc, Ol.*   star,] *Q, Q4;* star:
Dod iii.

---

124. *engine*] contrivance, device.

126. *Styx*] in Greek mythology, one of the rivers of the infernal regions.

132. *star,*—] Punctuation must show that it is not Vittoria who fears; she
is telling Flamineo to fear (cf. l. 130).

133. *springe*] snare (for catching small game, as birds, etc.).

134. *fox . . . home*] i.e., fails to return. This sounds as if it were proverbial
(cf. ''Tis . . . true', l. 135), but no such proverb is known; the implication is
probably that '*even* the cunning fox . . .'.

135. *with*] by.
    braches] bitches.

136–7.] Cf. W. Alexander, *Croesus*, IV. i. 1469–70: 'No fitter offering for
th'infernall Furies, / Then one in whom they raign'd, while as he stood'.

    Shall I have no company?
Vit.   O yes thy sins
    Do run before thee to fetch fire from hell,   140
    To light thee thither.
Flam.   O I smell soot,
    Most stinking soot, the chimney is a-fire,—
    My liver's parboil'd like Scotch holy bread;
    There's a plumber, laying pipes in my guts,—it scalds;
    Wilt thou outlive me?
Zan.   Yes, and drive a stake   145
    Through thy body; for we'll give it out,
    Thou didst this violence upon thyself.
Flam. O cunning devils! now I have try'd your love,
    And doubled all your reaches. I am not wounded: FLAMINEO
    The pistols held no bullets: 'twas a plot   *riseth.* 150
    To prove your kindness to me; and I live
    To punish your ingratitude,—I knew

141–2. O . . . a-fire] *so Dyce i; one line Q.*   142. stinking] *Q2;* sinking *Q.*
chimney is] *Q2* (chimnie); chimneis *Q;* chimney's *Haz.*   143. holy] *Q4;*
holly *Q.*   146. Through] *Q;* Thorough *Dyce ii.*

    141–4. *O . . . scalds*] Cf. Intro., p. xxi, n. 2.
    142. *chimney is*] Metrical considerations suggest this interpretation of
Q's muddled, ambiguous form.
    143. *holy bread*] normally the bread provided for the Eucharist, or that
blessed and distributed afterwards to those who had not communicated;
but cf. Cotgrave, *Dict.* (1611): '*Pain benist d'Ecosse*—A sodden sheepes
liuer' (quoted by Sampson).
    145–6. *drive . . . body*] Suicides were traditionally buried thus at cross-
roads; the custom sought to restrain their evil ghosts (so Lucas, quoting
Fraser, *Golden Bough,* ix, 15ff.).
    149–50. Flamineo riseth] There was no room in the text-space of Q at the
end of l. 148, so it might be argued that this direction should be placed one
line higher.
    149. *doubled . . . reaches*] i.e., 'matched, or been equal to, all your con-
trivances, or plots' (cf. *O.E.D., double,* 3, and Greene, *Defence of Conny-
Catching* (1592), *Wks,* XI, 58: 'hauing a further reatch in hir head').
    I . . . wounded] False deaths were fairly common occurrences on the stage
when *W.D.* was written; *The Honest Man's Fortune* (pf. 1613), and *The
Second Maiden's Tragedy* (pf. 1611) both have false pistols, Marston's
Malcontent (1604) has a feigned death by a false poison, and, in less hectic
ways, there are revivals from death in Shakespeare's *Pericles* and *Cymbeline.*
    151. *kindness*] natural affection.

One time or other you would find a way
To give me a strong potion,—O men
That lie upon your death-beds, and are haunted   155
With howling wives, ne'er trust them,—they'll re-marry
Ere the worm pierce your winding-sheet: ere the spider
Make a thin curtain for your epitaphs.

How cunning you were to discharge! Do you practise at
the Artillery Yard? Trust a woman?—never, never;   160
Bracciano be my precedent: we lay our souls to pawn to
the devil for a little pleasure, and a woman makes the bill
of sale. That ever man should marry! For one Hypermnestra that sav'd her lord and husband, forty-nine of
her sisters cut their husbands' throats all in one night.   165
There was a shoal of virtuous horse-leeches.

159. How . . .] *indented Q.*   161. precedent] *Dyce i;* president *Q.*

154-8. *O men . . . epitaphs*] Cf. *D.M.*, I. i. 302-5: '*Duchess*. . . . I'll never
marry:—*Cardinal*. So most widows say: / But commonly that motion lasts
no longer / Than the turning of an hour-glass, the funeral sermon, / And
it, end both together'; and *D.L.C.*, II. iii. 105-7: 'the flattery in the Epitaphs, which shewes / More sluttish farre then all the Spiders webs / Shall
euer grow vpon it'.

160. *Artillery Yard*] Under the leadership of Philip Hudson, a Lieu-
tenant in the Artillery Company, the 'weekely exercise of Armes, and
military discipline' for citizens and merchants was revived in the Artillery
Gardens (at Bishopgate) in 1610 (so Stowe, *Annals* (1631), pp. 995-6). The
Privy Council gave official recognition on 3 July 1612.

Flamineo alludes to the zeal and inexperience of the city soldiers; cf. the
'Websterian' first scene of *A.Q.L.*: 'at the Artillery-Garden, one of my
neighbors in courtesie to salute me with his Musquet, set a-fire my . . .
Breeches' (ll. 152-4).

161. *precedent*] Q's was an ambiguous current spelling; some trace of
mod. 'president' may be required here (but not at l. 179, where Q has the
same spelling).

163-5. *For one . . . night*] Cf. *Honour's Academy* (cf. App. IV), Ll3: 'For
one *Hypermnestra*, that remembred her husband, fortie nine of her Sisters,
cut their husbands throats'. *Hypermnestra* was one of the fifty daughters of
Danaus who were compelled to marry the fifty sons of their father's
brother, Ægyptus; Danaus, warned by an oracle that he would be killed by
one of his nephews, persuaded his daughters to murder their husbands on
their marriage night; all obeyed except Hypermnestra who spared her
husband Lynceus.

166. *horse-leeches*] blood-suckers.

~~Here are two other instruments.~~

Enter LODOVICO, GASPARO, [*disguised as Capuchins,*] PEDRO,
[*and*] CARLO.

Vit.   Help, help!
Flam. What noise is that? hah? false keys i'th'court!
Lod. We have brought you a masque.
Flam.   A matachin it seems,
     By your drawn swords. Churchmen turn'd revellers!   170
Car. Isabella, Isabella!
Lod. Do you know us now?   [*They throw off their disguises.*]
Flam.   Lodovico and Gasparo.
Lod. Yes and that Moor the duke gave pension to
     Was the great Duke of Florence.
Vit.   O we are lost.
Flam. You shall not take justice from forth my hands,—   175
     O let me kill her.—I'll cut my safety
     Through your coats of steel: Fate's a spaniel,
     We cannot beat it from us: what remains now?

---

167. Here . . . instruments] *so Q; as prose Scott.*   167.1–2.] *This ed.;*
Enter Lod. Gasp. Pedro, Carlo Q, (at end of line) Dyce ii subs.; Enter Lod.
Gasp Q3; Enter Lodovico disguised as Carlo, Gasparo disguised as Pedro
Samp.   169. masque] *Wheel;* Maske *Q.*   169–70. A . . . revellers] *so*
Q4; . . . seemes, / By . . . swords. / Chuch- . . . *Q; . . .* swords. / Church-
. . . *Dod ii.*   171. *Car.*] *Dyce i subs.;* Con. *Q;* Gas. *Q3;* Lod. *conj. Samp.*
172. *Lod.*] *Q;* Gasp. *conj. Samp.*   172. S.D.] *Samp; not in Q.*

---

167. *two . . . instruments*] i.e., two more pistols; presumably Flamineo is
overpowered before he is able to use them (for this, at least four conspirators should enter immediately; contemporary accounts of Vittoria's death
say that a *band* of masked men entered).

168ff.] For agreement with possible sources, cf. Intro., pp. xxvi–xxxiv.

169. *masque*] 'Mask' and *masque* were not differentiated in spelling.

In its basic form, a *masque* entailed a formal and, usually, a surprise
entry of disguised and masked revellers, who then invited those already
present to dance with them. See Introduction to Revels *D.M.*, p. xxxi.

matachin] sword-dance, in masks and fantastic costumes.

170.] Q's line-arrangement is explained by the desire to avoid confusion
with 'seemes', which was run-over from the previous long line.

177–8. *Fate's . . . us*] Lucas quoted Nashe, *Lenten Stuff* (1599), *Wks*, III,
196: 'Fate is a spaniel that you cannot beate from you; the more you thinke
to crosse it, the more you blesse it and further it' and Lyly, *Euphues* (1578),

Let all that do ill, take this precedent:
Man may his fate foresee, but not prevent.   180
And of all axioms this shall win the prize:
'Tis better to be fortunate than wise.

Gasp. Bind him to the pillar.

Vit.   O your gentle pity!—
I have seen a blackbird that would sooner fly
To a man's bosom, than to stay the gripe   185
Of the fierce sparrow-hawk.

Gasp.   Your hope deceives you.

Vit. If Florence be i'th'court, would he would kill me.

Gasp. Fool! Princes give rewards with their own hands,
But death or punishment by the hands of others.

Lod. Sirrah you once did strike me,—I'll strike you   190
Into the centre.

Flam. Thou'lt do it like a hangman; a base hangman;

---

179. precedent] president *Q*.   180, 182.] *italicized Q*.   187. would he
would] *Q; he would not Q3*.   191. Into] *Q; Unto Q3*.

Wks, I, 249: 'the kinde Spaniell, which the more he is beaten the fonder
he is'.

180.] Cf. W. Alexander (cf. App. IV), *Croesus*, III. ii. 1373–4: 'Man may
his fate forsee, / But not shunne heavens decree'. Cf. *D.M.*, III. ii. 77–9:
'O most imperfect light of human reason, / That mak'st us so unhappy, to
foresee / What we can least prevent'.

182.] Cf. W. Alexander, *A.T.*, III. i. 1107: 'It's better to be fortunate,
then wise'; it was a common proverb (cf. Tilley H140).

183. *pillar*] possibly part of the structure of the tiring-house façade of the
Red Bull; for *The Virgin Martyr* (pf. *c.* 1620), however, a special pillar was
erected on its stage (cf. G. Reynolds, *Staging* (1940), pp. 92–3).

184–6. *seen . . . -hawk*] Cf. *Honour's Academy*, Rr5ᵛ: 'chusing as the
Blackebird vseth, rather to commit himselfe vnto the mercie of a man, then
to endure the griping nailes of the Sparrow-hawke'.

188–9.] G. K. Hunter (*N. & Q.*, n.s., iv (1957), 54) compared Machia-
velli, *The Prince*, xix (anon. Eliz. tr., ed. Craig, pp. 82f.): 'princes shoulde
dispatch those thinges by their deputyes which will move envie, and execute
those thinges themselves which will merritt thanckes'; and Dent, Guevara,
Dial of Princes (tr. 1557), III. i (F5ᵛ): 'yᵉ prince oughte more to endeuour
him selfe to reward, then for to punishe. For the punishment oughte to be,
by the handes of a straunger: but the rewarde oughte to be, wᵗ his owne
handes proper.'

191. *centre*] i.e., the heart.

192. *hangman*] executioner.

Not like a noble fellow, for thou seest
I cannot strike again.
Lod.   Dost laugh?
Flam. Wouldst have me die, as I was born, in whining?   195
Gasp. Recommend yourself to heaven.
Flam. No I will carry mine own commendations thither.
Lod. O could I kill you forty times a day
And use't four year together; 'twere too little:
Nought grieves but that you are too few to feed   200
The famine of our vengeance. What dost think on?
Flam. Nothing; of nothing: leave thy idle questions,—
I am i'th'way to study a long silence,
To prate were idle,—I remember nothing.
There's nothing of so infinite vexation   205
As man's own thoughts.
Lod.   O thou glorious strumpet,
Could I divide thy breath from this pure air
When't leaves thy body, I would suck it up
And breathe't upon some dunghill.
Vit.   You, my death's-man;
Methinks thou dost not look horrid enough,   210
Thou hast too good a face to be a hangman,—
If thou be, do thy office in right form;
Fall down upon thy knees and ask forgiveness.
Lod. O thou hast been a most prodigious comet,

199. year] *Q;* years *Q4.*   200. grieves] *Dod i;* greeu's *Q;* greev's *Samp.*
209. death's-man;] *Q* (Deaths man); deaths-man? *Q4.*

196–7.] Cf. Florio, I, xl (p. 118ᵃ): 'To another that exhorted him to re-commend himselfe to God, he asked, "Who is going to him?" And the fellow answering, "Yourselfe shortly:" "If it be his good pleasure, I would to God it might be to morrow night," replied he. "Recommend but your selfe to him," said the other, "and you shall quickly be there." "It is best then," answered he, "that my selfe carry mine owne commendations to him." '

200. *grieves*] Q may represent an elided form of 'grieves us' (so Sampson), but cf. 'mouth's' at III. ii. 171 (also set by Compositor A).

202. *of nothing*] Sampson compared *Oth.*, v. ii. 303. See also the Duchess' death-scene in *D.M.*, IV. ii. 15–16: '*Cariola.* . . . What think you of madam? *Duchess.* Of nothing: / When I muse thus, I sleep'.

But I'll cut off your train:—kill the Moor first.   215
Vit. You shall not kill her first. Behold my breast,—
  I will be waited on in death; my servant
  Shall never go before me.
Gasp. Are you so brave?
Vit.   Yes I shall welcome death
  As princes do some great ambassadors;   220
  I'll meet thy weapon half way.
Lod.   Thou dost tremble,—
  Methinks fear should dissolve thee into air.
Vit. O thou art deceiv'd, I am too true a woman:
  Conceit can never kill me: I'll tell thee what,—
  I will not in my death shed one base tear,   225
  Or if look pale, for want of blood, not fear.
Car. Thou art my task, black Fury.
Zan.   I have blood
  As red as either of theirs: wilt drink some?
  'Tis good for the falling sickness: I am proud
  Death cannot alter my complexion,   230
  For I shall ne'er look pale.

220–1. As . . . way] *so Dod i; as prose Q; . . . weapon / Half way Q4.* 227.
Car.] Q; Gas. Q3.

---

215. *train*] (1) 'tail of a comet' (cf. *Ham.*, I. i. 117), and (2) 'retinue' (i.e.,
Zanche).

219. *Are . . . brave*] So Bosola asks the Duchess of Malfi: 'Doth not death
fright you?' (IV. ii. 210), and again, 'The manner of your death should
much afflict you, / This cord should terrify you?' (ll. 214–15).

224. *Conceit . . . me*] a quibble: (1) 'apprehension cannot kill me', nor (2)
'self-conceit, vanity', nor (possibly) (3) 'conception'. Lucas compared
Lyly, *Sapho* (1584), III. iii. 58: 'yet did I neuer heare of a woman that died
of a conceite'.

227–8. *blood . . . red*] Red blood was a sign of courage; cf. *Mer.V.*, II. i.
6–7.

229. *good . . . sickness*] Lucas quoted Pliny (tr. 1601), XXVIII, iv: 'if their
mouths bee rubbed with the said bloud, who being ouertaken with the
epilepsie, are falne downe, . . . immediatly thereupon they will rise and
stand upon their feet.'

231. *pale*] i.e., with fear. Q does not indicate when Zanche dies; it may
be supposed that the 'joint motion' of l. 232 despatches all three, and certainly Zanche is dead before l. 253. Vittoria does not die first as she wished
(cf. ll. 216–18 above).

Lod.   Strike, strike,
With a joint motion.   [*They strike.*]

Vit.   'Twas a manly blow—
The next thou giv'st, murder some sucking infant,
And then thou wilt be famous.

Flam.   O what blade is't?
A Toledo, or an English fox?   235
I ever thought a cutler should distinguish
The cause of my death, rather than a doctor.
Search my wound deeper: tent it with the steel
That made it.

Vit. O my greatest sin lay in my blood.   240
Now my blood pays for't.

Flam.   Th'art a noble sister—
I love thee now; if woman do breed man
She ought to teach him manhood: fare thee well.
Know many glorious women that are fam'd
For masculine virtue, have been vicious   245
Only a happier silence did betide them—
She hath no faults, who hath the art to hide them.

Vit. My soul, like to a ship in a black storm,
Is driven I know not whither.

Flam.   Then cast anchor.
Prosperity doth bewitch men seeming clear,   250

232. S.D.] *Luc; not in Q; They stab Vittoria, Zanche, and Flamineo Dyce ii; They strike. Zanche dies Sp.*   238–9. Search . . . it] *so Dyce i, Samp;* one line *Q.*   241. Th'art] *Q;* Thou'rt *Dyce ii.*   250–3. Prosperity . . . / But . . . / We . . . / Nay] „Prosperity . . . / „But . . . / „Wee . . . / „Nay *Q.*

235. *fox*] a kind of sword (*O.E.D.*, s.v., 6, suggests that the figure of a wolf on some sword-blades was mistaken for that of a fox).

238.] Both *Search* and *tent* = 'to probe', but there is probably a quibble on *tent* = 'to tend, care for the safety of'.

240–1. *blood . . . blood*] i.e., 'passion . . . life-blood' (cf. I. ii.292 and note).

247.] Cf. N. Breton, *Cornu-copiae* (1612), K4, where an 'old wife' advises a new-found cuckold: 'She is least faultie, that can faults best hide'.

250–1.] Cf. W. Alexander (cf. App. IV), *Croesus*, I. i. 65–73: 'Vaine foole, that thinkes soliditie to find / . . . The fome is whitest, where the Rocke is neare, / . . . The greatest danger oft doth least appeare. / Their seeming blisse, who trust in frothy showes, / . . .'

But seas do laugh, show white, when rocks are near.
We cease to grieve, cease to be Fortune's slaves,
Nay cease to die by dying. Art thou gone
And thou so near the bottom ?—false report
Which says that women vie with the nine Muses   255
For nine tough durable lives: I do not look
Who went before, nor who shall follow me;
No, at myself I will begin and end:
While we look up to heaven we confound
Knowledge with knowledge. O I am in a mist.   260

Vit. O happy they that never saw the court,
Nor ever knew great man but by report.   VITTORIA *dies.*

Flam. I recover like a spent taper, for a flash
And instantly go out.

259–60. While . . . / Knowledge] „While . . . / „Knowledge *Q.*   261. *Vit.*]
Q; Zan. conj. Samp.   262. Nor] „Nor *Q.*   man] *Q* (Man); Men *Q2.*
263–4. I . . . out] *so Q; one line Dod ii; as prose Scott.*

253–4. *thou . . . thou*] i.e., Zanche . . . Vittoria.

254. *so . . . bottom*] Cf. *D.M.*, v. v. 69–70, of Ferdinand before his death:
'He seems to come to himself, / Now he's so near the bottom'.

254–6. *report . . . lives*] Tilley (W652) traced a similar proverb back to
Heywood (1546), but always the lives of a woman (or wife) are compared,
less flatteringly, to those of a cat.

258.] Cf. W. Alexander, *Darius*, i. i. 177 and 182: 'Who on himselfe too
much depends, / . . . But at himselfe beginnes, and ends'.

259–60. *While . . . knowledge*] Cf. W. Alexander, *Croesus*, iv. ii. 2080–4:
'The Heau'ns that thinke we do them wrong / To trie what in suspence still
hings, / This crosse upon us justly brings: / With knowledge, knowledge is
confus'd, / And growes a griefe erè it be long'.

260. *mist*] Cf. *D.M.*, v. v. 93–6: 'How came Antonio by his death ? /
Bosola. In a mist: I know not how— / Such a mistake as I have often seen /
In a play: . . .' See also Marlowe, *II Tamburlaine*, ii. iv, which describes
Zenocrate 'All dazzled with the hellish mists of death'.

261–2.] Cf. W. Alexander, *A.T.*, v. i. 2767–70: 'Then when that I con-
ceuide with griefe of heart, / The miseries that proper were to Court, / I
thought them happie who (retir'd apart) / Could neuer know such things,
but by report'.

262. *man*] Q2's 'Men' is an attractive emendation in view of A's com-
parable error at iii. ii. 8, and the recurrence of the phrase 'great men'
throughout the play. But 'great men' is varied elsewhere as 'greatness' (iv.
iii. 144).

Let all that belong to great men remember th'old wives'　265
tradition, to be like the lions i'th'Tower on Candlemas
day, to mourn if the sun shine, for fear of the pitiful
remainder of winter to come.
　　'Tis well yet there's some goodness in my death,
　　My life was a black charnel: I have caught　　　270
　　An everlasting cold. I have lost my voice
　　Most irrecoverably: farewell glorious villains,—
　　This busy trade of life appears most vain,
　　Since rest breeds rest, where all seek pain by pain.
　　Let no harsh flattering bells resound my knell,　275
　　Strike thunder, and strike loud to my farewell.　　*Dies.*

English Amb. [*within*]　This way, this way, break ope the
　　　doors, this way.
Lod.　Ha, are we betray'd?—
　　Why then let's constantly die all together,
　　And having finish'd this most noble deed,　　　280
　　Defy the worst of fate; not fear to bleed.

　　　Enter Ambassadors and GIOVANNI [*with Guards*].

265. wives'] *Q2* (wiues); wides *Q*.　　273–4. This . . . / Since] „This . . . /
„Since *Q*.　　277. *within*] Dyce ii; not in *Q*.　　281.1.] *Wal; Enter
Embassad: and Giouanni* (after l. 276) *Q*, (*Embassador*) *Q3*, (*Embassadors*)
Dod ii; Enter . . . Giovanni Dyce ii.

　　266–8. *lions . . . come*] There was a small zoo in the Tower of London (cf.
Stowe, *Annals* (ed. 1615), p. 895).
　　Cf. Pettie, II, 211: 'And truely I know by proofe, that he which will long
injoy the favour of his Prince, must like the Beare, in faire wether, be sad to
think of the foule that is to come: whiche doubtfull thought, will keepe him
in such humilitie and lowlynesse as Princes like of'.
　　Candlemas is 2 Feb.; cf. the proverb (Tilley C52): 'If Candlemas day be
fair and bright, winter will have another flight'.
　　273. *trade*] habitual practice, employment (often without any idea of
commerce; cf. *O.E.D.*, s.v., 3 and 4).
　　274.] Cf. W. Alexander, *J.C.*, II. ii. 1013–14: 'Ease comes with ease,
where all by paine buy paine, / Rest we in peace, by warre let others raigne'.
See also, *D.M.*, II. v. 59–61: 'divers men . . . never yet express'd / Their
strong desire of rest, but by unrest, / By vexing of themselves'.
　　where = 'whereas'.
　　276.] Cf. I. i. 11–12.
　　279. *constantly*] resolutely.

Eng. Amb. Keep back the prince,—shoot, shoot,—

> [*They shoot, and wound* LODOVICO.]

Lod.   O I am wounded.

I fear I shall be ta'en.

Giov.   You bloody villains,
By what authority have you committed
This massacre?

Lod.   By thine.

Giov.   Mine?

Lod.   Yes, thy uncle,   285
Which is a part of thee, enjoin'd us to't:—
Thou know'st me I am sure,—I am Count Lodowick,—
And thy most noble uncle in disguise
Was last night in thy court.

Giov.   Ha!

Car.   Yes, that Moor
Thy father chose his pensioner.

Giov.   He turn'd murderer;   290
Away with them to prison, and to torture;
All that have hands in this, shall taste our justice,
As I hope heaven.

Lod.   I do glory yet,
That I can call this act mine own:—for my part,
The rack, the gallows, and the torturing wheel   295
Shall be but sound sleeps to me,—here's my rest—
I limb'd this night-piece and it was my best.

282.1.] *Samp subs.; not in Q; . . . and Lodovico falls Dyce ii.*   285–6.
Yes . . . to't] *so Dyce i; one line Q.*   289. *Car.*] *Q; Gas. Q3; Lod.
Haz.*   289–90. Yes . . . pensioner] *so Dyce i; one line Q.*   290. murderer;] *Q; murderer? Q2.*   297. I] „I *Q.*   limb'd] *Q; limn'd Q2*
(limm'd).

295.] possibly an allusion to the cruel deaths inflicted on the real-life
assassins (cf. App. I, pp. 191–2).

296. *rest*] (1) 'sleep', and (2) 'final hope, resolution' (cf. *H5*, II. i. 17).

297. *limb'd*] a 17th-century form of 'limned' (i.e., 'painted, portrayed'),
retained because it quibblingly associates 'limning' with the human body.

night-piece] painting representing a night-scene; cf. the entry of mas-
quers in Dekker's *Satiromastix* (1602), v. ii. 41–3: 'th'art ill suited, ill made

Giov. Remove the bodies,—see my honoured lord,
What use you ought make of their punishment.
Let guilty men remember their black deeds   300
Do lean on crutches, made of slender reeds.   [*Exeunt.*]

Instead of an epilogue only this of Martial supplies me:
Hæc fuerint nobis præmia si placui.

For the action of the play, 'twas generally well, and I dare affirm,
with the joint testimony of some of their own quality, (for the true
imitation of life, without striving to make nature a monster) the
best that ever became them: whereof as I make a general acknowledgement, so in particular I must remember the well approved
industry of my friend Master Perkins, and confess the worth of his
action did crown both the beginning and end.

FINIS.

298. *Giov.*] *Q; Eng. Amb. conj. Greg.*   lord] *Q, Q4;* lords *Dyce ii.*
299. you] *Q, Dyce ii;* we *Q4.*   ought] *Q;* ought to *Q4.*   300–1.]
italicized Q.   301. S.D.] *Dyce ii; not in Q.*

vp, / In Sable collours, like a night peece dyed, / Com'st thou the Prologue
of a Maske in blacke . . . ?'
      299. *ought*] 'to' was often omitted (cf. Abbott, *Shakespearian Grammar*
(ed. 1897), § 349).
      301.2. Hæc . . . placui] i.e., 'These things will be our reward, if I have
pleased you' (Martial, II, xci, 8).
      301.4. *quality*] profession, occupation.
      301.4–5. *true . . . monster*] Cf. *Ham.*, III. ii. 20–39 and 'An Excellent
Actor', *Characters* (1615): 'He doth not strive to make nature monstrous,
she is often seen in the same Scæne with him, but neither on Stilts nor
Crutches'.
      301.8. *Perkins*] Cf. Intro., p. xxiii.

Appendix I

Reprint from *The Fugger News-Letters*, ed. V. von Klarwill, tr. Pauline de Chary (G. P. Putman's Sons, New York and London; 1924), pp. 85–9.[1]

New tidings of a pitiful act of murder that took place on the 22nd day of December of the new calendar in the year 1585, at Padua in Italy, a town belonging to the Venetian rulers.

The Duke Paolo Giordano Orsini, Duke of Bracciano, scion of one of the noblest Roman families had for wife the sister of the now reigning Grand Duke of Florence, with whom he had as issue of the marriage-bed a young Prince of the name of Giovanni. But as the said Prince had but little sexual intercourse with the former Duchess of Florence, he was induced by fleshly desire to break his marriage vows.

He conceived a burning passion for the wife of the nephew of the now reigning Pope Sixtus. But she did not wish to turn unfaithful to her husband, and therefore told him that she was married and that no other man should approach her. Thereupon the said Duke forgot himself and had the husband of the lady (the nephew of the Pope) horribly murdered. He then once more approached the widow of the murdered man. But she curtly refused him because he was married and she a widow and not wishful to do such a thing. Thereupon the Prince Paolo Giordano forgot himself still further and had his own spouse, sister of the present Duke of Florence, put out of the way, in order to still his concupiscence for the above-named widow. Then, for the third time he paid his addresses to her. This time she made subjection to him but only on condition that he married her, which he did.

Meanwhile the Cardinal, the present Pope, did not rest in his desire to avenge the innocent blood of his nephew. But as he was not of much consideration, he has been placated. However, when he became Pope, the Duke wished to be reconciled with him. He knelt before him and begged for his blessing. Thereupon the Pope said:

[1] Being a translation of MS. 8959 (Nationalbibliothek, Vienna), ff. 247–8, 251–2.

'Duke Paolo Giordano, you insulted the Cardinal Montalto: but Pope Sixtus pardons you. Do not come again, however, of that we warn you.' The Duke was greatly alarmed at this speech and removed himself with his spouse to Padua, in Venetian territory, where he kept Court and had up to five hundred persons at his board. Nevertheless, before two months had passed, he died at Salo. Foul play was suspected. He left his spouse, who belonged to the noble Roman house of Accaramboni, a large property. The Grand Duke of Florence was by no means pleased with this testament, and took charge of the young forsaken Prince Giovanni, calling upon the widow at the same time to put aside the will. Should she marry again, he would deal handsomely by her: but he urged upon her to enter a convent or to remain a widow. Then also would he make handsome provision for her. But to this she would not agree, and wished to abide by the testament and to keep a retinue of one hundred persons. On the 22nd day of this month, at 2 o'clock at night, according to Italian time, her palace in Padua was found open. Fifty well-armed men thereupon entered and cruelly shot the brother of the Signora Accaramboni, a certain Duke Flaminio; as to the lady, they stabbed her where they found her at prayer. Although she pitifully entreated that she might be permitted first to conclude her orisons, the murderers fulfilled their deed. The most distinguished among them is Ludovico Orsini, the first chief of the Government here, cousin of the dead Paolo Giordano. Thereafter he entrenched himself with his assassins in his house. In the meanwhile the news was brought here and the Government has dispatched one of its Senators to Padua with authority to destroy the house of Orsini and to take the murderers alive or dead. The said Orsini surrendered himself with a dagger in his hand, and his house was fired upon from several large cannon. Thereby a number of his retainers perished, the remainder being taken prisoner.

From Venice, 27th day of December 1585.
Yesternight the Government here decided that the Colonel Ludovico Orsini was to be strangled three hours after the delivery of their letter. His accomplices were to be dealt with according to their deserts. Without doubt they will be hanged and quartered.

The chief culprit Orsini confessed that he had perpetrated this murderous deed at the command of great personages. The students in Padua have armed themselves and cried out 'Justice, Justice!'

From Venice, the 1st day of January 1586.
It has been recently reported that the Colonel of this Government, Ludovico Orsini, acted murderously and with his own hand slew in gruesome fashion the wife of the late Prince Paolo Giordano, Duke of Bracciano, and her brother, Duke Flaminio.

When the decision that he must die within three hours was made known to Ludovico Orsini, he confessed that although his years numbered but four-and-thirty, he had put to death with his own hands forty persons, believing that Justice would never lay hands upon him because he belonged to so illustrious a house. He had hoped likewise that he would not be publicly executed. But when he was informed that he was not to be strangled in a public place but in a chamber, he gave thanks for this judgment and penned two letters, one to his spouse and the other to the Government here. He commended to the latter's care his spouse and child, as well as his estate, so that they might not suffer on his account. He also made a will by which he bequeathed to the Government his armour, worth over and above six thousand crowns. The remainder of his property he left to his wife, who was at the time with child.

He gave fifty crowns to his executioner, in order that he might be dispatched quickly.

The brother of this Ludovico Orsini, Don Latino Orsini, is Governor of Candia under the Venetian rule. But shortly afterwards the Government sent a frigate to divest him of the command because they no longer put faith in him. And just as high as the house of Orsini had stood in esteem, as deep is now its fall.

After Ludovico Orsini had been strangled, his body was borne to the cathedral, the coffin decorated with tapestries and left lying there through the whole of this the 27th day of December. Then it was brought hither and interred in the Church of the Madonna dell'Orto, where Don Giordano and Don Valerio Orsini, the forbears of Ludovico, also lie buried.

The murdered Signora Accaramboni was a woman of great eloquence for as Ludovico Orsini was about to murder her, she was at prayer, and when the murderer said to her:

'Do you recognize me?' she made answer 'Yea, now it is time to prepare my soul. I beg of you by the Mercy of our Lord Jesus Christ, to let me make my confession and then do with me as you please.' 'Nay,' answered the enemy, 'now is not the time for confession.'

In Padua near on six hundred burghers paraded in arms and cried 'Justice, Justice!' Now follows the list of those who were publicly executed: Count Paganello Ubaldi and Captain Splandiano da Fermo. These two were the servants of the murdered lady, who did open her dwelling—the palace—and who were accomplices in the bloody deed. They were riven asunder with red-hot tongs, and killed with a hammer and then quartered. Buglion and Furio Savognano, two noblemen and secret advisers of Ludovico Orsini, have been secretly strangled.

Agrippa Tartaro de Monte Falco, the Comte de Camerion and

thirteen more, some of them nobles, others arrant scoundrels, were all hanged.

Colonel Lorenzo Nobile del Borgo, Liverotto, and da Fermo were torn to pieces by the mob as they were firing upon the house. Twenty of the people lie imprisoned. They also will probably be hanged.

Appendix II

Extracts from '*A Letter lately written from Rome, by an Italian Gentleman, to a freende of his in Lyons in Fraunce. Wherein is declared, the state of Rome: The suddaine death & sollemne buriall of Pope Gregory the thirteenth. The election of the newe Pope, and the race of life this newe Pope ranne before hee was aduaunced. Thereto are adioyned the accidentes that haue fallen out, not onely in Rome, but in Naples & other parts of the worlde also. Newely translated out of Italian into English by I.F.*' (1585).[1]

[After the election of Pope Sixtus V,] Contrary to the opinion of all men, the Lorde *Paulo Giordano Orsino*, Duke of *Brasciano*, came and kissed the Popes feete, who entertained him very curteously, and with all aduertised him to looke to the gouernment of his estate, and to the ouerthrowe and rooting out of the banished persons, or outlawes as we terme them; I sayde he did it contrary to the expectation of all men, because you shall vnderstand, that the Pope had not many yeeres agoe a Nephew, a young man of comely stature and personage, who viewing on a time a beautifull Damosell of *Corambonis de Augubbio*, fell so in loue with her, that in short space he won her and wedded her, but he enioyed her not long, for shortly after he was slaine with a gunne, and it was thought that Lorde *Paulo* had procured his death, for that not long after he became very familiar with the Gentlewoman, and meanyng to marrie her, Cardinall *Medici*, who is brother in law to him, and all his kinsmen of the house of *Orsini*, laboured to ye Pope very earnestly, that he should not suffer their kinsman to match with one of so base fortune, whereupon the Pope at their intreatie sent for him, and first by faire meanes sought to disswade him from his purpose, but seeing he could doo no good

---

[1] The translator was John Florio; cf. Frances A. Yates, *John Florio* (Cambridge, 1934), pp. 79–83, for the suggestion that Florio also wrote or compiled the letter.

thereby he grew to threatnings, saying, threatning him with excommunication, but Lord *Paulo* nothing terrified nor dismayed, sent the Gentlewoman to his house in the countrie, and the Pope as she was goyng thether, caused her to be apprehended and put into a monasterie of Nunnes, where she remayned certaine monethes, notwithstanding, that at the length Lord *Paulo* found meanes to get her at libertie, and in despight of al men maried her, and yet enioyeth her. For this cause it was thought, that hee would not haue submitted himselfe vnto the Pope, and trusted him, and that the Pope being now in that soueraigntie & dignitie, would haue reuenged the death of his Nephew. But see how vaine the iudgements of men are oftentimes, for now there is a marriage intreated of, betwixt the Popes Neece & Lord *Paulo* his sonne, & it is thought that he shall be general Standard bearer of the Church.   (B5ᵛ–6ᵛ)

[Later it is recorded that] The Lorde *Paulo Giordano* yesterday went to *Brasciano* with his wife, and al his Court, . . .   (B7ᵛ)

[Incidentally the letter recounts that] The other euening vnder the towre of *Corti Sr. Virgilio Orsino,* met L. *Chiappino Vitelli* and a gentleman of his company rose out of the coach of *Orsino,* and challenged another which was in *Vitelli* his coach, which was as they say, because the day before they met, and neither of them saluted other, but at that time they were not suffered to deale.   (C5ᵛ)

[The letter proceeds to recount Pope Sixtus' early life, how he was of obscure birth and poor upbringing, and how he was noted for his zeal and talents and made a cardinal, and] . . . howbeit he was so highly and so sodainely exalted, yet did he not degenerate from his first originall, for you should haue seene him heere in *Rome,* goe in a filthy great, and greasie Hat, al besmeared, and his hands foule and dyrtie. Yet is he very politike and patient, which was well perceyued in him not long agoe, when his Nephew (of whom I haue before made mention) was slaine, he neuer gaue showe of anger or alteration, which made all the citie to woonder at him. He is a man who will not easily be led, and gouerned of others, which maketh me to thinke, that he will not suffer himselfe to be robbed by others, and as the common Phrase is, to be drawen by the nose, wherein I pray God he still continue, for wee are long agoe wearie, and haue had to many Popes which haue beene thralls, and subiectes to yᵉ Spaniards. . . .

This man is of stature rather lowe then tall, but of a good complexion, leane and dry, vsed to endure labour, wherefore I thinke, that (if he bee not ouercome with such delicate and daintie meates as his degree requireth) hee will liue many yeares.   (E2–4ᵛ)

The letter is dated] From Rome the last of May. 1585.   (E4ᵛ)

Appendix III

Extracts from Hierome Bignon, '*A Briefe, but an Effectuall Treatise of the Election of Popes. Written by a French Gentleman, resident in Rome at this last Election. Faithfully translated according to the French Copie. . .*' (1605), B3–D1ᵛ.

Presently after the Pope is departed, yea and euen when they see, or that they haue aduertisement from the Physitions that hee is at the last cast, the Cardinalls which are then in *Rome*, assemble together in the priuy Consistory, to consult for the gouernment of the towne, and to prouide for the affaires of the vacancie: & then the seate being vacant, they are apparelled in *Rochettes*, & *Mozzettes*[1] without Copes, in signe of Iurisdiction, the people of the towne all in armes, guarde at the gates of the Cittie, the Cardinalls Pallaces, and in other quarters.

[The next day the Cardinals meet to arrange for the new election, and the deceased Pope is laid in state in St Peter's.]

In the daies following, the Cardinalls solemnize the Popes obsequies: and there is a convention in the vestrie of *Saint Peters*, wherin the Princes Embassadors do vse to enter, making their remonstrations, & motions touching the Election to be performed. During the vacancie, the great Chamberlain gouerns *Rome*. But so ther is no expedition nor dispatch of any thing admitted in the Apostolicall Chancerie, while there be a new Pope. And in briefe, as soone as the Pope hath yeelded vp his breath, the Vice-chanceler taketh the *Bulls* or *Seales*, causeth them publiquely to be broken, rased out, & that side to be taken away of them, wheron the deceased Popes name was written, so that they cannot be sealed withall. . . .

Nine dayes after the Popes death, they celebrate the *Masse of the Holy Ghost*, and beeing finished with singing the *Hymne, Veni sancte Spiritus*, they enter into the Conclaue.

The Conclaue at *Rome*, is in a place ioyning to Saint *Peters* Churche, within the Popes Pallace, in *Sixtus* his Chapell, as bigge as a great *Church*, where is portraied the last Iudgement, and it was the excellent worke-manship of *Michael Angelo*: . . . To the which Conclaue, the chappell of *Pauline*, & the great Royall Hall abutt, and

---

[1] I.e., in surplices and mantles. The text is corrupt here: the 1605 translation reads 'apparelled in *Coquests Rochettes*, & *Mozzettes*'; the French original reads 'sont vestus de roquests & Mozzetes'.

are adioyning, beeing as it were a part of the same. The gates, lower windows, and all accesses, are so mured, and closed vp, that one cannot talke, or communicate with any of those within.

When they are entred into the Conclaue, they assemble together in the chappell *Pauline*, where they consult of all things which concerns the gouernment of the Conclaue, & the same day, they take the oaths of the Officers, deputed for the guard of the Conclaue, as well of those without, as of them within.

At the beginning, after they are entred, the Conclaue remains open, for some little time, and then Princes Ambassadours vse to go in, and make their recommendations, and sollicitations in fauour of him, or them, whom they knowe to be best liked, and affected by their Princes.

After this, the Conclaue is shut, and then no man may any more goe in, nor communicate in any sort, with any one without, neither by letters, messengers, nor otherwise: nor likewise go out, till there be a new Pope created, ...

Euery day the necessarie prouision is brought them, which they giue them in at a window, or by the wicket of the gate, before which there is treble garde, wherof the neerest to the gate, consistes of the Prelates that are in *Rome*, who looke that none may communicate with those that are inclosed in the Conclaue, and for this cause, they searche the Vessells and platters, to see whether there bee not any letters hidden in the same.

Euery Cardinal within the conclaue, can haue no more, but two men to serue him, whom they call *Conclauistes*.

The conclaue being closed, the day following the Deane of the Cardinalls after the celebrating of Masse, administreth the holie Communion to all the Cardinalles... Euery daye in *Paules Chappell*, one of the Cardinalls celebrates the *Masse* of the *Holy Ghost*, and so they proceede to the election of the Pope: which for the most part also is performed after two manners, one by Scrutinie, & the other by Adoration.

The scrutenie is held after this sort: euery Cardinall writes within a certaine billet of paper, his voice and choice, and at the end of Masse, he putteth it into the great challice of Gold, which standeth vpon the Altar: ... There are three of the Cardinalls, which in the sight, and presence of all the rest, vnfold these little rolles, or billets, pronouncing aloude his name, who hath subscribed to euery of them, and the Cardinalls write & set downe in a sheet of paper, the number of the voices which euery one hath, to know who hath most.

Where by the way we must note, that to choose, & create a Pope, there must concurre two thirds of al the Cardinals voices in the Conclaue by the constitution of Pope Alexander, 3. ... For if in such a

scrutenie, ther is not any one, with whom the two thirds accur,[1] at the
same instant they cast al the billets into the fire, & by this means the
affaire is referred ouer to some other time, when they make and re-
commence an other scrutenie in the same forme: the which, by
reason of this, vseth to be repeated & reiterated many times, while
these two thirds occurre in one person. The which falls out very
seldome, by way of scrutenie: so as they are vrged to haue recourse to
adoration... [There are however some variations in the manner of the
scrutiny which may make a two-thirds' decision easier.]

The other maner, which is Adoration,[2] is, when the Cardinalles
being assembled together in the Chappell, turne towardes him, whom
they desire to be made Pope, doing reuerence vnto him, and bending
the knees very lowe, and when they see that the two thirds are gone to
this maner of Adoration, The Cardinall thus adored, is made Pope.

And though this maner of Election, be referred to that which is
called by the auncients, and in the cannon law, *per inspirationem,*
and that they say, it is the way of the holy Ghost, which was, when all
with one voice without any treatie, or precedent scruteny, and without any formalitie, concurre, as it were by diuine inspiration, to say,
that such a one must bee made Pope, it being thus equally designed
by euery one.

Notwithstanding this forme of Adoration is not esteemed by many,
so lawfull, and auaileable as scrutenie: because by meanes of con-
tentions, and partialities, there may be some fraude or violence committed therein, in that the weaker side may be drawne to Adoration
by the example of those more mightie, and those fearful, induced by
them more resolute. ...

When the two thirds of the voices concur in one person, be it by
scrutenie secret, or open, ... or by way of Adoration, he out of doubt
is truly Pope. .. And then the chiefe Cardinal Bishop, all the other
being set, pronounceth, and declareth in the name of all the Colledge,
that he chooseth such an one for Pope. .. [and then he is enthroned
and asked what name he will choose for himself.]

Hauing therfore declared what name he wil take vpon him, he
vseth to subscribe to the constitutions ... [and in] the mean while, the
chiefest of the Cardinal Deacons, opening a little windowe, from
whence the people which attend, may see, and be seene, he shewes
forth a Crosse, pronouncing these words, with a loud voice; *Annuncio
vobis gaudium magnum: Papam habemus. Reuerendissimus Cardinalis
Florentinus electus est in summum Pontificem, & elegit sibi nomen,
Leo 2.*

This being done, he is disvested of his common garments, ... and
revested with all the habits Pontificall, and causing him to sit vpon

---

[1] accur,] *ed.*; accur; *Q.*   [2] Adoration,] *ed.*; Adoration: *Q.*

the Aultar, all the Cardinalls a rowe doe him reuerence, in kissing his feete, hands, and mouth.

During this entercourse of Ceremonie, all the gates of the Conclaue are opened, the barres, and walls which closed and mured the passages, gates, and windows, are broken down, & ouerthrowen: & the Souldiers entering confusedly, as it were by force, take & pill whatsoeuer they meete withal in their way. And this is the reason, that when any one is declared Pope, the *Conclauistes* do all they can, to ramasse, & lay close vp, and get together, all the best things that belong to their Cardinall: And in[1] like maner the people vse to rush into his house that is chosen, & to pillage the same.

At the same time, the newe Pope is carryed into *Saint Peters* Churche, followed with the Channons and Singing men of the same Churche, which sing; *Ecce Sacerdos Magnus ?*

And after hee hath prostrated himselfe on the earth, and made his prayer, hee is placed vpon the great & high Pontificall Chayre, where, *Te Deum laudamus* is said: There againe before the holy assemblie, & multitude of people, which come thither in great preasse, hee is adored by the Cardinalls, Bishops, Prelates, and others. And then hee giueth generall Absolution, and his Benediction to euery one, with much Solemnitie, & Ceremonies, which graunt full Indulgence: and incontinently after he is carryed into *Saint Peters Pallace*, highly reuerenced by euery one, and whereof hee receiues such contentment, as euery one may easilie iudge. . . .

[The last election, in 1605, was of Leo II who followed Innocent IX who had 'held the seate' since January 1592.] The Cardinals [had] entred into the Conclaue, the fourteenth of . . . March, and there was of them to the number of three-score and one. The Scrutenie was diuerse times set on foote, and many Cardinals propounded. [For a long time a two-thirds' majority could not be obtained, but] the first day of Aprill, when they came to mention my Lord Cardinall of *Florence*, there was presently such a concurrence, & consent on all parts, that without making any scruple or doubt in the matter, they being in *Paules* Chappell, the place ordained for such elections euery one ran to adoration, . . .

And [it was] at so great a promptitude, alacritie, and harmonie of all willes, that we neede not to doubt but it was a verie diuine inspiration: . . .

---

[1] in] *ed.;* in in *Q.*

Appendix IV

Webster's Imitation; an index to passages cited in this edition.

<table>
<tr><td align="center">AUTHOR</td><td align="center">CORRESPONDING PASSAGES IN
'THE WHITE DEVIL'</td></tr>
<tr><td>Alexander, William
   The Alexandrean Tragedy
     (1607)</td><td>IV. iii. 103 and 152–3; V. i. 41–2; V.
iii. 201–4; V. iv. 103–4 and 122–3;
V. vi. (?) 182 and 261–2.</td></tr>
<tr><td>   Croesus (1604)</td><td>V. vi. 136–7, 180, 250–1, and 259–60.</td></tr>
<tr><td>   Darius (1604)</td><td>V. vi. 258.</td></tr>
<tr><td>   Julius Caesar (1607)</td><td>II. ii. 56–7; IV. iii. 58; V. vi. 116–18
and 274.</td></tr>
<tr><td>Ariosto, Ludovico
   Orlando Furioso, tr.
     J. Harington (1591)</td><td>III. iii. 1–2.</td></tr>
<tr><td>   Satires, tr. R. Tofte (1608)</td><td>(?) I. ii. 78–92.</td></tr>
<tr><td>Breton, Nicholas
   Cornu-copiae (1612)</td><td>(?) V. vi. 247.</td></tr>
<tr><td>Chapman, George
   Byron's Conspiracy (1608)</td><td>I. ii. 347–54; (?) V. ii. 24.</td></tr>
<tr><td>   Byron's Tragedy (1608)</td><td>(?) IV. iii. 150.</td></tr>
<tr><td>Dekker, Thomas
   If it be not Good (1612)</td><td>To the Reader, ll. 3–6; II. i. 49–51;
(?) V. i. 166; V. vi. 141–4.</td></tr>
<tr><td>   Whore of Babylon (1607)</td><td>III. ii. 80.</td></tr>
<tr><td>Erasmus, Desiderius
   Colloquia, Funus</td><td>V. iii. 135–46.</td></tr>
<tr><td>Guazza, Stefano
   Civil Conversation, tr.
     G. Pettie (1581)</td><td>(?) II. i. 101–5; V. i. 101–2, 106–9,
118–21, (?) 168, 172–4, 176, 191–2,
(?) 205–7 and 218; V. iii. 51–3 and
67–8; V. iv. 4–9 and 13–17; V. vi.
266–8.</td></tr>
<tr><td>Guevara, Antonio de
   Dial of Princes, tr.
     T. North (1557)</td><td>I. i. 2–4, 46–9; V. vi. 188–9.</td></tr>
</table>

Jonson, Benjamin
  Masque of Queens (1609)   III. ii. 135.
  Sejanus (1605)   To the Reader, ll. 13–24; III. ii. 225–
    6, 229, and (?) 270.

Lloyd, Lodowick
  Linceus Spectacles (1607)   To the Reader, ll. 28–33.

Marston, John
  Antonio and Mellida (1602)   (?) III. iii. 90.
  The Malcontent (1604)   (?) To the Reader, ll. 13–15.

Middleton, Thomas
  Michaelmas Term (1607)   (?) I. ii. 140–2.

Montaigne, Michel de
  Essays, tr. J. Florio (1603)   I. ii. 19–20, 21–3, 43–6, 90–1, 109–10,
    156–8, 196–7, 198–201; (?) III. i.
    43–5; (?) III. ii. 138–9; IV. ii. (?)
    91–2 and 102–4; IV. iii. (?) 82–4 and
    (?) 85–7; V. i. 25–7; V. iii. 195–6; V.
    vi. 68–72, 76–7, (?) 105, and 196–7.

Montreux, Nicolas de
  Honour's Academy, tr.   III. ii. 110–11 and 204–6; III. iii. 130–
    R. Tofte (1610)   1; IV. ii. 175–7 and 178–9; V. iii. 188–
    9; V. iv. 26; V. vi. 163–5 and 184–6.

Nashe, Thomas
  Lenten Stuff (1599)   (?) V. vi. 177–8.

Riche, Barnaby
  A New Description of Ire- IV. ii. 96–7.
  land (1610)

Saluste du Bartas, Guillaume de
  Judith, tr. T. Hudson (1584) I. i. 23; IV. i. 41–2.
  Divine Weeks, tr. J.   IV. i. 20–1.
    Sylvester (ed. 1608)

Shakespeare, William
  Hamlet (1604/5)   V. iv. 66 ff.
  King Lear (1608)   II. i. 219; V. ii. 36–40.
  Richard III (1597)   (?) IV. ii. 105.
  Troilus and Cressida (1609) (?) V. iii. 88–9

Sharpham, Edward
  Cupid's Whirligig (1607)   (?) III. i. 25–6; (?) IV. ii. 201–2; (?)
    V. i. 74.

Sidney, Sir Philip
Arcadia (1590)   (?) v. iii. 17–18.

Southwell, R.
St Peter's Complaint   iv. ii. 138 and 201–2.
(1595)

Stanyhurst, Richard
'Description of Ireland',   i. ii. 30–2.
Holinshed's Chronicles
(ed. 1577)

Topsell, Edward
History of Four-footed   (?) iv. ii. 222–35.
Beasts and Serpents
(1607–8)

The following imitations are noted by R. W. Dent, but are not cited in this edition.

Beaumont, F. and Fletcher, J.
Woman Hater (1607)   i. ii. 130–3.

Jonson, Benjamin
Sejanus (1605)   (?) iii. iii. 109–10.

Macchiavelli, Niccolo
Florentine History, tr.   (?) iii. ii. 257–61.
T. Bedingfield (1595)

Matthieu, Pierre
General Inventory, 'Sup-   i. i. 11–12, 24–6; i. ii. 142–4, 159–60
plement' by Jean de   (quoted in part in this ed.); (?) ii. i.
Serres, tr. E. Grimeston   73; iii. ii. 143–5, iv. ii. 63–5, (?) 186;
(1607)   v. iii. (?) 39, (?) 57–9; v. iv. 47–8;
                                    (?) v. vi. 79–81.

Mornay, Philip de
Discourse of Life and Death,   (?) iii. i. 43–5.
tr. Countess of Pem-
broke (1592)

Glossarial Index to the Annotations

An asterisk indicates that the annotation referred to contains information as to sense or usage not provided by *The Oxford English Dictionary*; where more than one reference is given for a word, the asterisk refers to the first reference. When a gloss is repeated in the annotations, only the first occurrence is indexed.